DATE DUE

PRINTED IN U.S.A.

GREAT ARTISTS OF THE WESTERN WORLD

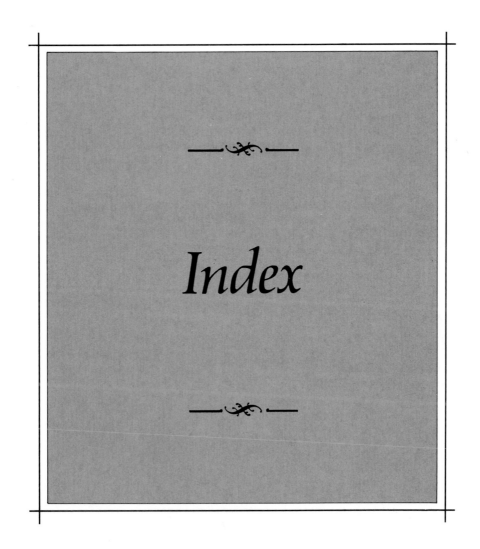

Index

GREAT ARTISTS OF THE WESTERN WORLD

Thirty-six of the great Masters of Western art in nine
thematic volumes:

1 Pre-renaissance in Northern Europe
The Limbourg brothers   Jan van Eyck
Rogier van der Weyden   Hieronymus Bosch

2 The High Renaissance
Leonardo da Vinci   Michelangelo Buonarroti
Raphael Sanzio   Titian Vecellio

3 The Old Masters
Peter Paul Rubens   Frans Hals
Rembrandt van Rijn   Johannes Vermeer

4 The French Classical Tradition
Nicolas Poussin   Claude Lorrain
Jacques-Louis David   Jean-Auguste-Dominique Ingres

5 The French Rococo
Antoine Watteau   Jean-Baptiste-Siméon Chardin
François Boucher   Jean-Honoré Fragonard

6 English Portraiture and Landscape
Joshua Reynolds   Thomas Gainsborough
John Constable   Joseph Turner

7 Impressionism
Edouard Manet   Edgar Degas
Claude Monet Pierre-Auguste Renoir

8 Modernism
Henri Matisse   Pablo Picasso
Umberto Boccioni   Amedeo Modigliani

9 American Artists
James McNeill Whistler   Mary Cassatt
John Singer Sargent   Edward Hopper

GREAT ARTISTS OF THE WESTERN WORLD

Index

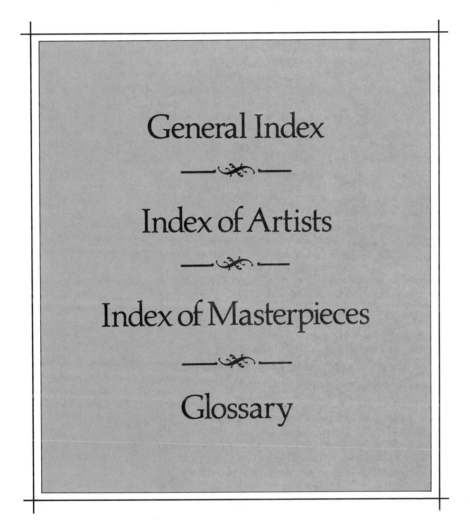

General Index

Index of Artists

Index of Masterpieces

Glossary

MARSHALL CAVENDISH·LONDON·NEW YORK·SYDNEY

Staff Credits

Editors	Clive Gregory LL B Sue Lyon BA (Honours)	**Picture Researchers**	Vanessa Fletcher BA (Honours) Flavia Howard BA (Honours) Jessica Johnson BA
Art Editors	Kate Sprawson BA (Honours) Keith Vollans LSIAD	**Production Controllers**	Steve Roberts Alan Stewart BSc
Deputy Editor	John Kirkwood B Sc (Honours)	**Secretary**	Lynn Smail
Sub-editors	Caroline Bugler BA (Honours), MA Sue Churchill BA (Honours) Alison Cole BA, M Phil Jenny Mohammadi Nigel Rodgers BA (Honours), MA Penny Smith Will Steeds BA (Honours), MA	**Publisher**	Terry Waters Grad IOP
		Editorial Director	Maggi McCormick
		Production Executive	Robert Paulley B Sc
		Consultant and Authenticator	Sharon Fermor BA (Honours) Lecturer in the Extra-Mural Department of London University and Lecturer in Art History at Sussex University
Designers	Stuart John Julie Stanniland		

Reference Edition Published 1990

Published by Marshall Cavendish Corporation
147 West Merrick Road
Freeport, Long Island
N.Y. 11520

Typeset by Litho Link Ltd., Welshpool
Printed and Bound in Singapore by
Times Offset Private Ltd.

Library of Congress Cataloging-in-Publication Data

Main entry under title:

Great Artists of the Western World.

    Includes index.
    1. Artists – Biography. I. Marshall Cavendish
Corporation
N40.G77 1987   709'.2'2 [B]   86–23863
ISBN 0–86307–743–9

ISBN 0–86307–743–9 (set)
ISBN 0–86307–753–6 (vol)

Contents

How to use the index —————————————— 6

General Index —————————————— 7

A Glossary in Pictures —————————————— 33

THE PLATES

The Bridge at Langlois (Van Gogh) —————————————— 33

The Coronation of the Virgin (Fra Angelico) —————————————— 34

The Resurrection and *Noli Me Tangere* (Giotto) —————————————— 35

The Murano Altarpiece (Bellini) —————————————— 36

The Adoration of the Magi (Leonardo da Vinci) —————————————— 37

The Calumny of Apelles (Botticelli) —————————————— 38

Ceiling of the Chapel of Eleonora of Toledo (Bronzino) —————————————— 39

Récréation Galante (Watteau) —————————————— 40

Are They Thinking of Grapes? (Boucher) —————————————— 41

Cornard Wood (Gainsborough) —————————————— 42

Boatbuilding (Constable) —————————————— 43

The Boyhood of Raleigh (Millais) —————————————— 44

Peace: Burial at Sea (Turner) —————————————— 45

In a Levantine Port (Sargent) —————————————— 46

Sunday, Port-en-Bresson (Seurat) —————————————— 47

The Good and Evil Angels (Blake) —————————————— 48

Index of Artists —————————————— 49

Index of Masterpieces —————————————— 65

Glossary —————————————— 75

How To Use
The Index

The following pages are a complete index to volumes 1
to 9 of **Great Artists of the Western World.** The
index is divided into three sections: a General Index, an
Index of Artists, and an Index of Masterpieces. This
volume also contains a Glossary of art terms, illustrated
by sixteen colour plates.

The General Index
This index includes entries on all topics – people,
countries, technical terms and historical events, as well,
of course, as art and artists – that appear in **Great
Artists of the Western World.** Where possible, people
are indexed under surnames; where this is inappropriate
(for example, Louis XIV, King of France), the person is
listed under his or her most familiar name. Works of art
(the fine arts of painting and sculpture, plus books, plays
and movies) are also indexed, with the artist's name
following in parenthesis. Portraits and self-portraits are
indexed under the sitter's name as appropriate. Famous
names in other fields of art are also listed in this index,
but for painters and sculptors, turn immediately to the
Index of Artists.

The Index of Artists
In this section, all fine artists (painters and sculptors)
appearing in the nine volumes are listed; other artists –
writers, architects, etc. – are not included here, but in
the General Index. Fine artists are indexed under their
main surname – for example: Hopper, Edward;
Constable, John; Eyck, Jan van – but where this does not
apply, the artists are indexed under their best-known
names – for example: Raphael Sanzio; Titian Vecellio.
Each entry is followed by detailed subentries on the

artist's life and works; the works themselves are listed
alphabetically at the end of the subentries.

The Index of Masterpieces
This index lists paintings and sculptures alphabetically
from Absinthe (Degas) to Ypres Salient at Night
(Nash); other works of art can be found in the General
Index. Portraits and self-portraits are listed
alphabetically by sitter under the entries, 'Portraits' and
'Self-portraits'. Each work of art is followed by the
artist's name in parenthesis.

The Glossary
In this section there are definitions of nearly two hundred
terms used in the art world, including explanations of
movements in, or Schools of, art, definitions of technical
terms, and descriptions of specialist equipment. Sixteen
of the Glossary entries are explained in greater detail and
are illustrated on pages 33 to 48 by colour plates of the
works of some of the great Masters of Western art.

Using the Index
The number immediately following an entry is the
number of the relevant volume. This is followed by a
colon and then the page numbers on which the entry
appears. If an entry can also be found in other volumes,
these volume and page numbers are printed in numerical
order and are separated by a semi-colon. Page numbers
which refer to illustrations are printed in italics in all
three indexes, as are titles of works of art. The thirty-six
artists who are featured in **Great Artists of the
Western World** are printed in **bold type,** both in the
General Index and in the Index of Artists.

General Index

A

Abbey, Edwin Austin *see*
  Artists' Index
Abdulla of Jordan 8:42
Abercrombie, General 5:106
Absinthe (Degas) 7:62
Absinthe Drinker, The (Manet)
  7:14, *18*
Abstract Impressionism,
  Hopper and 9:112
abstract painting
  forefather of 8:52
  Picasso and 8:48
*Academicians of the Royal
  Academy, The* (Zoffany) 6:41
Académie des Sciences 3:74, *74*
academies 6:36
  see also under individual
    names
Academy of La Lonja 8:45
Academy of Sculpture and
  Painting (French) 6:36
Accademia del Disegno 6:36
*Acrobat's Family with a Monkey,
  The* (Picasso) 8:55
Act of Seclusion (1654) 3:136-7
Actor, The (Fragonard) 5:116
Actors of the Comédie Française
  (Watteau) 5:30
Actors of the Comédie Italienne
  (Watteau) 5:31
Adam brothers 6:16
Adamites 1:109
Adams, John (USA President)
  5:137, 138
Addison, Joseph 4:69
  on 'landscape' 4:69
Admiral's House, The
  (Constable) 6:94
Adoration of the Golden Calf

(sketch, Claude) 4:*51*
Adoration of the Golden Calf, The
  (Poussin) 4:27
Adoration of the Magi, The
  (Fabriano) 1:76-7
Adoration of the Magi, The
  (Bosch) 1:122
Adoration of the Magi, The
  (Leonardo) 2:14
  study for 2:32
Adoration of the Shepherds, The
  (Van der Goes) 1:141
Adrianople, fall of (1878)
  9:72-3, 73
aerial perspective 4:54
Aertsen, Peter *see Artists' Index*
Aesthetic Movement 9:34-5
Africa, Zulu wars in (1879) 9:74
After the Bath (Degas) 7:64
After the Bath (Renoir) 7:129
Agony in the Garden, The
  (Bellini) 4:53
Agony in the Garden, The
  (El Greco) 2:140
Agony in the Garden, The
  (Mantegna) 2:33
Agincourt, Battle of (1415)
  1:40-41, 41
Aida (Verdi) 4:*138*
Air du Soir, L' (Cross) 8:13
Aire-sur-la-Lys, Siege of (1641)
  4:40
Aken, Jheronimous
  Anthonissen van *see* Bosch,
  Hieronymus
Albani, Francesco 5:77
Albergati, Cardinal Niccolò
  (Van Eyck) 1:56, *58*
Albert, Archduke, Regent of
  the Netherlands 3:*15*, 17, 68
  and Rubens 3:*15*, 68

Albert, Prince of Saxe-Coburg-
  Gotha (consort of Queen
  Victoria) 4:138
Albert Memorial, London 9:*38-9*
Alberti, Leon Battista 4:69
Alciati, Andrea 3:51, 59
  emblem-book 3:55
Aldobrandini Marriage, The
  (Roman fresco) 4:22
Alexander, King of the Serbs
  9:138
Alexander I, Tsar of Russia
  6:103
Alexander II, Tsar of Russia
  7:38-9
  attempt on life of 7:41
Alexander VI, Pope 2:36-9, *37,
  40, 41,* 47, 78, 101
  conduct of 1:133
  and crusade against Turks
    1:136
  declares a Jubilee Year 1:136
  divides the Americas 1:138
  French woodcut of 1:*138*
Alexander VI, Portrait of
  (Pinturicchio) 2:37
Alexander VII, Pope 4:37, 38
*Alexander Cassatt and his son
  Robert* (Cassatt) 9:46
Alexandre, Paul, and
  Modigliani 8:110, *120*
Alexei, Tsar of Russia 3:*137*
Alfonso, Duke of Bisceglie 2:37
Algeciras Conference (1906)
  8:*138*
Algiers, Dutch alliance with
  (1612) 3:69
All Quiet on the Western Front
  (Remarque) 9:137
Allegory of Faith (Vermeer)
  3:109-10, 114, *118*

Allegory of Grammar (La Hyre)
  4:141
Allegory of Holland (Visscher)
  3:71
Allegory of Wealth (Vouet) 4:141
altarpieces: carved 1:95
  see also individual artists
Altarpiece of the Sacrament, The
  (Bouts) 1:140
Altieri, Prince Gaspard 4:46, 47
Alva, Fernando Alvarez de
  Toledo, Duke of 1:140-42
'Amazons, The' 7:34
*Ambassadors of Agamemnon in
  the Tent of Achilles, The*
  (Ingres) 4:*109*, 110
Amboise, Charles d' 2:18-19
America 5:106
  discovery of 1:137-8
  and Kellogg-Briand Pact
    (1929) 9:136
  and Napoleonic Wars 4:106
  in the 1920s 9:68
  second President 5:*137*, 138
  and slavery 4:106
  the South surrenders 9:*40-41*
  transfer of power 5:138
  and World War I 9:104,
    104, 137
  see also Thirteen Colonies
American Academy of Arts
  and Letters, and Hopper
  9:111
American Civil War (1861-5) 7:15
'American Hogarth, The' *see*
  Sloan, John
American in Paris, An (Minnelli,
  1951) 9:71
American Revolution 4:106;
  5:72-3; 6:72-4
Amiens, Treaty of (1802) 6:111

Amsterdam 3:70, 71, 78, 104
  administrative body 3:101
  art public in 3:*102*, 102-103
  canals 3:102, *102*
  harbour 3:*101*
  history of the city 3:*103*
  16th-century 3:*100*
  17th-century 3:100-103
  Town Hall controversy 3:82
Amsterdam Couple, An (Codde)
  3:101
Anabaptists 1:135, *135*
Anarchist terrorists 7:*102*,
  103-104
Anatomy of a Horse (Stubbs)
  6:141
*Anatomy Lesson of Dr Sebastian
  Egbertsz, The* (de Keyser)
  3:86
Anatomy Lesson of Dr Tulp, The
  (Rembrandt) 3:79, 84, *84*
Andelys, Les, France
  4:*12*
Anderson, Hans Christian
  6:*138*
Andrée, Ellen: by Degas 7:*62*
  by Renoir 7:*118-19, 124-5*
Andrians, The (Titian) 2:111,
  114-15
*Angel and the Virgin of the
  Annunciation, The* (Van Eyck)
  1:*62*
Anglo-Dutch Treaty (1654)
  3:136, 138
Anglo-Dutch Wars
  (1652-4) 3:103
  (1655-7) 3:72-4
Anglo-French Treaty (1655)
  3:106
Anglo-Iranian Oil Company
  8:42
Anglo-Spanish Treaty (1630)
  3:40-41
Animal Locomotion (Muybridge)
  7:68
Anna and the Blind Tobit (Dou)
  3:140
Anna of Saxony 3:12
Anne, Queen of England, and
  Bath 6:69
Anne of Austria, Queen of
  France 3:73,138
Annunciation, The (Leonardo)
  2:20-21
  drapery study for 2:30
Antichrist, coming of the 1:*133*,
  134
Antiochus and Stratonice (David)
  4:76, *82*
Antiope (Correggio) 2:140
'Antiquity Smith' 6:77
antiseptic 7:40
Antwerp, Belgium 3:12, 16, 23, 44
Antwerp Cathedral 1:*138*; 3:23

painters' guild 3:13
  Rubens' house 3:*15*
  sack of 3:*68-9*
Apelles 2:111
Apollinaire, Guillaume 8:46
  and Cubism 8:69
  and Futurism 8:80
  and World War I 8:47
  calligrammes 8:71
Apollo and Daphne (sculpture,
  Bernini) 4:*38*
Apollo and Daphne (Poussin)
  4:*17*
Apollo Belvedere 2:*102*
  (sculpture)
  as inspiration for Reynolds
  6:14, 19, 24, 38
Apotheosis of Hercules
  (Lemoyne) 5:140
Apotheosis of Homer, The
  (Ingres) 4:112
Apotheosis of Napoleon, The
  (sketch, Ingres) 4:*131*
Apotheosis of Winckelmann
  (Vien) 4:141
apprentices
  assignments 1:100-101
  dependence on 1:102
  guild regulations for 1:103
  time to learn drawing 1:103
  training 1:102-103
  value of 1:101
apprenticeships
  Chardin's 5:44
  Claude's 4:44, *44*
  Fragonard's 5:108-109
  length of 1:101
  Manet's 7:12
  Modigliani's 8:111
  Poussin's 4:12
  Rembrandt's 3:77
  Renoir's 7:108-109
  Rubens' 3:13
  Sargent's 9:77
  Watteau's 5:12
Arc de Carrousel, Paris 4:133
Arc de Triomphe, Paris 4:133,
  133
Archduke Albert, Portrait of
  (Rubens) 3:*15*
Archer, Fred 7:*69*
Archers' Guild, Louvain,
  altarpiece for *see Deposition,
  The*
  commission for Van der
  Weyden 1:78-9
Arcola, Battle of (1796) 5:*136-7*
Aretino, Pietro 2:*113*, 116
Aretino, Portrait of (Titian) 2:*113*
Argenteuil, France 7:132
  Sunday trips to 7:133
Argenteuil, Jean Marcotte 4:111
Ariosto, Ludovico 2:121; 5:114
Aristotle Contemplating a Bust of

Homer (Rembrandt) 3:*94*
Arlecchino (Harlequin in
  Commedia dell'Arte) 5:37, *37*
Arlington, Lord 3:73
Armada, Spanish (1588) 2:135
Armory Show (1913) 9:11, 135
  Hopper and 9:109
  Matisse and 9:111, *111*
Arno Landscape (Leonardo) 2:*13*
Arnolfini, Giovanni: portrait
  by Van Eyck 1:*49*
  occupations 1:71
Arnolfini Wedding, The (Van
  Eyck) 1:*60*
  feeling of space in 1:50
  symbolism in 1:56, *60*
*Arrangement in Flesh Colour and
  Black: Portrait of Théodore
  Duret* (Whistler) 9:*33*
*Arrangement in Grey: Portrait of
  the Painter* (Whistler) 9:11
*Arrangement in Grey and Black:
  Portrait of the Artist's Mother*
  (Whistler) 9:26-7
  sale of 9:17
'Arrangements' 9:19
Art Institute of Chicago, and
  Hopper 9:111
Art Nouveau 9:37
Artist at Work, The (Van Loo)
  5:*81*
Artist's Daughters, The
  (Gainsborough) 6:46
Artist's Father, The (Constable)
  6:77
Artist's Mother, The (Constable)
  6:77
Artist's Mother, Portrait of the
  (Rembrandt) 3:76
Artist's Studio, The (Vermeer)
  3:114, 118-19, 126
  details 3:*118, 119*
Artist's Wife, The (Chardin) 5:47
artists and their wives 3:21, *21*
artists' colonies 9:100
Artois, Hotel d' 1:39
*Ascanius Shooting the Stag of
  Silvia* (Claude) 4:47, *67*
Ascent to Calvary (Bosch),
  reverse of 1:113
Ashcan School, The 9:*109*,
  132-5
  rejection of 9:133
Ashley, Anthony, Earl of
  Shaftesbury 4:74
Ashmole, Elias 4:74
Ashmolean Museum, Oxford
  4:74
Asquith, H. H. (British Prime
  Minister) 8:105, 106
assistants
  Claude and 4:44
  Hals and 3:47
  Rubens and 3:16, 17, 19-20

Assumption of the Virgin, The
  (Correggio) 2:140
Assumption of the Virgin, The
  (El Greco) 2:140
Assumption of the Virgin, The
  (Titian) 2:*109*, 110, 116, *124*
Astronomer, The (Vermeer)
  3:112, *129*
Atelier Carolus-Duran 9:77, 78
Atelier Suisse: Monet at 7:77
Attlee, Clement (British Prime
  Minister) 8:41
At the Piano (Whistler) 9:13, *18*
Attributs des Arts, Les (Chardin)
  5:48-9
Auberge Ganne, Chailly 7:132
Audiger, Jean 5:70
Audran, Claude *see Artists'
  Index*
Audubon, John James *see
  Artists' Index*
Augsburg, Peace of (1555)
  2:135
Aurelio, Niccolò, Chancellor of
  Venice 2:110, 118, 122
Austerlitz, Battle of (1805)
  6:136
Australia, gold in 7:*106*
Austria
  and First Coalition (1793) 4:104
  and Quadruple Alliance (1713)
  5:42
Austrian-French Alliance
  (1756) 5:*103*
Austrian Succession, War of
  the (1740-48) 5:105
Auteuil, France 7:66
Automat (Hopper) 9:*121*
Automobile Club (Italian),
  design by Boccioni 8:*77*
Autreau, Jacques 5:39
*Autumn Landscape with a
  View of Het Steen* (Rubens)
  3:*32*
Aved, Jacques *see Artists' Index*
Aved, Portrait of (Chardin) 5:47
Avignon Pietà, The 1:*85*
Awakening Slave, The
  (sculpture, Michelangelo)
  2:*51*

B

Babangi mask 8:52
Babeuf, 'Gracchus' 5:136, *137*
Baburen, Dirck van *see Artists'
  Index*
Bacchanal (Dossi) 2: *38-9*
*Bacchanalian Revel before a Term
  of Pan* (Poussin) 4:20-21
Bacchanals 4:20, 21, 26

Bacchantes 4:20
Bacchus, images of 4:21
Bacchus (sculpture, Michelangelo) 2:46
Bacchus and Ariadne (Titian) 2:111, *125*
background
    style of Limbourgs' 1:16
    in Van Eyck's work 1:49
Baker, The (Berckhyde) 3:134-5 *135*
Bakst, Léon 8:132, 134
    Schéhérazade 8:132-3
    programme design 8:134-5
Balanchine, George 8:135
Balcony, The (Manet) 7:17, *31*
Baldwin, Stanley (British Prime Minister) 8:73
Balfour, Arthur (British Prime Minister) 9:36
Balla, Giacomo *see Artists' Index*
Ballerina with a Bouquet, Curtseying (Degas) 7:50-51
Ballet Dancers in Butterfly Costumes (Degas) 7:52-3
    detail 7:52
Balletti, Manon 5:133
Ballets Russes 8:46, 47, 132-5
    influence of 8:132
    Matisse and 8:17
    and World War I 8:135
Balthasars, Digna 3:108
Banquet of the Officers of the St George Civic Guard Company (Hals) 3:45, 45, 52
Banquet of the Officers of the St Hadrian Civic Guard Company (Hals) 3:60-61
Banqueting House, Whitehall, London 3:16, 17, 40
Baptism of Christ, The (detail, Leonardo) 2:13
Bar at the Folies-Bergère, A (Manet) 7:21, 33
Barber of Seville (Rossini) 5:71, 73, 74
Barberini, Cardinal Francesco 4:14, 15, 24
Barbès, Armand 4:136
Barbier, Baron, by Renoir 7:118-19, 124-5
barges 6:98-9
Bario Chino, Barcelona 8:45
Barnard, Fred, and Broadway 9:101
Barnard, Polly and Dorothy, by Sargent 9:86-7
Barnes, Djuna 9:68
Barnes Foundation, Philadelphia 8:17
Barnum, P. T. 7:136
Barocci, Federico 4:20
Baroque, 3:19, 84; 4:15, 22, 36, 83

Barras, Paul François 5:136-7, *137*
Barry, Madame du 5:112, 124, 125
Barrias, Félix-Joseph 7:44
Bartholome, Paul, and Degas 7:49, *49*
Bas, Portrait of Agatha (Rembrandt) 3:85
Baseball League, founding of (1876) 7:70 ·
Basle, Treaty of (1795) 5:137
Basler, Adolphe 8:112-13
Bassano, Jacopo *see Artists' Index*
Bateau-Lavoir, Paris 8:46
Bath, England 6:68, 68-71, 70, 71
    Gainsborough in 6:46, 46, 47
Bath, The (Cassatt) 9:52
    detail 9:52-3
Bather, The (Lemoyne) 5:140
Bathers, The (Fragonard) 5:122
Bathers, The (Renoir) 7:114, 117
Bathsheba (Rembrandt) 3:95
Batoni, Pompeo 6:13
Battle of Anghiari, The (Leonardo) 2:30, 32, 77; 3:27
    copy by Rubens 2:18
Battle of Cascina, The (Michelangelo) 2:18
    preliminary study for 2:50
Battle of the Centaurs, The (Michelangelo) 2:45
Battle of Eylau (detail, Gros) 4:81
Battle of Spoleto, The (drawing, Titian) 2:114
Baudelaire, Charles 7:14, 34; 8:45
    on Ingres 4:117
Baudouin de Lannoy, Portrait of (Van Eyck) 1:56, 64
Baudouin, Portrait of Madame (Boucher) 5:80
Bazalgette, Joseph 9:41
Bazille, Frédéric 7:78, 140
    death of 7:80, 110
    and Gleyre 7:109
Beach, Sylvia 9:68, 70, 70
Beardsley, Aubrey 9:37
Beauchamp, Richard, Earl of Warwick 1:42
Beaumarchais, Pierre Augustin Caron 5:71, 73, 74
Beaumont, Sir George
    and Constable 6:76-7
    and Turner 6:112
beauty, ideal 4:117
Beauvais tapestry factory, Boucher and 5:78, 78
Beckett, Samuel 8:138
Beckford, William 6:110
Bed with Cupids (sketch,

Fragonard) 5:117
Bedford, Duke of (Gainsborough) 6:47
Bedouins (Sargent) 9:80
Beerbohm, Max, caricature of Whistler 9:16
Belgium, and the Congo 9:74
Belisarius Receiving Alms (David) 4:84
Bell, Alexander Graham 7:71, 104
Bell, Henry 6:105
Bellini Family, The (Degas) 7:44, 56
Bellini, Gentile *see Artists' Index*
Bellini, Giovanni *see Artists' Index*
Bellini, Jacopo *see Artists' Index*
Bellingham, John 6:103
Belshazzar's Feast (Rembrandt) 3:84-5
Bembo, Pietro 2:39, 112
Benedict XIII, Pope, and Great Schism 1:42
Benois, Alexander 8:132
Benton, Thomas Hart *see Artists' Index*
Bérard, Paul 7: 110, 111
Berckhyde, Job *see Artists' Index*
Bergson, Henri, 8:84
Bernhardt, Sarah 9:36
Bernini, Gian Lorenzo *see Artists' Index*
Bernis, Cardinal de 5:134
Berry and Burgundy, rivalry between 1:36
Berthe Morisot with a Bunch of Violets (Manet) 7:17, 140
Bertoldo di Giovanni 2:44
Betrothal of the Virgin, The (Raphael) 2:86
Betty, William 6:135
Between Two Fires (Millet) 9:100-101
Bevan, Aneurin 8:41
Biancolelli, Domenico 5:38, 39
Bicêtre, Château de 1:14, 16
    Limbourg murals in 1:14, 18
Bicknell, Maria (Mrs John Constable) 6:78, 79, 80-81
    tomb of 6:81
bicycles, first mass-produced 9:74
Billy Budd (Britten) 8:42
binding method, vellum books 1:20
Bingham, George Caleb *see Artists' Index*

Binnenhof 1:44
Biondi, Flavio 2:102
Birnie-Philip family 9:16-17
Birth of Bacchus, The (La Hyre) 4:141
Birth of John the Baptist (Ghirlandaio) 2:44
Birth of the Virgin, The (Murillo) 3:106
Bismarck, Otto von 7:138; 9:73
Black Death 1:133
'Black Thursday' (24 October, 1929) 9:136-7, 137
black paint, base for 1:21
    Hals' use of 3:52
Black Sun press, Paris 9:70-71
Blackwall Dock, London 6:131
Blake, Admiral Robert 3:106
Blake, William *see Artists' Index*
Blasco, José Ruiz 8:44
Blashfield, Edwin, and Broadway 9:101
Blenheim Park, Oxfordshire 4:71
Blessings of Peace (Rubens) 3:40
Blind Man's Buff (Fragonard) 5:112, 128
Blind Orion Searching for the Rising Sun (Poussin) 4:33
Bloemaert, Abraham
    Boucher and 5:83
Blois, Castle of, France 3:38-9
Blue Boy, The (Gainsborough) 6:47, 61
blue paint (ultramarine): base material for 1:21, 101
    Cassatt and 9:55
    in Limbourgs' work 1:20, 21
    Rubens' use of 3:20
    Van Eyck's method with 1:102-103
    Vermeer's use of 3:114
    Whistler's use of 9:14
Blue Period (Picasso) 8:45-6, 51
    greatest inspiration in 8:52
    painting from 8:54
Blue Room, The (Cassatt) 9:46, 53, 58-9
Blue Window, The (Matisse) 8:20, 27
Blum, Leon 8:73
Blum, Réne 8:135
Boatbuilding (Constable) 6:84, 88
Boating (Manet) 7:20-21
Boating Party, The (Cassatt) 9:48, 53, 66-7
Boating Party, The (Monet), Cassatt and 9:48-9
Boccioni, Amelia 8:76
Boccioni, Cecilia 8:76
    by Boccioni 8:76
Boccioni, Raffaele 8:76

Boccioni, Umberto *see Artists' Index*
Bockelson, Jan 1:135
Böhm, Hans, preachings on the 'Last Day' 1:134
Bois de Boulogne, Paris 7:34, *34-5, 35,* 67
Bois de Vincennes, Paris 7:67
Boit, Edward Darly 9:*90*
daughters painted by Sargent 9:*90*
Boldoni, Giovanni *see Artists' Index*
bole (paint primer) 1:100
Boleyn, Anne, Queen of England 2:74
Bolnes, Catharina 3:109
by Vermeer 3:*109*
Bolognese Academy 6:36
Bolt, The (Fragonard) 5:113, *130-31*
Bonaparte, Josephine 4:130, 131-2; 5:136-8
Bonaparte, Laetitia 4:*132*
Bonaparte, Louis-Napoleon (Emperor Napoleon III) 4:118, 136
Bonaparte, Napoleon *see* Napoleon Bonaparte (Napoleon I)
Bonaparte as First Consul (Ingres) 4:*120*
Bonnard, Pierre *see Artists' Index*
'Book of Truth' (Claude) *see Liber Veritatis*
Books of Hours
comparisons 1:21
contents 1:16, 21
Booth, John Wilkes 9:*38*
Booth, Sophia, Turner and 6:*112,* 113
Borghese, Cardinal Scipione 4:38
Borgia family 2:36-9, 40-41
Cesare 1:136; 2:18, 36-9, 41, 104
Juan 2:37-8
Lucrezia 2:36-9
Roderigo *see* Alexander VI, Pope
Borodino, Battle of (1812) 6:*106*
Borromini, Francesco *see Artists' Index*
Boscawen, Admiral 5:*105*
Bosch, Hieronymus *see Artists' Index*
'Bosie' *see* Douglas, Lord Alfred
Boston, Massachusetts 3:40; 6:40, 41-2
founding of 3:*40*
Library murals 9:79-80, *81,* 84-5

Boswell, James 6:14, 16, 42
Both, Andries 4:46
Both, Jan 4:46
Botticelli, Sandro *see Artists' Index*
Bottini, Francesco *see Artists' Index*
Bottle of Vieux Marc, Guitar, Glass and Newspaper (Picasso) 8:58-9
Boucher, François *see Artists' Index*
Boucher, Portrait of Madame (Boucher) 5:*79*
Boucher, Nicolas 5:76
Boudin, Eugène *see Artists' Index*
Boughton, George, and Broadway, England 9:101
Bougival 7:*132,* 133
Bouguereau, Adolphe 8:12, 9:132
Bouillon, Duc de 4:54
Boulevard des Capucines, exhibition in 7:47
Boulevard des Capucines (Monet) 7:*90*
Boulevard Montmartre, The (Pissarro) 7:*84*
'boulevardiers' 7:34
Boulton, Matthew 5:73
Bourges, France
cathedral 1:*13*
under siege 1:16, *39*
Bouts, Dirck *see Artists' Index*
Boy Dressed as a Pierrot (Fragonard) 5:*115*
Boy Playing a Flute, A (Leyster) 3:*47*
Boy with a Flute (Hals) 3:*52*
detail 3:*53*
Brabant, Duchy of 1:*12*
Brahe, Tycho 2:*136*
Bramante, Donatello d'Angelo *see Artists' Index*
Bramantino (Bartolomeo Suardi) 2:78
Bramer, Leonaert
and Vermeer 3:108, 109
Brancusi, Constantin *see Artists' Index*
Brant, Isabella 3:15
death of 3:17
Portrait of (Rubens) 3:*14*
Braque, Georges *see Artists' Index*
Braque Triptych, The (Van der Weyden) 1:*84*
right wing 1:*80*
use of landscape in 1:84
Brasserie des Martyrs, Paris 7:77
Brazil 3:136, *137*
Breakfast, The (Metsu) 3:*21*

Breakfast, in the Loggia (Sargent) 9:*83*
Brethren of the Common Life 1:109
Breton, André, on Picasso 8:48
Briand, Aristide 9:136
Bride and Groom, The (Modigliani) 8:*122*
Bridge, The (Boucher) 5:*94*
Bridge at Argenteuil, The (Monet) 7:*91*
Brighton, Sussex 6:79, 82, 96
Brighton Pavilion 6:79
Bril, Paul 4:44
Brioche, The (Chardin) 5:*67*
Brissot, Jacques 4:105
Britain 5:105-106, 138; 8:74
attacks on the monarchy 4:138
Chartism in 4:136-8
constitutional conflict (1911) 8:105-106
expansion of trade 6:130-33
Festival of (1951) 8:*40,* 41
and First Coalition (1793) 4:104
General Elections (1906) 8:138; (1865) 9:41-2
and Napoleon 6:135-6
plague (1665) 3:74
and Quadruple Alliance 5:42
and Russian invasion of Turkey 9:73
and Senegal 5:*106*
and Seven Years War (1756-63) 5:105
and Spanish Civil War (1936-9) 8:72, 73
state of visual arts in 6:36-7
and the Thirteen Colonies 5:72-3
Trades Disputes Bill (1906) 8:138
war with France 4:106, *106*
war with Holland (1652-4), (1655-7) 3:73, *73-4,* 103
war with USA (1812) 6:72-4, *106*
see also England
Britten, Benjamin 8:42
Broadway, Worcestershire 9:*100-101*
lifestyle in 9:101-103
Sargent and 9:79
Broadway Group 9:100-103
Brockman Family and Friends in the Rotunda at Beachborough Manor, The (Haytley) 4:70-71
Broken Pitcher, The (Greuze) 5:140
Bronzino, Agnolo *see Artists' Index*
Brook, The (Sargent) 9:*83*

Brooklyn Museum, and Hopper 9:110
Brooks, Louise 9: *138*
Brotherhood of Our Lady 1:110
Bosch altarpiece for 1:110-111
Brouwer, Adriaen *see Artists' Index*
Brown, Capability (Lawrence) 4:71, *71*
Bruegel, Jan *see Artists' Index*
Bruegel, Pieter, the Elder *see Artists' Index*
Bruges, port of, Belgium 1:45, 68-9, *71*
decline of 1:71
early history 1:68-9
figures on City Hall 1:*47*
finance in 1:70-71, *71*
merchandize 1:69-70, *70*
merchant class in 1:*70*
tournaments in 1:71
trade in 1:69, 69-70
wealth of 1:68
Brummell, George (Beau) 6:33, *102*
Brummel Children, The (Reynolds) 6:*33*
Brunelleschi, Filippo 2:102
brushes, for illuminating 1:21
Brussels official painter *see* Weyden, Rogier van der
Brutus Receiving the Bodies of His Sons (David) 4:78, 84, *84-5*
Buat, Seigneur de 3:73-4
Buen Retiro Palace, Madrid 4:45
Buchellm, Aernout van, on Rembrandt 3:78
Bugatto, Zanetto, and Van der Weyden 1:*78*
Bukharin Nikolay, expelled from Politburo 9:138
'Bulgarian massacre' (1878) 9:73
Bunker Hill, Battle of (1775) 5:71, *72-3*
'Bunthorne' 9:35
Buonarotti, Michelangelo *see* Michelangelo Buonarotti
Burckhardt, Charlotte Louise 9:81
by Sargent 9:81, *82-3*
Burgess, Guy 8:42, *42*
Burgundy
family conflict in 1:38-9
life at court of 1:*38-9*
territories 1:38
Burke, Edmund 6:16, 38
on Reynolds' funeral 6:17
Burlington House, Piccadilly, London 6:39
Burne-Jones, Sir Edward *see Artists' Index*

Buron, Jacques 4:76
Buseau, Marie-Jeanne 5:78, 78-9
Busoni, Portrait of Ferruccio (Boccioni) 8:99
Busoni, Portrait of Signora, (Boccioni) 8:80-81
Buttall, Jonathan 6:61
Buytewech, Willem *see Artists' Index*
Byrd, Richard 9:138
Byron, Lord George 6:104, 106
Byzantium (Istanbul, Turkey) 2:105

C

cabinets particuliers 7:35
Caboche 1:39
Cabral, Pedro Alvares, discovers Brazil 1:137, 138
'Cade's Rebellion' (1450) 1:106
Café Anglais 7:35
Café Guerbois 7:15, 32
Café Nouvelle Athènes 7:47, 62
Café Riche 7:34
Café Royal Set 9:37, 37
café society, 7:34-5, 35; 8:112, 112-13; 9:68-9, 69, 70
Caillebotte, Gustave, *see Artists' Index*
by Renoir 7:118-19, 124-5
Caine Mutiny, The (Wouk) 8:42
Cajoler, The (Watteau) 5:17
Calais Pier: an English Packet Arriving (Turner) 6:120
Calder, Alexander *see Artists' Index*
calligrames 7:71 (Apollinaire)
Calvin, John 2:106
Cambrai, League of (1508) 2:105, 106
camera obscura 3:114, 115
Limbourgs' use of 1:19
Vermeer and 3:116-17
Camille on her Deathbed (Monet) 7:83
Camoin, Charles 8:38
Campagna (sketch, Claude) 4:46-7
Campin, Robert *see Artists' Index*
Canada, Dominion of 7:40
Canaletto, Antonio *see Artists' Index*
Capello, Bianca 3:37
Capilla Real, Granada, works by Van der Weyden in 1:80
Capitano, Il 5:36-7, 37
Capitol, The, Rome 2:49

Capone, Al 9:137
Carline, Sidney *see Artists' Index*
Carlyle, Portrait of Thomas (Whistler) 9:17
Carnation, Lily, Lily, Rose (Sargent) 9:86, 91, 100, 103
Caroline Murat, Queen of Naples 4:111, 122
Carolus-Duran *see Artists' Index*
Carothers, Wallace H. 8:74
Carpaccio, Vittore *see Artists' Index*
Carracci, Annibale *see Artists' Index*
Carravaggio, Michelangelo Merisi da *see Artists' Index*
Carriera, Rosalba *see Artists' Index*
Carroll, Lewis 7:138
Cars, Jean-François 5:76-7
cartoons 2:26, 50, 66, 83, 84, 97
Carthusian Monk, A (Christus) 1:140
Caryatids (Modigliani) 8:111, 115
Casagemas, Carlos 8:45
Casanova, Giacomo 4:38; 5:86, 93, 132, 133-5, 135
Casati, Marchesa 8:103
Casimir, John, King of Poland 3:104
Cassatt, Alexander 9:49
Portrait of (Cassatt) 9:47
Cassatt, Gardner 9:49
Cassatt, Lydia 9:47
Cassatt, Mary *see Artists' Index*
Cassat, Robert Kelso, Portrait of (Cassatt) 9:50
Castel Sant 'Angelo, Rome 2:73, 48, 101
Castiglione, Baldassare 2:78, 82, 85
Portrait of (Raphael) 2:78
Catalonia, Spain 4:40, 41
Catanei, Vanozza 2:37
Catcher in the Rye (Salinger) 8:42
Catherine of Aragon, Queen of England 2:74, 104, 106
Catherine the Great, Empress of Russia 5:58, 74, 138; 6:40, 74
Cats' Rendezvous, The (Manet) 7:18
Cavalieri, Thomas 2:48
Caxton, William 2:42
Cazes, Pierre-Jacques *see Artists' Index*
Cellar Boy, The (Chardin) 5:68
Cenami, Giovanna 1:60
ceramics, Picasso and 8:52
Céret, Landscape of (Gris) 8:70

Ceuta, Morocco 1:42
Cézanne, Paul *see Artists' Index*
Chagall, Marc *see Artists' Index*
Chain Pier, Brighton (Constable) 6:96
Chamber of Assurance 3:101
Chamberlain, Neville (British Prime Minister) 8:73
Chambers, William 6:36, 37-9
Champaigne, Philippe de *see Artists' Index*
Champnol charterhouse 1:37
Channel tunnel, start of 7:74
Chantelou, Fréart de 4:17
Chantilly, Château de 1:17
Chapeau de Paille, Le (Rubens) 3:29
Chapel of the Rosary, Vence (Matisse) 8:16, 16, 17
technique for windows 8:16
Chapelle, Madeleine 4:110, 111
charcoal, Picasso and 8:50
Chardin, Jean 5:44
Chardin, Jean-Baptiste-Siméon *see Artists' Index*
Chardin, Portrait of (de la Tour) 5:48
Chardin, Jean-Pierre 5:46, 48-9
Chardin, Marguerite Agnès 5:46
Charge of the Lancers, The (Boccioni) 8:81
Chargot, Aline
and Renoir 7:111-12
by Renoir 7:111, 118
Charles the Bold, and Van der Weyden 1:77
Portrait of (Van der Weyden) 1:77
Charles, Duke of Orleans, imprisonment in England 1:41
Charles I, King of England 3:16, 17, 40, 41; 4:38, 40, 41-2, 74; 6:68
and Rubens 5:16, 16, 17
Charles I and Henrietta Maria Departing for the Chase (Mytens) 3:41
Charles I, Portrait of (detail, Van Dyck) 3:16
Charles II, King of England 3:41, 105, 106; 4:73-4
Charles III, King of Spain 5:74
Charles V, Emperor (Charles I of Spain) 2:48, 69, 72-4, 110-12, 117, 129, 132-5
Charles V on Horseback (Titian) 2:129, 135
Charles V, Portrait of (Titian) 2:132-3
Charles V, King of France, coronation 1:22
Charles VI, Emperor 5:42

Charles VI, King of France 1:36
Charles VII, King of France 1:104-105
coronation 1:74, 74
mistress of 1:106
Charles VIII, King of France 2:41, 46
Charles IX, King of France 2:136-7
Charles X, King of Sweden 3:104, 138
Charonton, Enguerrand *see Artists' Index*
Charterhouse, The (Gainsborough) 6:44, 45
Chartism 4:135, 136-8
Chastellain, Georges 1:70
'Chatelaine of the House Beautiful' 9:36
Château de Steen 3:17
Chateauroux, Duchesse de 5:101
Chatte, Le (Diaghilev) 8:135
Chaucer, Geoffrey 2:42
Chavannes, Puvis de *see Artists' Index*
Cheneau, Marie-Anne 5:68
Chevrot, Jean, Bishop of Tournai
altarpiece for 1:92-3
and Van der Weyden 1:78
Chicago, great fire of (1871) 7:135
'Chicago Whitey' *see* Luks, George
Chiesa Nuova, Rome 3:14, 15
childhood, images of 6:20-21, 32, 33
Chile, war with Spain (1866) 9:14
China, revolution in (1911) 8:105, 105
Chinese motifs 5:14
Boucher and 5:83-4
Chirico, Georgio de 8:134
Chocolatière, La (Liotard) 5:71
Chocquet, Victor
and Renoir 7:111
by Renoir 7:114
Choiseul, Duc de 5:104
Choisy, Château de 5:48, 49
cholera epidemic (1892) 7:103, 104
Christ Carrying the Cross (Bosch) 1:112-13
Christ and the Money-Lenders (Bassano) detail 2:112
Christ in the House of Martha and Mary (Aertsen) 5:52
Christ in the House of Mary and Martha (Vermeer) 3:112, 112
Christian I, King of Denmark, elected King of Norway 1:104, 105

Christiana, Queen of Norway 7:80

Christina, Queen of Sweden 3:*136*, 137-8; 4:*36*, 135, 136-8

Christus, Petrus *see Artists' Index*

Church Interior, Haarlem (Saenredam) 3:*47*

Church of England 2:106

City Art Museum of St Louis, and Hopper 9:111

City Rises, The (Boccioni) 8:84, 86, *86-7*, *92-3*
   colour studies 8:*87*

Civil War, English 3:41

Clain, Château de 1:*30*

Classical versus Romantic 4:112

Claude Lorrain *see Artists' Index*

Claude Monet Painting at the Edge of a wood (Sargent) 9:*84-5*
   detail *85*

Clavius, Christopher 2:138

Clemenceau, Georges
   death of 9:138
   and Monet 7:81

Clemens, Samuel Langhorne *see* Twain, Mark

Clement VII, Pope 2:48, 73-4, 134

Clement VIII, Anti-pope 1:*74*

Cleopatra's Needle, London 9:*72*

clergy, conduct of in Middle Ages 1:*132*, 132-3

Clermont, Comte de 5:104

Clinton, Sir Henry 6:73

Cluny, France 1:38

Clyde River, Scotland 6:105

coal gas 6:135

Coast Scene with a Fight on a Bridge (sketch, Claude) 4:*51*

Coast View of Delos with Aeneas (Claude) 4:*68-9*

Coastal Survey, Washington, Whistler at 9:18

Cochin, Charles-Nicolas, the Elder *see Artists' Index*

Cochin, Charles-Nicolas, the Younger *see Artists' Index*

Cocteau, Jean 9:*138*
   and the Ballets Russes 8:134
   Les Enfants Terrible 9:*138*
   in Paris 9:69
   and Picasso 8:46, 47
   Parade 8:*134-5*
   drop curtain for (Picasso) 8:*46*

Codde, Pieter *see Artists' Index*

Cold War, the 8:41-2

collage *see papiér-collés*

Collettes, Les 7:113, *113*

Collins, Lottie 7:*106*

Collioure, France 8:14, *14-15*

Cologne, Germany 3:*12*

Colombe, Jean *see Artists' Index*

Colonna, Lorenzo Onofrio 4:47

Colonna, Vittoria 2:49
   Portrait of (Piombo) 2:*49*

colours/pigments
   acquiring 1:100
   base materials for 1:21, *101*
   Cassatt's use of 9:52, 53
   Chardin's use of 5:53
   effect of light on 9:79
     in Mediterranean 8:14, 15, 36
   Fauves' use of 8:14
   Gauguin on 8:20
   making for illuminating 1:21
   Matisse and 8:18-19
   mixing 1:100
   Modigliani and 8:115
   Netherlandish technique 1:101
   Picasso and 8:52
   Rubens' use of 3:*20*
   Sargent and 9:79
   Vermeer and 3:114

colour harmonies 9:20, *20*

Columba Triptych, The (Van der Weyden) 1:*78*, *94-5*

Columbus, Christopher 1:136; 2:*40-41*, 41-2
   and New World 1:137

'Comanche' 7:73

Combing the Hair (Degas) 7:*65*

Comédie Française, The 5:30, 35

Comité d'Etudes du Haut Congo 9:74

Commedia dell'Arte 5:13, 14, *15*, 18, 19, 31, 32, *36-7*, *38-9*

Committee of Public Safety 4:105

Common Market (European Economic Community) 8:40

Communism, champion of 5:*137*

Company of Captain Roelof Bicker, The (Van der Holst) 3:*88-9*

Company of the St George Civic Guard, The (Van der Holst) 3:*70-71*

Compte rendu (Necker) 6:74

Comte de Turenne (David) 4:*83*

Comtesse d'Haussonville, The (Ingres) 4:*128*

Concert, The (Vermeer) 3:*125*

Concert in the Tuileries Gardens (Manet) 7:*14*

concerts, open-air 7:34

Concini, Carlos 3:*38*

Condé, Louis II de Bourbon, Prince of 3:138

Condor Legion 8:72

Confirmation (Poussin) 4:*28*

Congreve's rockets 6:137

Conjurer, The (Bosch) 1:*120-21*

Constable, Abram 6:76, 80

Constable, Ann 6:77

Constable, Golding 6:76, 77, 98

Constable, John *see Artists' Index*
   Portrait of (Reinagle) 6:*75*

Constantijn Huygens and his Secretary (de Keyser) 3:*79*

Constantine, Arch of, Rome 2:*101*

Constantine the Great, Roman Emperor 2:68, *69*, *101*

Constantini, Angelo 5:32

Conte, Jacopo del *see Artists' Index*

'Continental Congress' (1775) 5:73

contract, taking out a 1:101

contrapposto 2:52-3, *53*

'Convention of the Industrial Classes' (1839) 4:136-7

conversation pieces 6:*50*, 52, *52*

Cook, Captain James 2:72; 6:40, 42

Coote, Sir Eyre 6:73

Cope, Charles West *see Artists' Index*

Copley, John Singleton *see Artists' Index*

Corbusier, Le
   Villa Savoie 9:137

Corday, Charlotte 4:86, *87*, *102*, 102-103, 105

Corelli, Arcangelo 3:138

Coresus Sacrificing Himself to Save Callirhoé (Fragonard) 5:*110*, 111

Cornard Wood (Gainsborough) 6:*84*

Corneille, Pierre 4:20

Corneille, Thomas 5:14

Cornelius, Albrecht, contract agreements 1:101

Cornfield, The (Constable) 6:*95*

Cornwallis, General Charles 6:72, 73, 74

Coronation of the Virgin, The (Quarton) 1:*141*

Corot, Camille 7:17

Corot, Jean-Baptiste *see Artists' Index*

Corpore, De (Hobbes) 3:*106*

Correggio, Antonio *see Artists' Index*

Correspondence School of Illustrating, New York 9:108

Corsica 6:42; 8:12

Cosa, Juan de la, map of the known world 1:137, *137*

Cossacks 3:137, 138

Costa, Lorenzo 4:15

'Costume Book' (Rubens) 3:*13*

Cotman, John Sell *see Artists' Index*

Cottage Girl with Dog and Pitcher, The (Gainsborough) 6:*64*

Cotton Exchange, New Orleans, The (Degas) 7:*46*

cotton gin, invention of 4:106

Council of the Church 1:42
   and John Huss 1:42

Count Ugolino and his Children (Reynolds) 6:*17*

Counter-Reformation, Roman Catholic 4:36

Countess of Bressingham, The (Lawrence) 9:*84*

Country Dance, The (Watteau) 5:*16*

Courbet, Gustave *see Artists' Index*

court painter, duties of 1:45

Courtyard in Delft (de Hooch) 3:*135*

Courtyard Scene (de Hooch) 3:*103*

Couture, Thomas 7:12

Coypel, Nicolas 5:44

Coysevox, Antoine *see Artists' Index*

Cox, David *see Artists' Index*

Cozens, John Robert 6:109

Cracow, fall of (1655) 3:*104*

Cradle, The (Morisot) 9:*53*

Crane, Hart 9:68

Crane, Walter, *Shilling Toy Books* 9:*36*

crayon, Picasso and 8:50

Creation of Adam (Michelangelo) 6:*13*

'Creator of Baroque' 3:*19*

Credi, Lorenzo di *see Artists' Index*

Crefeld, Battle of (1758) 5:104

crinolines 7:36

Cromwell, Oliver 3:*105*, 105-106, 136

crop rotation 6:99, 100

Crosby, Caresse 9:71

Crosby, Harry 9:68, 71

Crome, John ('Old Crome') *see Artists' Index*

Cross, Henri Edmond *see Artists' Index*

Crowning with Thorns, The (Bosch) 1:*121*, 129

Crozat, Pierre 5:13, 14, 17

Crucifixion, The (Van der Weyden) 1:80, *96*
   use of landscape in 1:84
   technique in 1:81

Cruel Sea, The (Monsarrat) 8:42

Crystal Palace, London 9:40

Cubism 8:80
   aims of 8:69
   Analytical 8:69, 71
   methods 8:71
   development of 8:46, 68-71

first canvases 8:68
foundation stone of 8:56-7
importance to Boccioni 8:85
Modigliani and 8:110
Picasso and 8:52, *64-5*
Synthetic 8:71
Parade 8:134-5
Cuer d'Amour Espris, Le
(René Master) 1:141
Cumming, Dr John 7:39
cummings, e.e. 9:68, 69
Cunard, Samuel 4:137
Cup of Tea, The (Cassatt) 9:55
Cupid and Psyche (Gérard) 4:140
Cupid and Psyche (Natoire)
5:141
Cupid Seller (Vien) 4:141
Cure of Folly, The (Bosch) 1:*112*
symbolism in 1:114
Curtis family, and Sargent 9:78
Custer's Last Stand (Paxson)
7:*72-3*
Cut Melon, The (Chardin) 5:*65*,
66
Czechoslovakia 6:*136*
Czechowska, Lunia, on
Modigliani 8:117

D

Da Vinci, Leonardo *see*
Leonardo da Vinci
Daguerre, Louis-Jacques-
Mandé 4:*137*
Dammartin, Guy de 1:14
Dampierre, Château of,
France 4:*112-13*
Danaë (Titian) 2:115, 130
Danby, Sarah 6:110
dance, images of 4:20, *20*
Dance (Matisse) 8:15, 20, 21, *21*
Dance in the Country (detail,
Renoir) 7:*111*
Dance in the Town (Renoir)
7:*127*
Dance to the Music of Time
(Poussin) 6:22, *23*
Dancers at the Ball (Severini)
8:*103*
Dancing Class, The (Degas) 7:*54*,
60
details 7:*54*
perspective of 7:*55*
*Dancing Couple, Bagpiper and
Eight Other Figures* (Watteau)
5:*29*
'Dancing Mania' 1:*133*
Dancourt, Florence 5:22
Danton, Georges-Jacques 4:105
Daret, Jacques 1:76
and Campin's work 1:102

Darwin, Charles 7:*135*
Descent of Man 7:*135*
On the Origin of Species 7:*135*
Das Kapital (Marx) 7:42
Daughters of Edward D. Boit, The
(Sargent) 9:78, *90*
David (sculpture,
Michelangelo) 2:46, 52, *55*,
77
David, Gerard *see Artists' Index*
David, Jacques-Louis *see Artists'*
Index
Dawn after the Wreck (Turner)
6:*128*
'Day of Dupes' (1630) 3:39, 42
Dead Christ, The (Mantegna)
2:*140*
Dead Toreador, The (Manet)
7:*18-19*
Dead Wolf, The (Oudry) 5:*46*
Death of Dido, The (Reynolds)
6:17, *18-19*
Death of Germanicus, The
(Poussin) 4:15, *24-5*, 84
Death of Leonardo, The (Ingres)
2:19
Death of Marat, The (David)
4:84, *86-7*, 93
details 4:*86, 87*
Death of St Peter Martyr (copy,
Titian) 2:*111*, 116
Death of Socrates, The (David)
4:84, *90-91*
Death of the Virgin, The (Van
der Goes) 1:141
Debussy, Claude 7:74
Decline of the West (Spengler)
9:106
Dedham, Suffolk 6:*76-7*, 98
Dedham Lock and Mill
(Constable) 6:*82-3*
Degas, Achille, by Degas 7:*46*
Degas, Edgar *see Artists' Index*
Degas, René 7:46
by Degas 7:*46*
Defoe, Daniel 6:70
on Bath, England 6:70
Déjeuner, Le (Boucher) 5:*90*
Déjeuner sur l'Herbe (Manet)
see Luncheon on the Grass, The
Déjeuner sur l'Herbe (series,
Picasso) 8:49
Delacroix, Eugène *see Artists'*
Index
Delaunay, Robert and Sonia *see*
Artists' Index
Delektorskaya, Lydia 8:17
Delft, Holland 3:108-109, 110
destruction of 3:*110-11*
'hooftman' of painters' guild
3:110
Delftware 3:*109*
Delhi Durbar (1911) 8:*104*, 106
Delphi, excavations at 7:*103*

Demoiselles d'Avignon, Les
(Picasso) 8:*46-7*, 52, *56-7*, 68
Demuth, Charles *see Artists'*
Index
Denis, Maurice 8:36
Picasso and 8:45
Denis Diderot (Van Loo) 5:*81*
Denmark, alliance with Dutch
(1625) 3:70
Deposition, The (Van der
Weyden) 1:78, 80-81, *90-91*
details 1:*98-9*
levels of reality 1:80-81
Depression, The 9:137, *137*
Derain, Andre *see Artists' Index*
Derby Day (Frith) 7:68, *68-9*
Deruet, Claude 4:44, 45
Desboutin, Marcellin 7:62
Descartes, René 3:47; 4:40
Discourse on Method 4:40
Portrait of (Hals) 3:*47*
Descent from the Cross, The
(Campin) 1:78
Descent from the Cross, The
(Rubens) 3:15, *22-3*, *24-5*
details 3: *22-3*
modello 3:22
Deshayes, Jean-Baptiste 5:80,
109
Desmaisons, Pierre 4:76, *76*
Portrait of (David) 4:76
Desportes, Alexandre-François
see Artists' Index
*Destruction of the Turkish
Transport* (Carline) 9:*105*
Detroit Institute of Art, and
Hopper 9:111
Deutsch, Niklaus Manuel *see*
Artists' Index
Development of a Bottle in Space
(sculpture, Boccioni) 8:83, 85
Devis, Arthur *see Artists' Index*
Devotio Moderna 1:109
Diaghilev, Serge 8:46, 47, *132*
and artists 8:134
and the Ballets Russes
8:*132-5*
death of 9:138
Miro and 8:134
Diana, images of 5:*84-5*
Diana and her Companions
(Vermeer) 3:112
Diana after Bathing (Boucher)
5:*84*; 7:*117*
detail 5:*85*
Diana the Huntress (School of
Fontainebleau) 5:*85*
Diaz, Narcisse, on Renoir's
colour 7:114
Diderot, Denis 5:50, 54, 67, 80,
85, 111
on Chardin 5:53
on Fragonard 5:112
Portrait of (Van Loo) 5:*81*

Dido Building Carthage (Turner)
4:*53*
Dihau, Desiré 7:45, *57*
Dijon Cathedral 1:*37*
Diligent, Mother, The (Chardin)
5:*54*, *62*
Dilke, Sir Charles 7:*138*
Dining Table, The (Matisse) 8:*13*
Dircx, Geertge 3:80
Discourse on Method (Descartes)
4:40
Discovery of the Body of St Mark
(Tintoretto) 2:141
Disputà, The (Raphael) 2:84, 98
details 2:98
preliminary study 2:98
Disputation of St Catherine, The
(Pinturicchio) 2:36, 37
Disraeli, Benjamin (British
Prime Minister) 7:73
and India 7:73, 74
and Russian invasion of
Turkey 9:73
and the Suez Canal 7:73
Dissius, Jacob 3:111
distemper, Degas' use of 7:51
*Distribution of the Eagle
Standards* (David) 4:80
Divine Wrath, diverting the
1:133-4
Divisionism
Balla and 8:77
technique 8:83
Doctor's Visit, The (Steen) 3:*134*
Doge Loredano (Bellini) 2:140
Dogs, Dead Game and Fruit
(Desportes) 5:*46*
Dolce, Ludovico 2:82, 116
Dôme, The, Paris 8:*113-14*;
9:68, 70
domestic interiors 3:*116*, 135
domestic life 5:68-71
Donatello *see Artists' Index*
Donation of the Keys, The
(Perugino) 2:77, 83
Doni Tondo, The (sculpture,
Michelangelo) 2:50
Doni, Portrait of Agnolo
(Raphael) 2:87
Donne Triptych, The (Memlinc)
1:79
donors: in *Crucifixion* (Van der
Weyden) 1:84
in *Ghent altarpiece* 1:53
Dos Passos, John 9:68
Dossi, Dosso *see Artists' Index*
Dou, Gerard (Gerrit) *see Artists'*
Index
Doubleday, Abner 7:70
Douglas, Lord Alfred ('Bosie')
9:37
Dourdan, Château de 1:*27*
Downs, Battle of the (1639)
3:71

Doyen, Gabriel-François see
    Artists' Index
Drake, Sir Francis 2:136
drapery painters 6:21
'drawing in space' 8:52
Dream, The (Picasso) 8:63
Dream and Lie of Franco, The
    (Picasso) 8:48
Dream of Ossian (Ingres)
    4:111, 114
Dreamers (Moore) 9:20
Dreyfus, Captain Alfred
    8:136-7
Dreyfus Case 7:49; 8:136-7,
    136-7
driers, improvements in 1:50
'Drolleries' 3:133-4
Drouais, François-Hubert see
    Artists' Index
'Drummer of Niklashausen'
    see Böhm, Hans
Drury Lane Theatre, London
    6:104
Du Maurier, George
    and Aesthetic Movement
        9:35
    and Whistler 9:17
    Trilby 9:17
Dubrovska, Felia 8:135
Ducal Palace, Mantua art
    collection 3:14
Duchamp, Marcel see Artists'
    Index
Dufy, Raoul see Artists' Index
Dughet, Anne-Marie 4:16
Dughet, Gaspard see Artists'
    Index
Dughet, Jacques 4:15
Duke of Lerma (Rubens) 3:13
Dumas, The Lady of the
    Camellias 7:37
Duncan, Isadora 8:132
Dunthorne, John, and
    Constable
Dupont, Gainsborough 6:49,
    76, 80, 82
Duquesnoy, François 4:16
Durand-Ruel, Paul
    and the Impressionists 7:79
        exhibitions 7:80
    and Manet 7:16
    and Monet 7:79, 80
    and Renoir 7:110
    see also Galerie Durand-Ruel
Duranty, Edmond 7:16
Dürer, Albrecht see Artists'
    Index
Dutch Colony in Brazil, A (Post)
    3:136-7
Dutch East India Company
    3:101, 101
Dutch Exchange Bank 3: 100,
    101
Dutch Independence 3:68-71

Dyck, Anthony Van see Artists'
    Index
Dying Slave, The (sculpture,
    Michelangelo) 2:53
Dynamism of a Cyclist
    (sketch, Boccioni) 8:83
Dynamism of a Human Body
    (Boccioni) 8:97, 98

E

Eakins, Thomas see Artists' Index
Early Sunday Morning (Hopper)
    9:110, 122-3
East Bergholt, Suffolk 6:76-7,
    82, 83, 84, 100
    labourers from 6:101
East Bergholt House (Constable)
    6:76
East India Company 3:101;
    6:131, 132
East India Docks, London
    6:130
Ecce Homo (Bosch) 1:123
Eckener, Hugo 9:138
Ecole des Beaux-Arts 7:77; 8:12
    Ingres and 4:109, 113
    Japanese exhibition at 9:47-8,
        48
Ecole des Elèves Protéges,
    Fragonard at 5:109
Ecole Quentin de la Tour 8:12
Edict of Restitution (1629) 3:42
Edinburgh Festival 8:41
Edward VII, King of England,
    and the Wyndham sisters 9:95
Edward Jenner giving the first
    vaccinations (satirical cartoon,
    Gillray) 6:103
Effects of War, The (Rubens)
    3:69
Egremont, George O'Brien,
    3rd Earl of 6:110, 113
Egypt 6:138
    Khedive of 9:74
    and Suez Canal 7:70, 73
    Pasha of 7:38-9
Egyptian Curtain, The (Matisse)
    8:20, 33
'Eidophusikon', the 6:48, 51
Eiffel, Gustave, and Panama
    Canal scandal 7:106
'Eight, The' 9:133-4
El Greco see Artists' Index
Elasticity (Boccioni) 8:8
Elder, Louisine 9:45
Eleanora of Toledo and her Son
    Giovanni (Bronzino) 4:117
Eleven a.m. (Hopper) 9:120
Elgin, Thomas Bruce, Earl of
    6:105

Elgin Marbles, The 6:105
Eliot, Sir John 3:41
Eliot, T. S. 9:70
Elizabeth I, Queen of England
    1:137; 6:68
Elle, Ferdinand 4:12
Ellen Terry as Lady Macbeth
    (Sargent) 9:93
Elsheimer, Adam 4:50
    and Rubens 3:14
Eluard, Paul 8:48
Embarkation of St Ursula (sketch,
    Claude) 4:50, 51, 54
emblem book 3:55
emblems 3:50-51, 55
    in Hals' work 3:50-51
Emmie and her Child (Cassatt)
    9:51
Empire Style 4:132, 133
Enchanted Castle, The (Claude)
    4:53, 65
Endymion (Girodet de Roucy-
    Trioson) 4:140
Empress Isabella, Portrait of the
    (Titian) 2:133
England
    anti-German feeling in 7:138
    enthusiasm for Watteau 5:21
    grey squirrel reaches 7:74
    and Holland 3:69, 70, 103
    invasion of 1:36
    loss of French territories
        1:104-105
    and Napoleon III 7:40
    racecourses 7:67, 68
    re-admission of Jews
        3:104-105
    relations with France 7:72-3
    in 1641 4:41-2
    and Suez Canal 7:73
    and West Indies 3:106
Engels, Friedrich 7:42
English Civil War 4:74
English Navigation Act (1651)
    3:103
English Prayer Book, The (of
    Church of England) 4:42
engraving
    Boucher and 5:76-7,77
    Picasso and 8:50
Enquiry Concerning Political
    Justice (Godwin) 4:106
Enseigne de Gersaint, L'
    (Watteau) 5:14, 18, 34-5
entente cordiale 8:138
Entombment, The (Raphael)
    2:89
Entombment, The (Titian) 2:115
Entombment of Atala (Girodet de
    Roucy-Trioson) 4:140
Entombment of Christ, The (oil
    sketch, Rembrandt) 3:85
Equestrienne, The (Modigliani)
    8:120

Erasmus, Desiderius 2:104
Erebus 4:137
Ernst, Max see Artists' Index
erotic art 5:111, 112, 114-17,
    118-19, 135
Escorial Palace, Madrid 2:135
Espolio, El (El Greco) 2:141
Este, Alfonso I d', Duke of
    Ferrara 2:37, 109, 110-11,
    114, 125
Este, Beatrice d' 2:15
Este, Marquis Leonello, d' and
    Van der Weyden 1:75
Estrées, Gabrielle d' 3:36
Et in Arcadia Ego (Poussin)
    4:16, 18-19
Etampes, Château d' 1:31
etching 3:86, 87
    cartographic 9:18
    Degas and 7:51
    drypoint 9:53
        Cassatt and 9:53
    Hopper and 9:114, 115
    invention of coloured 9:53
    Matisse and 8:15
    Rembrandt and 3:81, 84, 85, 86
    Whistler and 9:17, 18, 19, 23
Eulenspiegel, Till 1:136
Evelyn, John 3:132; 4:38
Evening Wind (Hopper) 9:115
Execution of Maximilian, The
    (Manet) 7:29
Exhibition of Degenerate Art
    8:72-3
Exhibition of Independent
    Artists 9:135
Exposition de la Jeunesse,
    Chardin and 5:45
Exposition Universalle 8:14
Expressionism, Picasso and
    8:48
Extreme Unction (Poussin) 4:15,
    (1644) 4:29
Eyck, Hubert van see Artists'
    Index
Eyck, Jan van see Artists' Index

F

Fabri de Peiresc, Nicolas-
    Claude, on Rubens 3:14
Fabriano, Gentile da see Artists'
    Index
Fabritius, Carel see Artists' Index
Fagus factory (Gropius) 8:106
Fall of the Damned, The
    (Rubens) 3:19
Fall of the House of Usher, The (Poe)
    4:138
Falstolf, Sir John 1:73
Family Group (Hals) 3:52

Family Group in a Landscape (Hals) 3:*64, 65*
Family of George, 4th Duke of Marlborough, The (Reynolds) 6:*18*
fancy pictures 5:112, 114, 116
Fantin-Latour, Henri *see Artists' Index*
Farmland Views near East Bergholt (Constable) 6:*83*
Farnese, Alexander, Duke of Parma 3:68
Farnese, Cardinal Alessandro 2:*111*
Farnese, Giulia 2:41
Farnese Hercules, The 6:38
Farnese, Isabella 5:*40,* 42
Farnese, Portrait of Ranuccio (Titian) 2:*114*
Farriner, Thomas 3:74
Fascism, rise of 8:73-4
fashions
　French Court 7:36-7
　influence on male 7:37
　influence on women's 7:36-7, *37*
Fate of Tityus, The (Michelangelo) 2: *48*
Father of the Family Reading from the Bible (Greuze) 5:140
Fauvism 8:12, 14, *14-15,* 23
　birthplace of 8:*14-15*
　Braque and 8:68
　Matisse and 8:19
　use of colour 8:14
Fazio, on Van der Weyden 1:75
Feast of Venus, The (Rubens) 3:*34-5*
Feltham, Owen 3:70
'female gorilla' *see Olympia*
Femmes d'Algers, Les (Delacroix) 8:49
　series by Picasso 8:49
Ferdinand II, Holy Roman Emperor 3:40-41, 42
Ferdinand of Brunswick 5:104, 105
Ferdinand of Aragon, King of Spain 2:42, 105-106
Ferrara, Italy 2:15, 37, 39
Festival of Britain (1951) 8:40, 41
Fête Champêtre (Giorgionê) 5:*21, 28*
fête galante 5:13, 15, 16-21, 28
Fête in a Park (Watteau) 4:*20-21*
Fête at Rambouillet, The (Fragonard) 5:*114-15,* 118
Fêtes Venitiennes, Les (detail, Watteau) 5:*15*
Fichte, Johann 5:*137*
Fifer, The (Manet) 7:20, *78*
Fighting Temeraire, The (Turner) 6:113, *118-19, 124-5*

Figures de Différents Caractéres (after Watteau) 5:77
'figures de fantasie' 5:*116*
Fiorillo, Tiberio 5:38
Fire in the Borgo, The (Raphael) 2:*99*
　detail 2:*99*
fire brigades 9:39
　London's 9:*40*
Fire of London (1666) 3:72, 74
Firebird, The 8:134, *134*
First Cloud, The (Orchardson) 9:*116*
First Coalition (1793) 4:104
First Night Out, The (Renoir) 7:*122*
Fischer von Erlach, Johann, Karlskirche, Vienna 5:*42*
Fisher, Revd John 6:78, 80, 92
　Portrait of (Constable) 6:*78*
Fishermen at Sea (Turner) 6:110
Fishing for Souls (Van der Venne) 3:68
Fitting, The (Cassatt) 9:*64*
Fitzgerald, F. Scott 9:68, 69
flagellants 1:*132, 133*
Flanders
　Count of *see* Philip the Good
　importance of cloth industry 1:*68,* 69
'Flanders Fever' 9:105
Flatford Mill, Suffolk 6:*83,* 86, 88, 90, 98, *99*
Flatford Mill (Constable) 6:*89*
Flémalle, Master of *see* Campin, Robert
Fleury, Claude 5:70
Flink, Govert 3:82
Flitcroft, Henry 4:70
Floating Studio (Monet) 7:*78*
Florence, Italy 2:13-14, 32, 40-41, 44, 46-7, 51, 55, 73-4, 77; 6:36
flower paintings
　by Manet 7:19
　by Monet *see Waterlilies*
　by Renoir 7:115, 117
Flowers in a Vase (Chardin) 5:*51*
Foch, Marshal 9:138
Fokine, Mikhail 8:132-3
Folies Bergère, The 9:*74*
Fontainebleau, France 5:45, 46, 80-81, 85
　Château of 7:*130-31*
　　Chardin and 5:*45,* 46
　　French court at 7:32-3
　　Salle du Conseil 5:*80-81*
　Forest of 7:*108*
　　Impressionists and 7:114
　　inns of the 7:132-3
　School of 4:12
　　Diana the Huntress 5:*85*
　Sunday trips to 7:130-31, *130-31*

Fontana, Domenico 2:70
Forbes, General John 5:104, 106
foreshortening 2:50, 64
Forestier, Julie
　Portrait of (Ingres) 4:*109*
Forestier Family, The (sketch, Ingres) 4:*109*
Formigny, Battle of (1450) 1:105
Fornarina, La 2:*80,* 81
　Portrait of (Raphael) 2:*80*
Forum Romanum, Rome 2:*46-7, 100-101*
Fosse, Charles de la 5:14-15
Founding and Manifesto of Futurism, The 8:78, 100
Fountain of the Four Rivers, Rome 4:37, 38
Fountain of the Innocents, influence on Renoir 7:109
Four Arts Ball, Paris 9:71
Four Dancers (Degas) 7:*51*
Four Gallican Articles, The (1682) 4:72
Fouquet, Jean *see Artists' Index*
Fourment, Hélène 3:17
　Portrait of (Rubens) 3:*16-17*
Fournaise, Alphonsine
　Portrait of (Renoir) 7:*118-19, 124-5*
Fournaise, M.
　Portrait of (Renoir) 7:*118-19, 124-5*
Fournier, Edmond, and Manet 7:12
Fourth Discourse (Reynolds) 6:14, *15,* 16, 17
Fra Giocondo 2:69
Fraenger, Wilhelm, on Bosch's art 1:109
Fragonard, Alexandre-Evariste 5:113
Fragonard, François 5:108
Fragonard, Jean-Honoré *see Artists' Index*
France 4:104-106, 135-6; 5:40, 42, 102-103, 104-106, 136, 137-8
　attacks on the monarchy 4:138
　Cassatt on 9:44
　and Catholic Church 7:104-105
　Convention 4:101
　in 1839 4:134-8
　and Egypt 9:74
　and Germany 3:39
　and the Habsburg Empire 3:39, 41, 42
　invades Italy 5:*136-7,* 137-8
　and Morocco 8:104-105, 137
　Napoleonic coinage 4:*131*
　and North America 5:106
　pastimes for the rich 7:66-7

political instability 8:40
　and Quadruple Alliance 5:42
　racing in 7:67-8
　relations with England 7:72-3
　republicanism in 7:138
　religious conflict in 4:72-3
　Royalty in 7:*38-9*
　in 1796 5:136-8
　and Seven Years War 5:105
　and Spanish Civil War 8:72-3
　and Suez Canal 7:73
　territorial ambitions 7:40
　terrorists in 7:*102,* 103
　and Turkey 7:42
　and the United Provinces 3:69, 71
　see also French Republic, French Revolution, South of France
Francesco I, Grand Duke of Florence 3:37
Francis I, King of France 2:19, 72, 133, 134
Franco, General Francisco 8:48
Franco-Austrian Alliance (1756) 5:104
Franco-Prussian War (1871) 7:16, 46, *134*
　Renoir and 7:110
Frank K. M. Rehn Gallery, and Hopper 9:110
Franklin, Maud 9:15
　and Whistler 9:15, 17
Fréart de Chantelou, Paul 4:17, 28
Frederick, Elector Palatine of Bohemia 3:39, 42
Frederick the Great, King of Prussia 5:103, 104-105, 135
　and Watteau 5:21
Frederick, Prince of Wales, and his Sisters (Mercier) 6:*52*
Frederick Henry, Prince of Orange 3:78, 79, 85
Frederick William III, King of Prussia 4:81
Free Exhibition of Art, Milan 8:104
Free Trade, attack on 8:*136*
French Academy 4:76, 110, 111, 113; 5:47-8, 49, 77, 81
　Chardin and 5:45-6
　David and 4:78
　Ingres and 4:112
　Watteau and 5:14-15
French Government, and Matisse 8:17
French Republic 7:17, 135
　celebrations of centenary (1892) 7:105
　humiliation of 7:137-8
French Revolution (1789) 4:84, 85, 86, 92, 101-103, 104-105;

5:82, 83, *112-13*, 113, 135, 136
David and 4:*78*, 78-9
French Woman and her Maid, A (Liotard) 5:*68-9*
fresco 2:52-3; 3:20
Firth, W. P. *see Artists' Index*
Froment, Nicolas *see Artists' Index*
Fruits of the Midi (Renoir) 7:*126*
Fugitive Slave Act (1793) 4:106
Fulvio, Andrea 2:101, 103
Funeral of Phocion, The (Poussin) 4:32
Fust, Johann 1:*104*
Futurism 8:76, 100-103
  beginnings of 8:78-9
  Boccioni and 8:82, 83
  first exhibition 8:104
  French attitude to 8:80
  leaders of 8:*100*
  manifestos 8:78, 79, 82, *100*, 101, 102
  mass appeal of 8:101
  Paris exhibition 8:80
  success of 8:80
  'superman' 8:85
  themes 8:*78*, 100
  and women 8:102-103
  and World War I 8:103
Futurist Evenings 8:101, *101*
Futurist Manifesto of Lust (Saint-Point) 8:*103*
Futurist Manifesto of Men's Clothing (Balla) 8:*102*
Futurist music 8:*102*

G

Gaddi, Taddeo *see Artists' Index*
Gainsborough, Humphry 6:44
Gainsborough, Margaret 6:45, *46, 51*
Gainsborough, Mary 6:45, *46, 51*
Gainsborough, Thomas *see Artists' Index*
Gainsborough Family, The (Gainsborough) 6:*44*
Gainsborough Dupont *see* Dupont, Gainsborough
Galerie Durand-Ruel 9:45
  Cassatt exhibitions at 9:48, 49
Galigai, Leonora 3:*38*
Galileo Galilei 4:14, *39*
Gama, Vasco da, discovers new route to India 1:138
Gaming Act (1739) 6:71
Gamme d'Amour, La (Watteau) 5:25

Garden of Earthly Delights, The (Bosch) 1:117, 121, *126-7*
  details 1:*118-19*
  meaning of 1:109
Garden of Love, the 5:28
Garden of Love (Rubens) 5:*21*
Garden of the Hesperides, The (Burne-Jones) 9:*20*
Garden Study of the Vickers Children (Sargent) 9:*87*
Gardener, Isabella Stewart, and Sargent 9:79
Gardener, The (Fragonard) 5:*114*
Gardens of the Villa d'Este, The (Fragonard) 5:110, *120*
Gardiner, Luke (MP), commission for Reynolds 6:22, *22-3*
Gare St-Lazare (Monet) 7:*92*
gargoyles 1:*110*, 116-17
Garibaldi, Giuseppe 7:38, 42
Garrick, David 6:16, *28-9*
  Portrait of (Gainsborough) 6:*48*
Garrick Between Tragedy and Comedy (Reynolds) 6:*28-9*
Garter, The (de Troy) 5:*134-5*
Gas (Hopper) 9:*124-5*
Gas, Auguste de 7:44, 46
  Portrait of (Degas) 7:*45*
Gassed (Sargent) 9:*98-9*
Gatteaux, Edouard 4:*111*
Gaudi, Francesco 4:*106*
Gauguin, Paul *see Artists' Index*
Gautreau, Madame Pierre, by Sargent 9:78, 92
Geertgen tot Sint Jans *see Artists' Index*
Gellée, Claude *see* Claude Lorrain
Gelosi troupe 5:37
genre painting 3:50-51, 52, 53, 112, 114, 116, 132-5; 5:16, 44, 45, 46-7, 50-52
  single-figure 3:53, *53*
  see also individual artists
Geographer, The (Vermeer) 3:112, *128*
George III, King of England 6:36, 38, 40, 41, 73, 102, 103, 136
  Portrait of (Reynolds) 6:*36*
George V, King of England 8:*104*, 106
Georgiana, Countess Spencer, and her Daughter (Reynolds) 6:*26*
Georgiana, Duchess of Devonshire, and her Daughter (Reynolds) 6:20-21
Gérard, Baron François-Pascal *see Artists' Index*
Gérard, Marguerite *see Artists' Index*
  Portrait of (sketch,

Fragonard) 5:*113*
Gérard, Marie-Anne 5:*112*
Géricault, Théodore *see Artists' Index*
Germany 4:41
  and French Republic 7:135-8
  military manoeuvres 8:*138*
  and Morocco 8:105, 137
  Prussia and First Coalition 4:104
  Swedish invasion 3:42; 4:41
  and World War I 9:105-106
Gersaint, Edme 5:14, 15, 34, *35*
  on Watteau 5:20
Gershwin, George 9:71
Gervex (Rolla) 5:*117*
Ghent Altarpiece (Van Eyck) 1:46, 49
  details 1:*52-5*
  exterior paintings 1:*52-3*
  history 1:56
  interior paintings 1:*54-7*
Ghirlandaio, Domenico *see Artists' Index*
Giacomo Casanova (portrait, Mengs) 5:*132*
Gibbon, Edward 5:70
Gide, André, in Paris 9:69
Gilbert and Sullivan 9:*34*
  operetta 9:34, 35
Gilles (Watteau) 5:33, 39
Gillot, Claude *see Artists' Index*
Gillray, James *see Artists' Index*
Gilot, Françoise 8:47, 49
Ginevra de' Benci (Leonardo) 2:22
Giorgione da Castelfranco *see Artists' Index*
Giotto *see Artists' Index*
Giovanni Arnolfini and his Wife (Van Eyck) *see Arnolfini Wedding, The*
Gipsy Girl (Hals) 3:62
Girl in a Chemise (Picasso) 8:54
Girl Making her Dog Dance on her Bed (Fragonard) 5:*123*
Girl Returning from Market (Chardin) 5:*61*
Girl Running on a Balcony (Balla) 8:*100,140*
Girondins 4:105
Girton, Thomas 6:109
Giulio Romano 4:13
Giverny, Monet in 7:80-81, *81*
  garden at 7:*98*, 98-101, *99, 100, 101*
Girodet de Roucy-Trioson, Anne-Louis *see Artists' Index*
Girtin, Thomas *see Artists' Index*
Glackens, William Jones *see Artists' Index*
Glacier Valley of Chamonix (Turner) 6:*115*

Gladiateur (racehorse) 7:67, *69*
  Portrait of (Herring) 7:*69*
Gladstone, William (British Prime Minister) 9:39-40 42, 73
Glanvill, Joseph 3:*73*
Glass of Wine, The (Vermeer) 3:*120*
Glassco, John 9:68
glazes, technique of Jan van Eyck 1:50
Gleyre, Charles *see Artists' Index*
Gloria, La (Titian) 2:135
Glorious Stone, The (ben Israel) 3:*104*
Gobelins tapestries 5:109
  Boucher and 5:*78*, 81, 83
Godwin, Beatrix 9:17
Godwin, Edward 9:*14*, 34
Godwin, William 4:106; 9:16
Goes, Hugo van der *see Artists' Index*
Goethe, Johann Wolfgang von 5:72, 73-4
Gogh, Vincent van *see Artists' Index*
gold, use in illuminating 1:21
Golden Fleece, Order of the
  foundation of 1:76
  insignia 1:64
Golden Gate Bridge, San Francisco 8:73
Golden Legend 1:117
Goldfinch, The (Fabritius) 3:*110*
Goldfish and Sculpture (Matisse) 8:26
Golding Constable's Flower Garden (detail, Constable) 6:*83*
Goldsmith, Oliver 6:15, 16
  Portrait of (copy, Reynolds) 6:*14*
goldsmith's work, 14th-century 1:12
Goncourt, Edmond and Jules de 5:23, 44, 49, 82, 83, 87, 114, 117, 119; 7:132
  on Fragonard 5:*115*
  on genre painters 5:*44*
Gonzalès, Eva *see Artists' Index*
Gonzalez, Julio, and Picasso 8:52
Goodbye to all That (Graves) 9:37
Good Government in the Countryside (Lorenzetti) 1:16-17
Good Government in the Town (detail, Lorenzetti) 4:20
Gonzaga, Elisabetta 2:78
Gonzaga, Federico II, Marquis of Mantua 2:*110*, 111, 117
  Portrait of (Titian) 2:*110*
Gonzaga, Francesco 2:38
Gonzaga, Vincenzo, Duke of

Mantua 3:13, 14, 15
Goodyear, Charles 4:134
Gorky, Arshile *see Artists' Index*
Gossart, Jan *see Artists' Index*
gouache découpée 8:16-17, 20, 34-5
Gounod, and Renoir 7:108
Governess, The (Chardin) 5:60
Goya, Francisco de *see Artists' Index*
Grace, Dr W. G. 9:39
Graf Zeppelin (air ship) 9:138, *138*
grain farming 6:98-101
Grancourt, Bergeret de 5:112, *112*
'grand manner' 3:15
Grande Odalisque, The (Ingres) 4:111, 112, 114, 116, 117 122-3; 8:20
'Grand Remonstrance, the' (1642) 4:42
Grand Tour, the 6:13, 14, 15, 37
grandes cocottes 7:37
Grant, General Ulysses S. (USA President) 9:40
Grapes and Pomegranates (Chardin) 5:66
Grasse, Admiral de 6:73, *73*
Grasse, France 5:108, 112
Gravelot, Hubert *see Artists' Index*
Graves, Robert 9:137
Graziano, Doctor (in *Commedia dell'Arte*) 5:37
Great Exhibition, England (1851) 8:41
Great Fire of London (1666) 3:74
Great Illusion, The (Cocteau) 8:72
Great Northern War (1700-21) 5:41
Greco, El *see* El Greco
Greek Girl at the Bath (Vien) 4:141
Greek vases 4:116, *117*
green paint, base material for 1:21, *101*
Gregorian Calendar 2:138
Gregory XII, Pope, and Great Schism 1:38
Gregory XIII, Pope 2:138
Grenouillère, La 7:110, 133
Grenouillère, La (Renoir) 7:*120*, *125*
grenouilles 7:133
Greta Bridge (Cotman) 6:140
Greuze, Jean-Baptiste *see Artists' Index*
Griffier, J.
  View of Potrel Manor 5:70
Gris, Juan *see Artists' Index*
grisaille 1:62; 4:84
  Boucher and 5:84

Groote, Gerhard, and Brethren of the Common Life 1:109
Gros, Baron Antoine-Jean *see Artists' Index*
group portraits 3:52, *86*
Guardi, Francesco *see Artists' Index*
Guébriant, General 4:41
Guelders, Duke of 1:12 and England 1:12, *12*
Guerick, Otto von 3:136, *136-7*, 138
Guérin, Pierre-Narcise *see Artists' Index*
Guernica (Picasso) 8:48, 49, 64-5
Guernica, bombing of 8:49, 72
Guild of Fullers and Shearers, contract with Albrecht Cornelius 1:101
Guild houses 1:*101*
  Guild regulations, for apprentices 1:103
Guild of St Luke 1:44, 2:12
  Chardin and 5:44
  Hals and 3:45, 47
Guillaume, Paul, and Modigliani 8:112
Guillaumin, Armand *see Artists' Index*
Guimard, Sophie 5:*111*, 132
  Portrait of (Fragonard) 5:*111*
guingettes 7:133, *133*
Guitar (sculpture, Picasso) 8:52
Guitar Player, The (sculpture, Lipchitz) 8:118
Guitar Player, The (Vermeer) 3:*131*
'gunboat diplomacy' 8:105, *105*
Gustavus Adolphus, King of Sweden 3:41, 42
Gutenberg, Johann 1:*104*
Gypsy Woman with Baby (Modigliani) 8:117
  detail 8:*116-17*

H

Haarlem, Holland 3:44-5, 48
  militia companies in 3:45-6
Habsburg Empire
  challenge to 3:39
  disintegration of 9:106
  in 1641 4:41
Halévy, Ludovic 7:48
Half-naked Woman Bending Over (sketch, Boucher) 5:*83*
Halifax, Lord 8:73
halletoren, Bruges 1:65
Halley, Edmond 4:*73*

Halley's Comet 4:73
Hals, Dirck *see Artists' Index*
Hals, Franchoys 3:44
Hals, Frans *see Artists' Index*
Hals, Joost 3:47
Halsmuseum, Haarlem 3:46
Hamar, Portrait of Mrs Joseph (Reynolds) 6:13, *13*
Hamilton, Gavin 4:77
Hammerstein's Roof Garden (Glackens) 9:133
Hampstead, London 6:*81*, 84, *94*
Hannibal 6:121
Harbour at Middleburg, The (Van der Venne) 3:69
Harfleur, siege of (1415) 1:40
'Harlem Spider, The' *see* Luks, George
Harlequin (in *Commedia dell'Arte*) 5:31, 37, 38, 39
Harmansdr, Annetje 3:45
'Harmonies' 9:19
Harmony in Pink and Grey: Portrait of Lady Meux (Whistler) 9:32
harrowing 6:*100*
Harvest Wagon, The (Gainsborough) 6:52-3
harvesting 6:*101*
Hastings, Beatrice 8:111-12
  Portrait of (Modigliani) 8:*110*, *111*
Haviland, Portrait of Frank Burty (Modigliani) 8:*121*
Hawaii 2:72
Hay Wain, The (Bosch) 1:121, *124-5*
  derivation of theme 1:125
  symbolism in 1:116
Hay Wain, The (Constable) 6:80, 81, 83, *86-7*, *90-91*
Hayman, Francis *see Artists' Index*
Haystacks, The (Monet) 7:80, *83*
Haytley, Edward *see Artists' Index*
Hayward, Edward 4:138
Head of a Child (Rubens) 3:28
Heads (drawing, Watteau) 5:*18-19*
Heads and Figures (studies, Rembrandt) 3:*81*
Heathfield, Lord (Reynolds) 6:34
Heberden, Dr 6:49
Hébuterne, Jeanne 8:112, 113
  Portrait of (Modigliani) 8:*112*, *130-31*
Heffernan, Joanna 9:13-14, 17, 22, *22-3*
  Portrait of (Courbet) 9:14
  Portrait of (Whistler) 9:23
Hell/Hellfire
  medieval fear of 1:132-3

visions of 1:*114*, *134*
Hemingway, Ernest 8:*74*; 9:68, 70, *70*, 137
  on Paris 9:68
  A Movable Feast 9:70
  The Sun Also Rises 9:70
Heneage Lloyd and his Sister (Gainsborough) 6:*50-51*
Henley Regatta 4:*134-5*
  by Tissot 4:*124-5*
Henri, Robert *see Artists' Index*
Henrietta Maria, Queen of England 3:*41*
Henry the Navigator, Prince of Portugal, captures Ceuta 1:42
Henry V, King of England 1:*38*, 39
  divine mission 1:*41*
  invades France 1:38, 39, 40-41
Henry VI, King of England 1:*73*
  and 'Cade's Rebellion' (1450) 1:105-106
  claims on French crown 1:72
Henry VIII, King of England 2:74, 104, 106, 133
Henry IV, King of France 3:*36*, 36-7, *37*; 4:41, 73
Herculaneum, Italy 4:77
Hercules and the Horses of Diomedes (Lebrun) 4:141
Herinnes, Charterhouse of, gifts from Van der Weyden 1:79
Herring, J. F. *see Artists' Index*
Herschel, William 6:73
Herz, Cornelius 7:106
Heylhuyzen, Willem van
  Portrait of (Hals) 3:49
High Road (Hopper) 9:112-13
Hippolytus and Phaedra (Guérin) 4:141
Hippopotamus and Crocodile Hunt (Rubens) 3:26-7
History of the Emperor Constantine (tapestries, Rubens) 3:17
Hitler, Adolf 3:126
  and the Depression 9:137
HMS *Dreadnought* 8:138
HMS *Victory* 6:112, 115-16, 118, 132, 138
Hoare, Henry 4:70, 71
Hobbes, Thomas 3:*106*
Hoccleve, Thomas 1:*38*
Hoche, General Lazare 5:138
Hochkirch, Battle of (1758) 5:*102-103*, 105
Hogarth, William *see Artists' Index*

Holland
and First Coalition 4:104
painting in the 17th century
3:84
and the Quadruple Alliance
5:42
and war with Spain 3:68, 69
see also Netherlands, The;
United Provinces
Holst, Bartholomeus van der
see Artists' Index
Holy Cross, Confraternity of
the 1:79
Holy Family on the Steps, The
(Poussin) 4:22-3, 30-31
details 4:23
preparatory drawing 2:43
Holy Family with Six Putti
(Poussin) 4:19
Homer, Winslow see Artists'
Index
Honthorst, Gerrit van see
Artists' Index
Hooch, Pieter de see Artists'
Index
Hood, Admiral Samuel 4:105
Hooft, Pieter 3:102
Hopper, Edward see Artists'
Index
Hopper, Elizabeth Griffiths
Smith, Portrait of (Hopper)
9:108
horse racing 4:137; 7:35, 35,
66-9
Degas and 7:47
Horse and Rider (bronze,
Leonardo) 2:30
horses
artistic convention 7:68
photographed action 7:68-9
Horses of Monte Cavallo, The
(drawing, Raphael) 2:103
Hoschedé, Alice see Monet,
Alice
Hoschedé-Monet, Blanche
7:81, 82, 83
Hôtel-Dieu, Beaune, altarpiece
1:10, 77, 77, 81
Houbraken, Arnold
on Hals 3:47
on Rembrandt 3:80, 83, 85-6
Hours of the Duchess of Burgundy
1:21
House by the Railroad (Hopper)
9:114
Hudson, Thomas see Artists'
Index
Hugo, Victor, on the Paris
Commune 7:72
Huguenots 2:36-8; 4:40, 72-3
Humbert, Marcelle, and
Picasso 8:47
Hunt Breakfast, The (de Troy)
5:141

Hunt Luncheon, The (Van Loo)
5:69
Hunter, Mrs Charles 9:81
hunting, painting by Herring
7:67
Huss, John 1:40, 42
Huygens, Constantijn 3:79
on Rembrandt and Lievens
3:78, 79
Hyder Ali, Maharajah of
Mysore 6:73

I

Iberian votive sculpture 8:52
Ibsen, Henrik 8:138
Iconologia (Ripa) 3:116
idealization 4:117, 121
Idris I, King of Libya 8:42
illustrations, methods of
working 1:20-21
images, stylized 8:116, 116
impasto 3:84; 5:53
Rembrandt and 3:85
Imperial Academy, St
Petersburg 9:12
Whistler at 9:18
Impression: Sunrise (Monet)
7:78, 79
Impressionism 6:20, 116; 7:78,
78-9, 80
first canvases of 7:110
Hopper and 9:114, 115-16
Matisse and 8:13-14
Impressionists
exhibitions 9:46, 74
first 7:47
greatest 7:82
greatest drawbacks to 7:84
last exhibition 7:48
painting at speed 7:84-5
second exhibition 7:71-2
In a Levantine Port (Sargent)
9:8
'Independents' 9:46
indulgences, Papal 2:68
Industrial Revolution 5:73
Infant Academy, The (Reynolds)
6:39
Infanta Isabella, Portrait of
(Rubens) 3:15
influenza epidemic 7:103
Ingres, Jean-Auguste-
Dominique,
see Artists' Index
inks, Picasso and 8:50
Inquisition, Spanish 2:42
inscriptions, in Van Eyck's
work 1:51
Inspiration (Fragonard) 5:110
Interior of a Hospital Tent, The

(Sargent) 9:80
International Exhibition,
Picasso and 8:49
Intervention of the Sabine
Women, The (David) 4:80, 83,
94-5
preliminary sketch 4:83
intonaco 2:52
Iris (Watteau) 5:16
Irish Land League 9:73, 74
Iron and Steel Community
(1952) 8:40
Isaac Massa (Hals) 3:55
Isabella, Infanta, Regent of the
Netherlands 3:15, 17, 68
and Rubens 3:17
Portrait of (Rubens) 3:15
Isabella of Bavaria, employs
Jean Matouel 1:12
Isabella of Castile, Queen of
Spain 2:42
and Van der Weyden
triptych 1:80
Isabella Coymans (Hals) 3:52, 67
Islamic Exhibition 8:15
Isle of Wight, England 6:110
Israel, Manasseh ben 3:104,
104-105
Istanbul, Turkey 2:105
Italian Comedians, The
(Watteau) 5:39
Italy 5:137
invasion of Tripoli 8:104, 104
trends in painting 8:82
unification of 7:42, 135-6

J

Jackson, General Andrew
(USA President) 6:106
Jacob, Max, and Picasso
8:45
Jacobin Club 4:78
Jacobins 4:105
Jaleo, El (Sargent) 9:78, 88-9
Jamaica 3:104, 106
James, Duke of York 4:74
James, Henry 9:103, 103
and Broadway, England
9:101
and Sargent 9:78-9
James I, King of England 3:16
James, 7th Earl of Lauderdale
(Reynolds) 6:25
Jan de Leeuw, Portrait of (Van
Eyck) 1:65
Jansenism 5:42
Janszoon, Reynier 3:108
Japan, invades China (1937)
8:73, 74
Japanese artefacts/prints

cult of 9:34, 35, 35
Liberty and Co. and 9:35, 35
Manet and 7:20, 21, 21
Matisse and 8:19
prints 9:48
exhibition of 9:47-8
Ukiyo-e school 9:47-8, 48
Whistler and 9:14
Jar of Apricots, The (Chardin)
5:64
Jar of Olives, The (Chardin)
5:52-3
detail 5:53
Jazz (Matisse) 8:19
Jealous Husband, The (Titian)
2:109
Jean, Duc de Berry 1:14, 14-15,
15
and aggression between
Orleans and Burgundy 1:38
alliance against Burgundy
1:39
châteaux 1:14
coat of arms 1:14-15
curios/works of art 1:14
death of 1:17
emblems 1:14-15, 19, 21, 21
employs Limbourgs 1:9, 14
influences on 1:19
presents to/from 1:16
and invasion of England 1:36
in 'January' (Très Riches
Heures) 1:24
presented with book 1:14-15
and St Ursine 1:14, 21
tomb 1:15
Jeanneret, Charles-Edouard see
Corbusier, Le
Jefferson, Thomas (USA
President) 5:138
Jehan, Shah 3:74
Jenner, Edward 6:103
Jesuit Church ceiling, Antwerp
(Rubens) 3:16, 17
Jesuits 5:105
Jewish Bride, The (Rembrandt)
3:99
Jews 3:101, 105-106
re-admission into England
3:104-105
Joan of Arc 1:72, 72-4
Jockeys before the Start, with
Flag-pole (Degas) 7:51
John, Duke of Bavaria 1:44
and Jan van Eyck 1:44
John the Fearless, Duke of
Burgundy 1:37, 38, 39
symbols 1:38
and war with England 1:38,
39
John II, King of Castile, and
Van der Weyden triptych
1:80
John XXIII, Pope (Pisan

obedience) 1:42
and Great Schism 1:42
Johnson, Dr Samuel 6:14, 16, 38
Portrait of (Reynolds) 6:15
Johnston, General Joseph E.
9:40
Joie de Vivre (series, Picasso) 8:49
Jongkind, Johan Berthold 7:141
and Monet 7:78
and painting out of doors
(*plein-air*) 7:82
Joseph II, Emperor, and *Ghent
Altarpiece* 1:56
Josephine, Empress of France
5:136, 137, 138
journeymen 1:101
financial resources 1:102
wage 1:13
Jouvenet, Noel 4:12
Joyce, James 9:70
Judgement, Day of 7:39
Judgement of Paris, The
(engraving after Raimondi)
2:78
Judgement of Paris, The
(Raphael) 2:78
Judgement of Solomon, The
(Mantegna) 2:140
Judith (Mantegna) 2:140
Julie Forestier (drawing, Ingres)
4:109
Julienne, Jean de, and Boucher
5:76-7
Julius Caesar 4:131
Julius II, Pope 2:38, 46-7, 49,
64, 67, 68-9, 78, 79, 94, 98,
99, 101-102, 104-108
Portrait of (Raphael) 2:79
July Monarchy (France, 1830-
1848) 4:113, 135, 136
July Revolution (France, 1830)
4:111
Juno Discovering Jupiter with Io
(Lastman) 3:77
Jupiter, loves of 2:117; 3:18
Jupiter and Io (Correggio) 2:117
Jupiter and Thetis (Ingres) 4:111,
116
detail 4:116
*Justice and Divine Vengeance
Pursuing Crime* (Prud'hon)
4:141
Justice of Emperor Otto, The
(Bouts) 1:140
Justice of Trajan and Herkinbald
(detail, tapestry) 1:75

K

Kahnweiler, Daniel-Henry,
and Picasso 8:46

Kant, Immanuel 6:74
Karlskirche, Vienna 5:42
Karsavina, Tamara 8:134
Kauffmann, Angelica *see Artists'
Index*
Keats, John 4:53, 65
Keir Hardie, James 7:104-105
Kellogg-Briand Pact (1928)
9:136
Kenilworth Castle, England
1:106, *106*
Kent, Rockwell 9:108
Kent, William 4:68-71
sketch for the Shell Temple,
Chatsworth 4:70
Kepler, John 4:14
Keppel, Commodore
Augustus 6;13, 14, 19
Portrait of (Reynolds) 6:24
Key, Francis Scott 6:137
'keyhole nudes' (Degas) 7:52, 64
Keyser, Thomas de *see Artists'
Index*
Khnopff, Fernand *see Artists'
Index*
Kim Il Sung, General 8:40-41
King's Painter 5:81
*Kitchen Still-Life with Cooking
Pots and Eggs* (Chardin) 5:56
*Kitchen Still-Life with Pestle and
Mortar* (Chardin) 5:57
Kitchenmaid, The (Moitte) 5:69
Klenze, Leo von 4:136
Kloveniersdoelen, Amsterdam
3:89
Kneeling in an Armchair
(Cassatt) 9:51
Kneeling Man (drawing,
Watteau) 5:19
Knox, John 2:137
Koch, Robert 7:71
Koëlla, Léon-Edouard 7:13
Koklova, Olga 8:46, 47
influence on Picasso 8:48
Korea, war in (1950-53) 8:41, 42
Kosciuszko, Tadeusz 4:105
Ku Klux Klan 7:137

L

L'Air du Soir (Cross) 8:13
L'Ami du Peuple (Marat) 4:101,
101
La Hire (Etienne de Vignolles)
1:72
La Hyre, Laurent de *see Artists'
Index*
La Marfée, Battle of (1641) 4:41
La Tour, Georges de *see Artists'
Index*
La Tour, Maurice-Quentin de

see Artists' Index
La Vallière, Louise de 3:73
Labour Representation
Committee 8:138
Lacemaker, The (Vermeer) 3:114,
130
Lady Agnew (Sargent) 9:79, 94
Lady Betty Hamilton (Reynolds)
6:18
Lady of the Camellias, The
(Dumas) 7:37
Lady Caroline Scott (Reynolds)
6:32
*Lady Governors of the Old Men's
Home at Haarlem* (Hals) 3:86
Lady, Portrait of a (Van der
Weyden) 1:97
*Lady Reading a Letter at an Open
Window* (Vermeer) 3:10
Lady Seated at the Virginals
(Vermeer) 3:113
Lady Standing at the Virginals
(Vermeer) 3:117
Lady at a Tea Table (Cassatt)
9:53, 54-5, 62
details 9:55
Lady at her Toilet (Terborch)
3:135
Lady Walking to the Right, A
(sketch, Gainsborough) 6:50
Lady with a Parasol (Monet) 7:83
Lady with an Ermine (Leonardo)
2:23
Lady with the Rose (Sargent)
9:81, 82-3
Laer, Pieter van 4:46
Lagrange, Comte de 7:67
Lakeshore Drive, Chicago 8:41
Lalaing, Countess of, page to
3:13
Lallemand, Georges 4:12
Lally, Comte de 5:105
Lamb, Lady Caroline 6:104
lamentation, comparison of
scenes of 1:85
Lamentation over Christ, The
(Christus) 1:140
Lamothe, Louis 7:44
Lancret, Nicholas *see Artists'
Index*
landscape gardening 4:16,
68-71
landscape painting 2:33; 4:44-7,
48-53, 69; 6: 77, 84, 85,
114-17
Bosch's treatment of 1:117
Boudin on 7:76
Claude and 4:45
earliest 'snow' in art 1:25
in English gardens 4:68-71
Monet on 7:77
Rembrandt and 3:82
Renoir and 7:116
in *Très Riches Heures* 1:17

by Van der Weyden 1:81, 84
see also background
*Landscape with Ascanius
Shooting the Stag of Silvia*
(Claude) 4:67
Landscape at Cagnes
(Modigliani) 8:115
*Landscape with Figures Gathering
Cherries* (Boucher) 5:82
Landscape with a Goatherd (copy
after Claude by Constable)
4:48, 50
*Landscape with Hagar and the
Angel* (Claude) 4:52-3
*Landscape with the Landing of
Aeneas at Pallanteum* (Claude)
4:46, 52
*Landscape with Man Killed by a
Snake* (Poussin) 4:19
*Landscape with the Marriage of
Isaac and Rebekah* (Claude)
4:54, 62-3
*Landscape with Narcissus and
Echo* (Claude) 4:58-9
*Landscape with the Nymph Egeria
Mourning over Numa* (Claude)
4:66
*Landscape with Psyche at the
Palace of Cupid* (Claude) 4:53
*Landscape with Samuel Anointing
David* (Claude) 4:48-9
*Landscape with a Shepherd and
his Flock* (Rubens) 3:33
*Landscape with St George Killing
the Dragon* (sketch, Claude)
4:50
Landscape with Watermill
(Boucher) 5:82-3
Lange Leizen, The (Whistler)
9:18
Langlois
portrait of David 4:81
Langtry, Lily 9:36
Laocoön, The (Greek sculpture)
2:46, 47, 103; 3:23
drawing by Rubens 3:23
Lapin Agile, Le (Utrillo)
8:108-109
Largillière Nicolas, and
Chardin 5:45, 46
Lascaux, Judge, and Renoir
7:112
'Last Day', interpretations of
1:134, 134
Last Judgement, The (Bosch)
1:111
details 1:114-5
Last Judgement, The
(Michelangelo) 2:48, 51,
60-63
Last Judgement Altarpiece, The
(Van der Weyden) 1:77, 81
detail 1:116
emotion in 1:84-5

Last Supper, The (Leonardo)
2:16, 18, *24-5, 32, 34-5*
  details 2:*35*
  restoration of 2:*34*
Lastman, Pieter *see Artists' Index*
Lateran Treaties (1929) 9:138
Laud, Archbishop 4:42
Laugh, The (Boccioni) 8:*84*
  detail 8:*84*
Laughing Boy (Hals) 3:*48*, 49
Laughing Cavalier, The (Hals)
3:50, *51*
  detail 3:50, *51, 57*
Laughing Madonna and Child
(sculpture, Rossellino) 2:*85*
Laurentian Library, Florence
2:*51*, 52, *24-5, 32, 34-5*
  restoration of 2:*34*
Lavinia, Countess Spencer
(Reynolds) 6:20, *21*
Law, John 5:40, *41*, 42
Lawrence, Commander 5:*105*
Lawrence, Sir Thomas *see
Artists' Index*
lay figures 6:46, 51
Lazarus Triptych (Froment) 1:140
Le Nôtre, André 4:68
Le Sueur, Eustache de *see
Artists' Index*
Leaping Horse, The (Constable)
6:*85*
Lebrun, Charles *see Artists'
Index*
Lecadre, Sophie 7:76
LeCoeur, Jules 7:109
  Portrait of (Monet) 7:*109*
Leczinska, Marie, Queen of
France 5:78
Leda (Rubens) 3:*18*
Lee, General Robert E. 9:*40*
Leenhoff, Suzanne 7:13, *13,*15
Leeuw, Jan de, Portrait of (Van
Eyck) 1:*65*
Leeuwenhoek, Anthonie van
3:102, *115*
  and Vermeer 3:117
Legal Quays, Port of London
6:130
Legends of the Saints (de Voragine)
1:*117*
Léger, Fernand *see Artists' Index*
Légion d'Honneur 7:*17*, 67
  awarded to Ingres 4:112, 113
  awarded to Manet 7:17
  awarded to Matisse 8:17
  awarded to Whistler 9:17
Leicester Fields (now Square),
London 6:*14*
Leiden, Holland 3:*76, 77*
Lemonnier, Isabelle 7:16
Lemoyne, François *see Artists'
Index*
Lending Bank (1614,

Amsterdam) 3:101
lenses 3:114, 115, 117
Leo IV, Pope 2:99
Leo X, Pope 2:19, 69, 79, *80*,
81, 99, 102-103, 109
  *Leo X and Two Cardinals,
    Portrait of* (Raphael) 2:*80*
Leonardo da Vinci *see Artists'
Index*
Leopold II, King of Belgium
7:38-9
Lepelletier de Saint-Fargeau
4:78
  Portrait of (David) 4:*86-7*
Leroy, Louis, on *Impression;
Sunrise* (Monet) 7:78
Les Andelys, Normandy 4:*12*
Leslie, C. S., on Gainsborough
6:64
Lesseps, Ferdinand de 7:73, 103,
106
  Portrait of (Renoir) 7:*118-19,
    124-5*
Letter, The (Cassatt) 9:*49*
levée en masse, A (French
  universal conscription, 1793)
  4:105
Leyland, Frederick, and
  Whistler 9:15
Leyster, Judith *see Artists' Index*
Lhote, Paul, by Renoir
7:*118-19, 124-5*
Liber Veritatis (Claude) 4:46, 49,
50-51, 55
Liberation of Arsinoe, The
(Tintoretto) 2:*141*
Liberty (sloop), seizure of 6:64
Liberty, Arthur 9:34
  shop in Regent Street,
    London 9:*34-5, 35*
Libya, independence of 8:42
Lichtenstein, Roy *see Artists' Index*
Liddell, Alice 7:*138*
Liebermann, Max, on
  Rembrandt 3:86
Lieve Vouvre Broederschap *see*
  Brotherhood of Our Lady
Lievens, Jan *see Artists' Index*
Lifar, Serge 8:135, *135*
life below stairs 3:68-71
Life of Johnson (Boswell) 6:42
Life of St Bruno (Le Sueur)
4:*141*
Life of St Genevieve (Chavannes)
9:*74*
light: Boccioni and 8:83
  Cézanne and 8:36
  Claude and 4:52
  Van Gogh and 8:36
  Hals and 3:50, *52*
  Matisse and 8:15, *30*
  qualities of Mediterranean
    8:14, *14*, 15, 17, 36, 37, 38-9
  Rembrandt and 3:*87*

Vermeer and 3:114
Lighthouse at Two Lights
(Hopper) 9:*114-15*
Lima, Peru 2:72
Limbourg, Herman de *see
Artists' Index*
Limbourg, Jean de *see Artists'
Index*
Limbourg, Marguerite de 1:*12*
Limbourg, Mechteld de 1:*12*
Limbourg, Paul de *see Artists'
Index*
Limbourg, Roger de 1:*12*
Limbourg brothers *see Artists'
Index*
Lincoln, Abraham (USA
  President) 9:*38*
linocutting, Picasso and 8:52
Liotard, Jean-Etienne *see
Artists' Index*
Lipchitz, Jacques *see Artists'
Index*
  Portrait of Jacques and his Wife
    8:*118-19, 123*
Lister, Joseph 7:40
lithography
  Degas and 7:51
  Picasso and 8:50
'lines of force' 8:84
Little Girl in Blue, The
(Modigliani) 8:*129*
Little Girl with Cherries
(Chardin) 5:*48*
  engraving after, by Cochin
    5:*48*
Little Girl with a Shuttlecock
(Chardin) 5:*58*
Little Juniper Bud (Whistler)
9:*19*
Little Mermaid, The (Andersen)
6:*138*
Little Peasant, The (Modigliani)
8:*128*
Little Sisters, The (Cassatt) 6:20,
21; 9:*10*
Little Street, The (Vermeer)
3:*122*
Little White Girl, The (Whistler)
9:*19*
Livingstone, David 7:42
  found by Stanley 7:*137*
Livorno, Italy 8:*108-109*
Livy 4:19
Lloyd, Constance 9:36
Lloyd George, David (British
  Prime Minister) 8:105; 9:106
Lloyds of London 6:*131*, 132
Lock, The (Constable) 6:81
locomotor ataxia, Manet and
7:16
Lodovico Gonzaga and his Family
(Mantegna) 2:140
Loge, La 7:133
Loge, La (Renoir) 7:*121*

London, Great Fire of (1666)
3:*72*, 74
London Dock Company, The
6:130
Longchamp 7:35, *35, 66*
  Racehorses at (Degas) 7:*58-9*
Longed-For Moment, The
(Fragonard) 5:112, *114*, 115
Loo, Carle van *see Artists' Index*
Loo, Jean-Baptiste, Chardin
  and 5:*45*, 46
Lord of the Harvest 6:100
Lorenzetti, Ambrogio *see
Artists' Index*
Lott, Willie 6:81, 83, 86, 90
Louis II, Duc d'Anjou 1:*15*
Louis XII, King of France 2:16,
  19, 36, 104-105
  and capture of Milan 1:*137*
Louis XIII, King of France 3:17,
  36, 37, 38, 39, 40, 42; 4:17,
  40, *41*
Louis XIV, King of France 3:39,
  71, 72, 73, 138, *138*; 4:68,
  72-4; 5:12, 13, 30, 38, 39, *40*,
  42, 116
  and Academie des Sciences
    3:74
Louis XIV on Horseback (relief
  carving, Coysevox) 5:*40*
Louis XV, King of France 5:21,
  42, 46-7, 48, 49, 54, 72, 79,
  82, 83, 86, 93, 99, *100*, 101,
  112, 117, 134
  and Chardin 5:46, 47
Louis XVI, King of France
  4:101, 104, 106, 130-31;
  5:72
Louis Philippe, King of France
  4:*113*, 135, 136, 138
Louisbourg 5:*104-105*, 106
Louise Ulrique, and Chardin
  5:47
Louisiana, founding of 4:73
Loutherbourg, Philippe James
  de *see Artists' Index*
Louvre, the 1:*22, 33*; 5: *46-7, 76*
  creation of museum in 4:105
  Ingres commissions for 4:113
love, symbols of 3:*55*
Love Letter, The (Fragonard)
5:*126*
Love Letter, The (Vermeer) 3:*127*
Lucas, E. V., on Broadway,
  England 9:100
*Lucca Madonna see Madonna in
  Her Chamber, The* (Van Eyck)
Ludd, Ned 6:104, 105
Luddite Riots 6:104, *105*
Luigi, Russolo 8:79
Luks, George *see Artists' Index*
Lunch of Oysters, A (de Troy)
5:*70*
Luncheon of the Boating Party

(Renoir) 7:111-12, *124-5*
Luncheon on the Grass, The
    (Manet) 7:15, 19, 20, *24-5;*
    8:49
Lusignan, Château de 1:*26*
Luther, Martin 2:73, 74
Lux, Margot 9:*48*
Luxe, Calme et Volupté (Matisse)
    8:*13*, 14, 18, *18*, 37
Luxembourg Palace, Paris 3:17,
    38; 4:13; 5:14
Lycée Louis-le-Grand 7:44
*Lydia Crocheting in the Garden at
    Marly* (Cassatt) 9:*46*, 47
*Lydia Leaning on her Arms seated
    in a Loge* (Cassatt) 9:*50*
Lydia and her Mother at Tea
    (Cassatt) 9:*54*
Lytton, Lord, on Edward, Prince
    of Wales 7:74

M

Maar, Dora 8:*48*
MacArthur, General Douglas
    8:*41*, 42
Macbeth Galleries, and 'The
    Eight' 9:133-4
MacDowell Club, New York
    9:109
Machiavelli, Niccolò 2:38-9,
    39, 74
Machuca, Pedro 2:72
Maclean, Donald 8:42, *42*
*Madame Charpentier and her
    Children* (Renoir) 7:*110*
Madame Matisse (Matisse)
    8:*23*
Madame Monet and her son Jean
    (Renoir) 7:*77*
Madame de Pompadour
    (Boucher), (1758) 5:*98*, (1759)
    5:*99*
Madame de Senonnes (Ingres)
    4:*124*
*Mme (Vigée-Lebrun) and her
    Daughter* (Vigée-Lebrun) 9:*53*
*Madame X (Madame Pierre
    Gautreau)* (Sargent) 9:*78*, 92
Mademoiselle O'Murphy
    (Boucher) 5:*86-7*, 92-3
    details 5:*86*, *87*
    early sketch for 5:*87*
Mademoiselle Rivière (Ingres)
    4:*114*
Madeleine, La, Paris 4:132-3
Maderno, Carlo 2:70-71
Madonna and Child, Cassatt
    and 9:45, 51
Madonna and Child, The
    (Giorgione) 2:140

Madonna del Granduca
    (Raphael) 2:*84*, 85
*Madonna with Canon van der
    Paele, The* (Van Eyck) 1:*49*
    66-7
Madonna in Her Chamber, The
    (Van Eyck) 1:*63*
*Madonna with Chancellor Rolin,
    The* (Van Eyck) 1:*61*
    back views in 1:*50*
Madonna in a Church, The (Van
    Eyck) 1:*48*
Madonna of the Fish (Raphael)
    4:*22*
Madonna by the Fountain, The
    (Van Eyck) 1:*50*
Madonna of the Goldfinch, The
    (Raphael) 2:*84*, 88
Madonna with Jan Vos, The (Van
    Eyck) 1:*47*
    Petrus Christus and 1:*47*
Madonna with the Long neck
    (Parmigianino) 8:*116*
Madonna of the Meadow (Bellini)
    2:*85*
Madonna della Sedia (Raphael)
    2:*80*, *82*; 4:*117*
*Madonna with Three Female
    Saints* (David, G.) 1:*140*
Madras, India, struggle for
    5:*105*
Maes, Nicholas *see Artists'
    Index*
Mafarka Futurista (Marinetti)
    8:*78*
Magdeburg Hemispheres
    3:*136-7*, 138
Magdalen with a Lamp (La Tour)
    3:*40*
Maggioli, by Renoir 7:*118-19*,
    124-5
'Magistro Rogel' *see* Weyden,
    Rogier van der
magnifying glasses 1:*21*
Mahal, Mumtaz, tomb of 3:74
Mahler, Gustav 8:*105*
mahlstick 3:*116*
Maid with a Milk Jug (Vermeer)
    3:*114*, *115*
    detail 3:*115*
Maintenon, Madame de
    5:38, 39
maiolica pottery 1:*138*
Maison Reglée, La (Audiger) 5:70
Málaga, Spain 8:*44-5*
Malagrida, Gabriel 5:*105*
Mallarmé, Stéphane 7:*74*; 8:45;
    9:*16*
    Matisse and 8:17
    and Whistler 9:16
Malle Babbe (Hals) 3:*49*, *63*
Malouel, Jean *see Artists' Index*
Malplaquet, France 5:14
Malton, Thomas 6:109

Man Carrying a Scythe (sketch,
    Constable) 6:*87*
Man with a Blue Sleeve (Titian)
    2:*121*
Man with a Red Turban (Van
    Eyck) 1:*43*
Mander, Karel van *see Artists'
    Index*
Manet, Auguste 7:12
    Portrait of, and Mme (Manet)
    7:*13*
Manet, Edouard *see Artists'
    Index*
Manet, Eugène 7:17
Manguin, Henri 8:38
Manifesto of Futurist Painters
    8:79, *100*
Mannerism 4:12, 36
Mantegna, Andrea *see Artists'
    Index*
map of the known world (1500)
    1:137, *137*
Marat, Jean-Paul 4:78, 85, *86-7*,
    93, *100*, 100-103, 105
    Death of (David) 4:*86-7*, 93
Marche, La 7:67
Marcus Aurelius, Column of
    4:*18*
Margaret of Flanders, and Philip
    of Burgundy 1:38
Margaret Tyers and her Husband
    (Hayman) 6:*54*
Marguerite Pouget (pastels,
    Chardin) 5:*47*
Marie-Antoinette (sketch,
    David) 4:*79*
Marie-Antoinette, Queen of
    France 5:95
    death of 4:104-105
    sketch by David 4:*79*
Marie de' Medici cycle (Rubens)
    3:17, 30, 31, 36-9
Marinetti, Filippo Tommaso *see
    Artists' Index*
Marino, Giovanni Battista 4:*13*,
    14
    and Poussin 4:*13*, 14
'Marino' drawings (Poussin)
    4:*13*
Market Cart, The
    (Gainsborough) 6:*66*
Markova, Dame Alicia 8:*135*
Marlborough House, London
    9:39
Marquand, Henry, and
    Sargent 9:79
Marquet, Albert 8:12
    and Salon d' Automne 8:15
Marquise de Pastoret, The
    (David) 4:*92*
Marriage of Figaro
    (Beaumarchais) 5:73
Marriage at Cana (David, G.)
    1:*140*

Married Couple in a Garden
    (Hals) 3: *54-5*, *58-9*
Mars and Minerva (David) 4:*76*,
    88
Mars and Venus (David) 4:*83*, 85
'Martyr of Equality' (English
    satirical cartoon, 1793) 4:*104*
Martyrdom of St Erasmus
    (Poussin) 4:14, 15, *18*
Martyrdom of St Symphorian
    (Ingres) 4:*113*
Marx, Karl 7:42
Mary, Countess Howe
    (Gainsborough) 6:*60*
Mary Cassatt in the Louvre
    (etching, Degas) 9:*47*
Mary of Hungary, and Van der
    Weyden *Deposition* 1:80
Mary, Queen of Scots 2:*137*
Masaccio *see Artists' Index*
Mass of Bolsena, The (Raphael)
    2:*99*
Massa, Isaac 3:54, *55*
Massacre of Chios (Delacroix)
    4:*112*
Masses, The (U.S. political
    journal) 9:*134*
Massimi, Camillo, Prince of
    Pamphili 4:*46*, *47*
Matthys, Jan 1:135
Matisse, Anna 8:*122*
Matisse, Emile 8:12
Matisse, Henri *see Artists'
    Index*
Matisse, Jean 8:14
Matisse, Marguerite 8:13
Matisse, Pierre 8:14
Maupassant, Guy de
    attempted suicide 7:103
    on *grenouilles* 7:*133*
Maurice, Prince of Nassau 3:*70*
Maximilian, Elector of Bavaria
    3:42
Maximilian, Emperor of
    Mexico, execution of 7:29,
    39, 41
Maximilian I, Emperor
    2:105-106, 132
Mayan architecture 4:*135*
Mazarin, Cardinal Jules 3:138
Medici, in Bruges 1:70
Medici, Alessandro de' 2:48
Medici, Catherine de' 2:136-8
Medici, Cosimo de' 6:36
Medici, Francesco I de', Grand
    Duke of Tuscany 3:36, 37
Medici, Lorenzo de' 2:13-14,
    19, 40-41, 44, *45*, 51; 6:36
    tomb of 2:48, *51*
Medici, Marie de' 3:17, 30, 31,
    36, 36-9, *39*, 42
    as Regent of France 3:37
    Marie de'Medici cycle
    (Rubens) 3:17, 30, *31*, 36-9

Medici, Piero di Lorenzo de'
2:181
Medici Chapel, Florence 2:48,
51, 52, 73
Medici tombs (sculpture,
Michelangelo) 2:48, 51, 52
Meditations on First Philosophy
(Descartes) 4:40
Meegeren, Van, and Vermeer
3:111
Meervenne, Aleyt Goyaerts
van den 1:110
Meissen porcelain 5:53, 67, 78
Melancholy (Degas) 9:45, 51
Melun Diptych (Fouquet) 1:140
Melusine 1:26
Melzi, Francesco 2:18, 19
Memling, Hans see Artists'
Index
Memoirs (Casanova) 5:133, 133
Mengs, Anton Raphael see
Artists' Index
Meninas, Las (Picasso) 8:49
Meninas, Las (Velàzquez) 8:49
Mentana, Battle of (1867)
7:42
Merchant of Loves (Vien) 4:77
Merchant Shipping Act (1876)
7:72
Mercier, Gillette de 1:10
Mercier, Philippe see Artists'
Index
Mérode Altarpiece (Master of
Mérode 1:51, 51
symbolism in 1:51, 51
'merry company' 3:132, 133,
134, 135
Merry Company (Hals, D.) 3:46,
110
Merry Company in the Open Air
(Buytewech) 3:132
Merry Drinker, The (Hals)
3:48
Merry Fiddler, The (Honthorst)
3:53
Metamorphoses (Ovid) 4:50
Metsu, Gabriel see Artists' Index
Meurent, Victorine-Louise
7:20, 22-3
Mexico, France and 7:39-40
Mezzetin, The (Watteau) 5:18,
19, 32
Michelangelo see Artists' Index
Portrait of (del Conte) 2:43
Micheli, Guglielmo 8:109
Middle Ages
Church doctrine in 1:132
life in late 1:132
Middle East, changes in (early
1950s) 8:42
Middleburg Castle, Holland
1:83
Mignard, Pierre see Artists'
Index

Milan, Italy 2:15, 16-17, 18, 36
militia companies in Haarlem
3:45-6, 88-9, 92, 95-6
Mill, The (Boucher) 5:91
Millais, John Everett, praises
Whistler 9:13
Millennium, theory of the
1:134-5
Millet, Frank see Artists' Index
Millet, Kate 9:86
Mill Stream, The (sketch,
Constable) 6:83
Milton, John 3:106
Miner, The (Luks) 9:135
miniaturist's art 1:16
Miraculous Draught of Fishes,
The (cartoon, Raphael) 2:83
Miraflores Triptych (Van der
Weyden) 1:80, 88-9
Miro, Joan see Artists'
Index
Mississippi Company, The
5:40, 42
Mistinguette 9:69
modello 3:19, 22
for Descent from the Cross
(Rubens) 3:22
models
Boucher's 5:78, 78-9
Cassatt's 9:48, 50
Manet's 7:17, 20-21, 22-3
Matisse's 8:14, 16, 17, 18
Modigliani's 8:116, 117
Renoir's 7:109, 109
wax 4:20
Poussin and 4:19, 20
Whistler's 9:13-14
modern art, Manet and 7:21
Modern Idol (Boccioni) 8:83,
96
Modern Movement 9:69
Modern Painters (Ruskin) 6:113
'Modern Woman' (Cassatt)
9:48
Young Girls Pursuing Fame
9:48
Young Women Plucking the
Fruits of Knowledge and
Science 9:48
Modigliani, Amedeo see
Artists' Index
Modigliani, Eugenia 8:108, 108
on Modigliani's drawing
8:109
Modigliani, Flaminio 8:108
Modiste, La (Boucher) 5:91
Mohammed Ali, Pasha of
Egypt 6:138
Moitte, Pierre Etienne see Artists'
Index
Molenaer, Jan Miensz 3:46
Molière (Jean-Baptiste
Poquelin) 5:38, 39, 71, 100
Molyn, Pieter de 3:64, 65

Mona Lisa (Leonardo) 2:18, 28
stolen 8:106
Monet, Adolphe 7:76, 76-7
and Monet's career 7:77
Monet, Alice 7:79
in Venice 7:80
Monet, Camille 7:77, 78, 79,
88-9
on her Deathbed (Monet) 7:83
Monet, Claude see Artists'
Index
Monet, Jean 7:77, 79, 88-9, 100
Monet, Michel 7:100
Monforte Altarpiece, The (Van
der Goes) 1:141
monotype 7:51
Monro, Dr, sketch of Turner
6:109
'Monro School', The 6:109
Monserrat, Nicholas 8:42
Monsieur Bertin (Ingres) 4:125
M. et Mme Auguste Manet
(Manet) 7:13
monsters, in Bosch's paintings
1:114-15, 116-17
Montague, Lady Mary 4:118
Montauban, France 4:108
Montcalm, General 5:106
Montconys, Balthasar de, on
Vermeer 3:110-11
Monte, Deodatus del 3:14
Montefeltro, Guidobaldo da,
Duke of Urbino 2:77, 82
Montereau, murder of John
the Fearless at 1:39, 39
Mont-Sainte Victoire (Cézanne)
8:68
Montespan, Madame de 3:73
Montpensier, Portrait of the duc
de (Boucher) 5:83
Moonlight Landscape with Figure
at the Door of a Cottage
(Gainsborough) 6:50
Moore, Albert see Artists' Index
Moore, George
on Degas 7:47
on Manet 7:20
Mor, Anthonis see Artists' Index
Moreau, Gustave
class of '97 8:12
style of teaching 8:12
Moretus, Balthasar 3:17
Morgan, Daniel 6:73
Morisot, Berthe see Artists'
Index
Morning, The (Boccioni) 8:90
Morning Toilet, The (Chardin)
5:51
Morning Walk, The
(Gainsborough) 6:65
Morocco, Dutch alliance with
(1608) 3:69
Moser, Wolfgang Amadeus 6:42
Moss Roses (Renoir) 7:115

Mother Antony's Inn (Renoir)
7:109
motion, poetry of, Futurists and
8:85, 85
Moulin de la Galette, Le (Renoir)
7:114-15, 116-17
Moulins, Master of see Artists'
Index
Mountain Stream (Sargent) 9:97
Mousehold Heath (Crome) 6:140
Movable Feast, A (Hemingway)
9:70
movement
Boccioni and 8:82-3, 84
comparisons 8:85, 85
Futurists and 8:102
Mr and Mrs Robert Andrews
(Gainsborough) 6:54-5, 56-7,
65
'Mr Rubens' 7:109
Mrs Joseph Hamar (Reynolds)
6:13, 13
Mrs Philip Thicknesse
(Gainsborough) 6:59
Mrs Richard Brinsley Sheridan
(Gainsborough) 6:53, 62
Muette, Château La, France 5:14
Munday, Peter 3:132
Muñoz, Gil Sanchez
see Clement VIII
Munster, Treaty of (1648) 3:70,
71
Murat, Queen Caroline
(drawing, Ingres) 4:111, 111
Murders in the Rue Morgue, The
(Poe) 4:138
Murillo, Bartolomé see Artists'
Index
Musée Condé, Chantilly 1:17
Musée Ingres 4:108, 113
Muses, The (Le Sueur) 3:119
Museum of Fine Arts, Boston
and Sargent 9:79-80
Museum of Modern Art,
New York
and Hopper 9:110
opening of 9:138
Museums Commission
(French) 5:113
Music (Russolo) 8:102
Music Lesson, The (Metsu) 3:141
Music Lesson, The (Vermeer)
3:124
Music Party, A (sketch,
Gainsborough) 6:47
Music Party, The (Watteau)
5:17, 20
changes to 5:20
Musician, Portrait of a
(Leonardo) 2:31
Musician's Table, The (Braque)
8:68-9
Mussadeq, Dr 8:42
Musson, Célestine 7:44

Musson, Michel 7:46
Muybridge, Eadweard 7:69
  research into motion 7:68-9
Mycenae, Greece, excavating
  7:74
Mytens, Daniel *see* Artists'
  Index

N

Nadar 7:15
  and independent exhibitions
    7:47
Nana (Zola) 7:37
Nancy Cathedral, riot in (1892)
  7:104
Nantes, Edict of (1598) 4:72
Naples, Italy 7:45
  Degas in 7:44-5
Napoleon Bonaparte,
  (Napoleon I) Emperor of
    France 4:79, *80, 81,* 85, *98,*
    99, 105, 106, 110-11, 118,
    120, 130-33, 136; 5:113, *136,*
    136-8; 6:101, 103-106, *106,*
    111, 135, 136, 137, 138
  at Austerliz 6:*136*
Napoleon Crowning Himself
  (sketch, David) 4:*80*
Napoleon as Emperor (Ingres)
  4:*130*
Napoleon as First Consul (Ingres)
  4:110, *120*
Napoleon at the Pass of St Bernard
  (David) 4:80, *98*
Napoleon in his Study (David)
  4:*99, 111*
Napoleon III, Emperor of
  France (Louis-Napoleon
    Bonaparte) 7:15, *36, 38-9*
  as Antichrist 7:39
  and Belgium 7:40
  defeat at Sedan (1870) 7:*134,*
    135
  and Garibaldi 7:42
  and horse racing 7:67
  and Luxembourg 7:40
  and Mexico 7:39-40
Napoleonic Wars 6:101,
  103-106, 135-8
Naseby, launching of (1655) 3:106
Nash, John 6:79
Nash, Paul *see* Artists' *Index*
Nash, Richard (Beau) 6:*68,*
  69-71
Nassau, Prince Maurice of 3:70
National Academy of Design,
  New York 9:109
  and the Ashcan School 9:133
  and Bellows 9:135
  and Hopper 9:111

Nativity (Campin) 1:*101,* 102,
  141
Nativity (Christus) 1:140
Nativity with Cardinal Jean Rolin
  (Master of Moulins) 1:141
Nativity at Night (Geertgen tot
  Sint Jans) 1:141
Nativity Triptych (Van der
  Weyden) 1:102
  right wing 1:*81*
Natoire, Charles-Joseph 5:110
  on Fragonard 5:114
Natoire, Jean-Marc *see* Artists'
  Index
Nazis
  and Picasso 8:49
  and Spanish Civil War 8:72-3
  bomb Guernica 8:49
Necker, Jacques 6:74
'Negro' Period (Picasso) 8:52
Nelly O'Brien (Reynolds) 6:27
Nelson, Horatio 5:138; 6:112,
  118, 131, 132, 135, 137, *138*
  Death of (Maclise) 6: *134-5*
Neo-Classicism 4:76, 77, 82,
  83, 110, 112, 113, 114, 116,
  117; 5:113
Nero, House of, Rome 2:*102*
Nesle, Hôtel de 1:22, *34*
Netherlands, The 2:136-8; 3:12,
  48, 72-4, 92, 100-103, 133;
  4:40, 41, 42
  and Brazil 3:136, *137*
  Islamic alliances 3:69
  revolt in 3:68
  in 1654 3:136-8
  and Spain 3:44
  truce with Spain 3:68, 69
  truce in 3:16
  see also United Provinces
New Jerusalem, the 1:135, *135*
New Orleans
  Degas in 7:46
  The Cotton Exchange, New
    Orleans (Degas) 7:46
New York School of Art 9:108
Newby Hall, Yorkshire, and
  Boucher's tapestries 5:82, 83
Newlyn, Cornwall 9:100
Niagara Falls 9:*76-7*
Nicholas II, Tsar of Russia
  and his family 9:*106*
  killed by the Bolsheviks
    9:105, *106*
Nicholas V, Pope 1:*105;* 2:68,
  100-101
  declares Holy Year 1:104
Nicholas of Montenegro,
  deposed 9:106
Nietzsche, Friedrich, on artists
  8:109
Night Watch, The (Rembrandt)
  3:*88-9, 92-3*
  details 3:*88, 89*

watercolour copy 3:*89*
Night Windows (Sloan) 9:134
Nighthawks (Hopper) 9:118-19,
  118-19, 126-7
Nijinsky, Vaslav 8:*132-3, 133-4,*
  135
Nijmegen, Holland 1:12
  Limbourgs in 1:12
  Treaty of (1678) 5:12
Nivison, Josephine Verstille
  9:110, *113*
  Portrait of (Hopper) 9:*111*
Nocturne in Black and Gold: The
  Falling Rocket (Whistler) 9:14,
  15, 15-16
  Ruskin and 9:73-4
Nocturne, Grey and Gold – Chelsea
  Snow (Whistler) 9:21, *29*
Nocturne: Grey and Gold –
  Westminster Bridge (Whistler)
  9:*28*
'Nocturnes' 9:15, 19
  preparations for painting
    9:21
Nogent-sur-Marne, France
  5:*15*
Noli Me Tangere (Titian) 2: *120*
nonconformist artists 7:15
Norham Castle; Sunrise (Turner)
  6:*122-3*
Normandy, collapse of English
  rule in (1450) 1:104, 106
Normant de Tournehem, Le
  5:100
North, Lord 6:74
North America Act (1867) 7:40
North Briton, The, and John
  Wilkes 6:40
North Foreland, Battle of (1666)
  3:72
Northcote, James 6:15
Nude descending a Staircase
  (Duchamp) 8:85
Nude in a Red Armchair
  (Picasso) 8:62
Nude in the Bath (Bonnard) 7:52
nudes
  reclining 7:21, *21*
  Renoir on 7:111, 117, *129*
Nureyev, Rudolf 7:*105*
Nurse and Child (Hals) 3:*56*
Nutcracker Suite, The
  (Tchaikovsky) 7:*105*
nylon, development of 8:74
Nymphs of Diana Surprised by
  Satyrs, The (Rubens) 5:84-5

O

O'Brien, Nelly, *Portrait of*
  (Reynolds) 6:27

O Mistress Mine (Abbey) 9:*102*
O'Murphy, Louise 5:86-7, 92-3,
  134, 135
  Portrait of (Boucher) 5:*86-7,*
    92-3
Oath of the Horatii, The (David)
  4:77, 84, *89,* 91, *132*
Oath of the Jeu de Paume (sketch,
  David) 4:*78,* 82
Oath of Julius Civilis, The
  (Rembrandt) 3:*82*
Oberto (Verdi) 4:138
Odalisque (Boucher) 5:*87*
Odalisque, The (Renoir)
  7:*109*
Odalisque with Red Bloomers
  (Matisse) 8:*31*
Odalisque with Slave (Ingres)
  4:*126-7*
odalisques, rediscovery of 8:15,
  20, *20*
Offenbach, Jacques 7:37, 43
Office at Night (Hopper)
  9:*116-17*
oil, for mixing pigments 1:100
oil painting 1:43, 44, 50; 2:31-2,
  108-109; 3:84, 137-8
  in 15th-century Italy 1:79
  Picasso and 8:50
  see also paints
'oiling out' 5:21
O'Keefe, Georgia *see* Artists'
  Index
Old Man and a Youth, A portrait
  of an (Leonardo) 2:15
Old Masters
  Boccioni and 8:76
  Fragonard and 5:109
  importance of copying 7:44
  Ingres and 4:111, 114
  as inspiration 7:20, *21,* 23, 50
  Matisse and 8:12, 17
  Picasso and 8:47
  Renoir and 7:109, *111,* 112,
    117
  Watteau and 5:17
Old Savoyard (drawing,
  Watteau) 5:*19*
Old Star, The (Turner's pub)
  6:*112-13*
Oldenbarnevelt, Johan van
  3:70
Oliver Goldsmith (copy,
  Reynolds) 6:*14*
Olivier, Fernande 8:46, 47
  on Matisse 8:17
Olympia (Manet) 7:15, 20, 21,
  22-3, 26-7; 9:82
  Matisse on 8:20
  sketch for 7:23
Omval, The (etching,
  Rembrandt) 3:*81*
On the Balcony during the
  Carnival (Cassatt) 9:*56*

On the Origin of Species
(Darwin) 7:*135*
Open Window, The (Matisse)
8:15, 19
Open Window, Collioure
(Matisse) 8:22
Opening of the Fifth Seal (El
Greco) 2:140
Opéra Orchestra, The (Degas)
7:45, *57*
Opium War, The First (1839-42)
4:*134*
Orange, House of (Dutch royal
house) 3:68-9, 71, 73-4
Orleans, Duke of 1:*38*
assassination of (1407) 1:38, *38*
symbols 1:38
Orlers, Jan, on Rembrandt 3:77
Orry, Philibert 5:54
Otello (Verdi) 4:*138*
Ottoman Empire
disintegration of 9:72-3
Dutch alliance with (1611) 3:69
war with Austria (1682) 4:74
Otway, Thomas 4:73
Oudenarde, Battle of (1708) 5:14
Oudry, Jean-Baptiste *see*
Artists' Index
Ovens, Juriaen 3:82
Ovid (Publius Ovidius Naso)
2:117 125, 130; 4:13, 17, 50,
52, 59, 65, 66; 5:84
Oyster Gatherers at Cancale, The
(Sargent) 9:82
sketches for 9:78

P

Pabst, G. W. 9:*138*
Paes, General Sidonio 9:106
Pagan Deities: Astarte and Neith
(Sargent) 9:*81*
Paganini, Nicolo 6:137
Pagans, Lorenzo 7:45
Portrait of (Degas) 7:*45*
*Painter's Daughters Chasing a
Butterfly, The*
(Gainsborough) 6:*51*
painters' guild, length of
apprenticeship 1:76
see also Guild of St Luke
painter's trade, depicting 1:*100*
paintings
keeping references 1:102
selling 1:103
paints 1:100, 101, 102-3
Palais de la Cité, Paris 1:*28*
Palazzo Barbaro, Venice 9:*78*
Palazzo Crescenzi, The, Rome
4:44, *45*
Palladianism 4:68-71

Pallas, Peter 6:42
Palma, Giovane 2:114, 117
Palma Vecchio 5:21
Palmer, Mary, on Reynolds
6:17
Palmerston, Lord (British
Prime Minister) 9:39-40
re-elected 9:41-2
Pamphili, Cardinal Camillo
4:52
Panama Canal scandal 7:*103*,
105-106
Panama Company, bribes from
7:105-106
Pancake Baker, The (Brouwer)
3:*133*
panels, preparing wooden
1:100
Pansies (Boldoni) 8:*85*
Pantalon (in *Commedia
dell'Arte*) 5:37
Pantheon, Rome 2:*81*, 100-101,
102
Stourhead 4:*69*
Paoli, General Pasquale 6:42
Papaver moneti (poppy), Monet's
bleeding of 7:100
paper cut-out technique *see*
gouache découpée
'paper museum' 4:14
papier-collés, Cubist use of 8:71
Picasso and 8:52
Parade (Cubist burlesque) 8:47,
134
drop-curtain (Picasso) 8:*46*
Paracelsus, Philippus
Aureolus 2:73
Portrait of (Rubens) 2:*73*
Parayre, Amélie (Madame
Matisse) 8:14, 17
Parental Admonition (Terborch)
3:*141*
Paris 4:*76*, 132-3; 7:*77*; 9:44-5
Americans and 9:68-71
Armistice Day (1918) 9:*106*
balls in 7:36, *36-7*
behind the scenes 7:50-53
café society 7:34-5, *35*, 109;
9:*68-9, 69*, 70
the Commune in 7:72, 110,
110-11, 134, 136-7
day trips from 7:*131*
fashionable 7:34-7, *44-5*
horse racing 7:67, 68
Napoleon I and 4:132-3
by night 7:35-6
nightclubs 9:69, *69*
pastimes in 7:34
Siege of (1870) 7:46, 136-7
end of (1871) 7:71-2
sixth *arrondisement* 9:69
the streets of 7:84, *84*
uprisings in 4:135-6

Paris Exposition (1878) 9:72
Paris Opéra 7:37, *37*, 46, *46, 47,
55*
Degas and 7:46, 47
Watteau and 5:12
Paris Salon 5:*48-9*, 79, 80, 85,
110, 111, 112, 118
Boucher and 5:79, 85
Cassatt and 9:45
David and 4:77
first artist to market
successfuly in 5:85
Fragonard and 5:111,
112
Ingres and 4:113
and Renoir 7:111
and Sargent 9:82, *88*
and Whistler 9:78
Paris World Fair (1867) 7:16
Park, Merle 7:*105*
Park, Mungo 6:135
Parmigianino *see Artists'
Index*
Parnassus (Raphael) 2:*98*
Parnell, Charles 9:73, 74
Parsons, Alfred, and
Broadway, England 9:101
Parthenon, Athens 6:105
Partie Quarrée, La (Watteau)
5:24
Parting of Hero and Leander, The
(Turner) 6:*115*
Pascal, Blaise 3:*137*
pastels
Cassatt and 9:49, *51*
technique with 9:53
Chardin and 5:49
Degas and 7:51
*Pastoral Caprice with the Arch of
Constantine* (Claude) 4:*64*
Pastoral Landscape (drawing,
Claude) 4:*49*
Pasture, Rogier de la *see*
Weyden, Rogier van der
Patenier, Joachim *see Artists'
Index*
Pater, Jean-Baptiste *see Artists'
Index*
Paterson Children, The
(Raeburn) 6:*21*
Patience (Gilbert and Sullivan)
9:34, 35-6
patronage
of Bosch 1:*110*, 111
of Boucher 5:78, 79, 80
of Chardin 5:47
of Claude 4:46-7, *47*
of Van Eyck 1:44-6
of Fragonard 5:110, *112*
French royal family and
1:9-10
of Limbourg brothers
1:13-14, 19
of Matisse 8:15

of Poussin 4:14, 15, *15*, 17
Reynolds and 6:13
of Rubens 3:14
of Vermeer 3:111
of Van der Weyden 1:*76,
76*-7
of Whistler 9:15
Paul I, Tsar of Russia 5:*138*
Paul III, Pope 2:48, 49, 61,
69-70, 71
Portrait of, and his Grandsons
(Titian) 2:*111*
Paul IV, Pope 2:71
Paul V, Pope 2:70, 71, 4:36
Pavillon d'Armide, Le (Fokine)
8:*133*
Pavlova, Anna 8:135
Peace, Burial at Sea (Turner)
6:*113*
Peacock Room, The (Whistler)
9:15, *36*
Pearl Earring, The (Vermeer)
3:*113*
Pearl Necklace, The (Vermeer)
3:*113*
Peasants' Revolt, Russian
(1773-4) 5:74
Pécoul, Charlotte 4:77
Portrait of (David) 4:*79*
*Peasants Smoking at a Cottage
Door* (Gainsborough) 6:*67*
Pedrolino (in Commedia
dell'Arte) 5:37
Peiresc, Nicolas-Claude Fabri de
3:14
Pelletier, Le (copy, David) 4:*87*
Pels, Andries, on Rembrandt
3:87
Penn, William 3:104, 106; 4:72
Penni, Gianfranco
finishes Vatican
appartments 2:81
Pennsylvania Academy of the
Fine Arts
Cassatt and 9:44
and Hopper 9:111
Penruddock, Colonel John
3:105
Pepys, Samuel 3:72, 73, 74
Perceval, Spencer (British
Prime Minister) 6:104
assassination of (1812) 6:*103*
Père Lathuille's, At (Manet) 7:*32*
Perrot, Jules, sketch of (Degas)
7:*55*
Perseus and the Origin of Coral
(sketch, Claude) 4:*50-51*
perspective
Claude and aerial 4:50
Cubism and 8:69
development of science of
1:50
in *The Dancing Class* (Degas)
7:*55*

Poussin and 4:19
Peru 2:72
Perugino, Pietro *see Artists' Index*
Peruzzi, Baldassare 2:69, 79
Pesaro Madonna, The (Titian) 2:10
Pestalozzi, Johann 6:137
Peter the Great, Tsar of Russia 4:74, 5:41
Petites Heures, Les 1:15
Petrushka (Stravinsky) 8:134
Petworth House, Sussex 6:100, 110-11, 113
square dining room 6:110-11
Philadelphia, founding of 4:72-3
Philip the Bold, Duke of Burgundy 1:13
attacks Guelders (1388) 1:12
funeral of (1404) 1:37
interests 1:37
and invasion of England 1:36
and Limbourgs 1:11, 13, 19
marriage 1:38
relationship with England 1:38
tomb 1:37, 37
Philip the Fair, Duke of Burgundy 1:110
patron of Bosch 1:110, 111
Philip the Good, Duke of Burgundy 1:45, 68, 76
changes allegiance 1:73
and Van Eyck 1:77
founds Order of the Golden Fleece 1:73
marriage 1:46-7, 68, 69
Portrait of (Van der Weyden) 1:76
and Van der Weyden 1:77
Philip II, King of Spain 2:112, 113, 114, 130, 135; 3:12, 13, 68
and Bosch 1:117
Escorial inventory 1:80
Portrait of, in Armour (Titian) 2:114, 135
Philip III, King of Spain 3:13, 14
Philip IV, King of Spain 3:17; 4:42, 65
Philip V, King of Spain 5:40, 42
Philip Egalité, Duke of Orleans 4:104; 5:83
Portrait of, as duc de Montpensier (Boucher) 5:83
Philosophical Endeavour Towards the Defence of the Being of Witches and Apparitions, A (Glanvill) 3:73
Philostratus 4:17
photography 4:137
Degas and 7:51

use in motion research 7:68-9, 69
Piazza Navona, Rome 4:36-7, 38, 39, 46
Picasso, Claude 8:49, 49
Picasso, Maia 8:48
Picasso, Pablo Ruiz *see Artists' Index*
Picasso, Paloma 8:49, 49
Picasso, Paolo 8:47
Picasso López, Mará 8:44
Portrait of (Picasso) 8:44
Picture of Dorian Gray, The (Wilde) 9:37
Picturesque 4:16; 6:114
Pierre, Jean-Baptiste 5:49
Pierrot (in *Commedia dell'Arte*) 5:33, 37, 39
Pietà (Bellini) 2:140
Pietà (Botticelli) 1:85
Pietà (Titian) 2:113, 116
Pietà Duomo (sculpture, Michelangelo) 2:49
Pietà, St Peter's (sculpture, Michelangelo) 2:46, 54; 4:87
Pietro da Cortona *see Artists' Index*
Pietro da Verona 1:19
Pig (study, Rembrandt) 3:80
Pigot, Governor 5:105
Piles, Roger de 3:23, 33
Pilgrimage to the Island of Cythera, The (Watteau) 5:15, 22-3, 26-7
Pink and Grey: Three Figures (Whistler) 9:30-31
Pinks and Clematis (Manet) 7:19
Pinturicchio, Bernardino *see Artists' Index*
Piombo, Sebastiano del *see Artists' Index*
'pipes' 1:16
piracy 6:132-3
Pissaro, Camille *see Artists' Index*
Pissaro, Lucien *see Artists' Index*
Pithecanthropus, discovery of 8:74
Pitt, William, the Elder (British Prime Minister) 5:105, 106; 6:42, 135, 138
Pitt, William, The Younger (British Prime Minister) 4:106
Pitti Palace, Florence 3:38
Pius III, Pope 2:38
Pius V, Pope 2:138
Pius VII, Pope 4:130
Pizzaro, Francisco 2:72
Place du Théâtre Français, La (Pissarro) 7:140
Plague at Jaffa, The (Gros) 4:140
Plantin Press 3:17
Plato 6:36

Plimsoll, Samuel 7:72
Plimsoll mark 7:72
Pliny the Elder 2:51
ploughing 6:99-101
Plutarch 4:17, 57
Poe, Edgar Allan 4:138, 7:74
Poesia (Marinetti's magazine) 8:79, 101
Poland 3:104, 137, 138; 4:105
Pole, William de la, Duke of Suffolk, banishment of 1:106
Polish Rider, The (Rembrandt) 3:84
Pollock, Jackson *see Artists' Index*
Pomegranates (Sargent) 9:96
Pomeranian Dogs (Gainsborough) 6:47
Pompadour, Madame de 5:48, 78, 79-80, 81, 84, 98, 99, 100-103, 104, 109, 112
Portrait of
by Boucher (1758) 5:98, (1759) 5:99
by Drouais 5:103
by La Tour, Maurice-Quentin de 5:100
Pompeii, Italy 4:77
murals, Renoir and 7:112
Poniatowski, Stanislaus, King of Poland 6:40
Pont Neuf (Renoir) 7:84
Ponte Vecchio, Florence 2:13
Ponts-de-Cé, Battle of (1620) 3:38
Pool of London (Derain) 8:14
Pope, A. A. 9:74
Poplars (Monet) 7:94
Port of London, The 6:130, 130-31
Porta, Giacomo della 2:70, 71
Portinari Altarpiece, The 1:141
(detail, Van der Goes) 1:103
portraits
aristocratic 9:84, 84
demand for lifelike 1:49
Van Eyck's contribution to 1:51, 51
individual sitters *see:*
Artists' Index under individual artists
General Index under name of sitter or title of painting
Works' Index under title of painting or **Portraits of**
Portugal 5:105; 6:103, 106
loses Brazil 3:136, 137
Post, Franz *see Artists' Index*
'Postlethwaite' (caricature of Wilde) 9:35
Potter Palmer, Mrs, and Cassatt 9:48
Pouget, Marguerite 5:47
Portrait of (Chardin) 5:47
Pound, Ezra 9:68

Portrait of (Wyndham Lewis) 9:68
Poussin, Gaspard *see* Dughet, Gaspard
Poussin, Nicolas *see Artists' Index*
'Poussinistes' 4:21
power struggles, Burgundian 1:36-9
Poynter, sketch of Whistler 9:12
Pozzo, Cassiano dal and Poussin 4:14, 15, 15
Pozzo, Andrea del 6:12
Prado, Picasso and 8:49
Premier Peintre, David as Napoleon's 4:80
Pre-Raphaelite Brotherhood, The 6:39
Presentation in the Temple, The (Rubens) 3:23, 25
Presentation of the Virgin, The (Gaddi) 1:17
press-gangs 6:132
Previati, Gaetano 8:83
Prince Igor (Borodin) 8:133
Prince Regent, the (George IV of England) 6:79, 102, 103-105
Prince of Wales, Edward
and fire brigades 9:39
and international understanding 9:40-41
Princesse du Pays de la Porcelaine, La (Whistler) 9:25
printing 2:42
in Amsterdam 3:103
Cassatt and 9:48, 53
Degas and 7:51
Prisoners, The 5:36
Prix de Rome 4:76
Boucher and 5:77, 77
J-P Chardin and 5:48-9
David and 4:110
Fragonard and 5:109, 109
Ingres and 4:109, 109-10
Watteau and 5;14
prize fighting 7:39; 9:134-5, 135
Procuress, The (Van Baburen) 3:111, 112, 114, 125
Procuress, The (Vermeer) 3:112, 112, 128
Prodigal Son, The (Diaghilev) 8:135
Prodigal Son, The (Rubens) 3:18-19
Prodigal Son in a Tavern, The (Hals) 3:51
Protestantism 2:106, 134-5; 3:44, 47, 58, 100, 103, 106
Proust, Antonin, and Manet 7:17, 17
Proust, Marcel, on Ballets Russes 8:132

Prussia: and Franco-Austrian
alliance (1756) 5:104-105
King of 7:38-9, 135
war with Austria 7:40
Pugachov, Emelyan 5:74
'Puggy Booth' (Turner) 6:112
Pulcinella (in Commedia dell'
Arte) 5:37, 38
Pullman, George Mortimer
9:38
Pullman Car 9:38
Punch (in Commedia dell'Arte)
5:37, 38
Pursuit of Love, The (Fragonard)
5:112, 124-5
Pynas, Jan 3:77

Q

Quadruple Alliance (1720) 5:40,
42
Quarrel of the Cabmen (Gillot)
5:14
Quarton, Euguerrand see
Artists' Index
Quatremère de Quincy 4:77
Queen Caroline Murat (sketch,
Ingres) 4:111, 111

R

Racehorses at Longchamp (Degas)
7:58-9
Racine, Jean 4:20
Radcliffe, Dr John 6:69
Radek, Karl 8:83
Raeburn, Sir Henry see Artists'
Index
railways in France, Sunday
trips on 7:130, 130-31
Raimondi, Carlo, Cassatt and
9:45
Rain, Steam and Speed (Turner)
6:113, 117, 129
Raising of the Cross, The
(Rubens) 3:15, 20, 22
Raising of Lazarus, The (Lievens)
3:78
Rake's Progress (Stravinsky) 8:42
Ramel, Portrait of Delphine
(Ingres) 4:113
Rape of Europa (Titian) 2:131
Raphael Sanzio see Artists'
Index
Raphael and La Fornarina
(Ingres) 2:80
Rauber, Die (Schiller) 6:72
Raven, The (Poe) 4:138
Ray, Man see Artists' Index

Reader, The (Fragonard) 5:115
Realism, Cassatt and 9:45, 51
Reality (journal of U.S.A.
Representational painters)
9:122
Récamier, Julie
Portrait of (David) 4:85, 96-7
Portrait of (Gerard) 4:140
Reclining Nude (Modigliani)
7:21
Reclining Nude with Necklace
(Picasso) 8:66-7
Red Horseman (Carrà) 8:101
Red Interior, Still-Life on a Blue
Table (Matisse) 8:32
red paint (vermilion)
base material for 1:21, 101
Jan Gossaert's method with
1:102-103
Rubens' use of 3:20
Vermeer's use of 3:14
Red Studio, The (Matisse) 9:111
Redshirts (in Italian
unification) 7:38
Reformation, The 2:68, 73, 74,
106, 134-5, 137; 4:36
Regatta at Argenteuil (Monet)
7:84-5
Regentesses, The (Hals) 3:47, 49,
50, 86
Reggio Calabria, Italy 8:76-7
Rehn, Frank K. M., and
Hopper 9:110
Reign of Terror (1792-3) 5:113
Reinach, Baron de 7:106
Reinagle, Ramsay see Artists'
Index
relief sculptures 2:51-2
Remarque, Erich Maria
9:137
Rembrandt van Rijn see
Artists' Index
Renard, Gabrielle 7:112, 112
René Master see Artists' Index
Reni, Guido see Artists' Index
Renoir, Claude 7:112
Renoir, Edmond 7:110
Renoir, Jean 7:112, 113
Renoir, My Father 7:113
La Grande Illusion 8:72
Renoir, Léonard 7:108
Renoir, Marguerite 7:108
Renoir, My Father (Jean Renoir)
7:113
Renoir, Pierre-Auguste see
Artists' Index
repoussoir technique 4:52
Repton, Humphrey 4:71
Resistance (copy, Fragonard)
5:119
Rest on the Flight into Egypt
(Patenier) 1:141
Restaurant Fournaise 7:118,
118, 133

restoration (of paintings) 2:34,
67
Return of Marcus Sextus
(Guérin) 4:84
Reyniers, Lysbeth 3:46
Reynolds, Frances 6:14
Reynolds, Revd Samuel 6:12, 12
Reynolds, Sir Joshua see
Artists' Index
Rhineland, Germany 6:110
Rhudde, Dr 6:78, 80
Rhyl Sands (Cox) 6:140
Ribera, Jusepe de 4:76
Riccoboni, Luigi 5:39
Rice, Elmen 9:112
Richard Wagner (Renoir) 7:112
Richardson, Jonathan 6:12
Richelieu, Cardinal Armand de
Wignerod 3:38, 39, 42, 71;
4:15, 16, 17, 26, 40-41
Portrait of (de Champaigne)
3:39
Richtofen, Baron Manfred von
9:104-105
Rigoletto (Verdi) 4:138
Rijn, Cornelia van 3:76
Portrait of (Rembrandt) 3:76
Rijn, Harmen van 3:76
Portrait of (Rembrandt) 3:76
Rijn, Rembrandt van
Harmenzoon see
Rembrandt van Rijn
Rijn, Titus van 3:80, 83
Portrait of (Rembrandt) 3:82
Rimbaud 8:45
Rinaldo and Armida (Boucher)
5:78-9
Riot in the Galleria (Boccioni)
8:83, 91
Ripa, Cesare 3:116, 118, 119
Rising of the Sun, The (Boucher)
5:84, 96
Rivals, The (Sheridan) 5:73
Robert, Hubert see Artists'
Index
Robert Kelso Cassatt (Cassatt)
9:50
Robertson, Mary Anne
(Grandma Moses) see Artists'
Index
Robespierre, Maximilian 4:75,
79, 104
Rochambeau (French
commander) 6:72
Rockets and Blue Lights (Turner)
6:127
Rockwell, Norman see Artists'
Index
Rococo 4:76, 82, 83, 88; 5:13-14,
40, 46, 76; 6:45, 46
Fragonard and 5:116-17
Rocques, Joseph-Guillaume
4:109
Rodin, on Sargent 9:79

Roger Freeing Angelica (Ingres)
4:8-9, 111, 115, 115
Rohan Book of Hours, The 1:21
Rohan Hours, Master of the see
Artists' Index
Rohe, Mies van der 8:41
Rolin, Chancellor Nicholas
and Van Eyck 1:47
and Van der Weyden 1:77,
77
Rolla, Henry see Artists' Index
Roman virtue 4:84
Romano, Giulio 2:81
Romanticism 3:87; 4:53, 80, 84,
112, 113, 114; 5:73-4; 6:115,
121
Rome 2:37, 46-7, 48, 64, 68-71,
72-4, 79, 81, 100-103; 3:14;
4:36-9, 46, 83-4; 5:77;
6:12-13
Sack of (1527) 2:47, 48, 69,
72-4, 112-13, 135; 4:36
Romney, George see Artists'
Index
Romulus and Remus and the She-
Wolf (Rubens) 3:8
Roque, Jacqueline 8:49
Rose Period (Picasso) 8:46, 51
greatest inspiration 8:52
work from 8:55
Ross, James Clark 4:137
Rossellino, Antonio see Artists'
Index
Rothenstein, William, on
Sargent 9:85
Rotherhithe (etching, Whistler)
9:19
Rothko, Mark see Artists' Index
Rotonde, Le, Paris 9:68-9, 70
Roualt, Georges 8:135
Rouart, Henri 7:48
Rouen Cathedral 7:86
series (Monet) 7:86-7
Rouen Cathedral in Full Sunlight
(Monet) 7:95
detail 7:87
Rouge et le Noir, Le
(Shostakovich) 8:17
Rousseau, Jean-Jacques 6:72,
72
Rovere, Guidobaldo della II,
Duke of Urbino 2:111, 127
rowing parties, from Paris in
19th century 7:132-3
Rowlandson, Thomas see
Artists' Index
Royal Academicians, The
(Sanders) 6:37
Royal Academy, The (British)
6:8-9, 14, 15, 16, 17, 36-9, 38,
39, 40, 47, 48, 77, 78, 80-81,
85, 109, 110, 111, 113
first exhibition 6:39
life class at 6:109

Sargent and 9:79, 85, *94*
Whistler and 9:13, 22
Royal Albert Hall, London 7:*40*
Royal Festival Hall, London 8:41
Royal Navy (British) 6:*133*
warships for 6:132
Royal Theatre, London 9:39
'Rubenistes' 4:21
Rubens, Maria 3:12
Rubens, Clara Serena 3:15-16
Portrait of (Rubens) 3:*28*
Rubens, Jan 3:12
Rubens, Peter Paul *see Artists' Index*
Rubens and Isabella Brandt in a Honeysuckle Bower (Rubens) 3:*18*
Ruche, La 8:*111*
Rue Montorgueil Decked with Flags, The (Monet) 7:*93*
Rueil, Country House at (Manet) 7:*16*
Ruisdael, Jacob van *see Artists' Index*
Rupert, Prince, of the Rhine 4:74
Ruskin, John
attack on Whistler 9:*14*, 14-16; 9:73-4
on Reynolds 6:20
and Turner 6:*112*, 113, 117
Russell, Lord John (British Prime Minister) 9:42
Russia 4:74; 5:74, 78; 6:103, 106, 136, 138
changes in (1796) 5:138
epidemic in (1892) 7:103, *104*
'freedom' in 5:74
invasion of Turkey 9:72-3
new dynasty in (1689) 4:74
peasant revolt (1773-4) 5:74
see also Soviet Union
Russolo, Luigi, *Music* 8:*102*
Rustici, Giovanni Francesco 2:32-3
Ruts, Nicholaes, and Rembrandt 3:79
Ruysbroeck, Jan van 1:109
Ryder, Albert Pinkham *see Artists' Index*

S

s'Hertogenbosch 1:*108, 109*
religious influence in 1:108
Sack of Rome (1527) 2:47, 48, 69, 72-4, 112-13, 135; 4:36
Sacre, Le (David) 4:80
Sacré Coeur, Paris 7:71
Sacred and Profane Love (Titian)

2:110, *118-19, 122-3*
Sade, Marquis de 5:133
Saducismus Triumphatus (Glanvill) 3:73
Saenredam, Pieter *see Artists' Index*
'Sailor's Friend, The' (Samuel Plimsoll) 7:*72*
St Barbara (Van Eyck) 1:*49*
St Bartholomew's Eve Massacre (1572) 2:136, 138
St Bavon Cathedral 1:*47*
Altarpiece *see Ghent Altarpiece*
St Botolph Club, Boston 9:79
St Cecilia Altarpiece, The (Raphael) 2:*83*
St Charles Borromeo 5:42
St Christopher (Bosch) 1:*113*
St Christopher (Patenier) 1:*141*
St Donat, Church of, Van Eyck buried in 1:47
St Eligius Weighing the Rings of a Bridal Couple (Christus) 1:*140*
St Erasmus Altarpiece (Poussin) 4:*14*
St Francis Receiving the Stigmata (Van Eyck) 1:*48-9*
St Francis Xavier 4:13
St George and the Dragon (Rubens) 3:*19*
St George's Guard, Amsterdam 3:*70-71*
headquarters 3:*45*
St Gudule, Cathedral of, Brussels 1:*79*
St Ignatius Loyola 4:13
St-Jacques-sur-Coudenberg, fraternity in 1:79
St James (study, Leonardo) 2:*34*
St Jerome (Bellini) 2:*140*
St Jerome (Leonardo) 2:*31*
St John, Cathedral of, s'Hertogenbosch 1:108, 110, *111*
Bosch works for 1:110-11
gargoyles 1:*110*, 116-17
St John the Baptist between a Pharisee and a Levite (sculpture, Rustici) 2:32-3
St John the Baptist with Sts Andrew and Peter (Domenichino) 4:*44-5*
St John the Baptist in the Wilderness (Bosch) 1:*121, 128*
landscape in 1:117
sources for 1:117
St Joseph (school of Campin) 3:*116*
St Luke Drawing the Virgin (details Van der Weyden) 1:*80*
St Luke Painting the Virgin (Deutsch) 1:*102*

St Mark (sculpture, Donatello) 2:*52*
St Mark Freeing a Christian Slave (Tintoretto) 2:*141*
St Martin's Lane Academy, The 6:44, 45, 46, 54
St Mary Magdalen (Titian) 2:*115*, 116
St Michael and the Dragon (Raphael) 2:*82*
St Paul's Cathedral, London 6:*17*
St Peter's Basilica, Rome 2:*37*, 41, 47, 49, 53, *68-71*, 80, 81, 102; 4:*37*, 38
St Peter's Church, Sudbury 6:*55*
St Petersburg 9:*12-13*
St Saviour, Church of, altarpiece 1:*46*
St Sebastian (Perugino) 2:*141*
St Sulpice, Paris 3:*106*
St Tropez 8:37-8, *38*
Saint-Julien, Baron, and Fragonard 5:111, 118, *119*
Saint-Non, Jean-Claude Richard, Abbé de 5:*110*, 112, *116*, 120, 129
Saint-Point, Valentine, and Futurism 8:103
Saintard, Marguerite 5:54
Portrait of (Chardin) 5:*45*
Sainte-Chapelle, Paris 1:*29*
Sainte Geneviève des Ardents (Doyen) 5:*119*
Salai, Giacomo 2:*15*, 16, 18, 19
Salinger, J. D. 8:42
Salisbury Cathedral 6:*78*
by Constable 6:*92-3*
Salle du Conseil, The (Boucher) 5:*80-81*
Salmon, André 8:46
Salome (Titian) 2:*112*
Salon d'Automne
Boccioni and 8:80
and 'Fauves' 8:15
Matisse and 8:37
and Modigliani 8:112
Russian paintings at 8:132
Salon des Refusés 7:14, *14*, 15
Whistler and 9:22
Salon of the Société Nationale des Beaux Arts, Matisse and 8:13
see also Société Nationale des Beaux Arts
Salons, private 7:37
Salvation Army, founding of 9:41
Samary, Jeanne, by Renoir 7:*118-19*, 124-5
Samuel Johnson (Reynolds) 6:*15*
San Carlo alle Quatro Fontane, Rome 4:42

San Georgio Maggiore (Guardi) 4:*106*
San Lorenzo, Florence 2:48, 49, 50
Sanders, John *see Artists' Index*
Sandrart, on Claude 4:45
Sandycombe Lodge, Twickenham 6:*111*
Sangallo, Antonio da 2:70, 71
Sangallo, Giuliano da 2:69
Sanger, 'Lord' 7:*136*
Sansovino, Jacopo 2:113
Sant'Andrea al Quirinale, Rome 4:39
Sant'Elia 8:*80*
Sant'Ivo alla Sapienza, Rome 4:37
Santa Maria in Vallicella, altarpiece, (Rubens) 3:15
Sanzio, Raphael *see Raphael Sanzio*
Sarah Siddons as the Tragic Muse (Reynolds) 6:*19*, 35, 49
Sardinia, and First Coalition (1793) 4:104
Sargent, Dr Fitzwilliam 9:76
Sargent, Emily 9:76, 80, 81
Sargent, John Singer *see Artists' Index*
Sargent, Mary Newbold 9:76, *76*
Sargent, Violet 9:76, 80
Saskia as Flora (Rembrandt) 3:*91*
Saskia, Portrait of (Rembrandt) 3:*78*, 79
Satie, Eric 8:135
Saumur, Château de, France 1:*11, 32*
Savonarola, Girolamo 2:40-41, 45-6
Savoy, Duke of 3:69
Savoy Hotel, London 7:*80-81*
Savoy Theatre, Sheffield, England 9:39
Saying Grace (Chardin) 5:*54-5*, 63
details 5:*55*
Rotterdam version 5:54
sketch of lost original 5:54
Saying Grace (Maes) 3:*133*, 134
Scaramouche (in *Commedia dell'Arte*) 5:*37*, 37
Scarlatti, Alessandro 3:138
Schéhérazade (Bakst) 8:*134*
designs for 8:*132-3*
Scheut, Charterhouse of gifts from Van der Weyden 1:*80*
sells Van der Weyden painting 1:80
Schiller, Johann Christoph Friedrich von 6:72
Schomberg House 6:48, *48*

Schönbein, Friedrich 4:*136*
School of Athens, The (Raphael)
2:78, 84, *90-91, 96-7,* 98
cartoon (full-scale) 2:*96-7*
details 2:*97*
preliminary study 2:*97*
Schoolmistress, The (Chardin)
5:*50*
Schooten, Joris van 3:77
Schrevelius, Theodorus 3:48
Schuman, Robert 8:40
Schuman Plan (1952) 8:40
Science of Rights (Fichte) 5:*137*
Scott, Sir George Gilbert
9:38
Screen with Old Battersea Bridge
(Whistler) 9:*19*
Scullery Maid, The (Chardin)
3:*117*
sculptural form 2:*52*
sculpture 2:52-3
Cubist 8:71
Degas and 7:*50,* 51
first 'assembled' 8:52
Futurist 8:79, *79,* 83
Lipchitz and 8:118, *118*
Matisse and 8:18, 20, 26
Modigliani and 8:110-11, *110*
115-16
Picasso and 8:50, 52, 71
primitive 8:52, *52*
Renoir and 7:113, 117
see also individual pieces
Scupstoel (drawing, Van der
Weyden) 1:*77, 106*
sea trade, British 6:130-33
*Seaport with the Embarkation of
the Queen of Sheba* (Claude)
4:50, *54-5, 60-61,* 63
details 4:*54-5*
preliminary sketch 4:*55*
*Seaport with the Landing of
Cleopatra in Tarsus* (Claude)
4:*57*
Seaport with Setting Sun
(Claude) 4:*56*
seascapes 6:136
Seasons (series, Watteau) 5:14
Spring 5:*13*
Seated Man Leaning on a Table, A
(Modigliani) 8:*126-7*
Seated Persian (drawing,
Watteau) 5:*18*
Seated Woman (Picasso) 8:53, *53*
Seated Woman, Portrait of a
(Hals) 3:48, *49*
Seated Nude (Modigliani) 8:*114*
Second Coming of Christ 1:134
Second-Storey Sunlight (Hopper)
9:*131*
Seine, boating on 7:*132-3,*
133
Seisinegger, Jacob 2:134
Select, The, Paris 9:68, 70

self-portraits 3:*21*
individual sitters *see:*
Artists' Index under
individual artists
Works' Index under
Self-portrait of
Senegal, British attack (1758)
5:*106*
Servant Reading to his Master
(Robert) 5:*71*
servants 5:68-71
Setting of the Sun, The (Boucher)
5:*84, 97*
Seven Deadly Sins, The (Bosch)
1:*112*
Seven Sacraments Altarpiece, The
(Van der Weyden) 1:78, *92-3*
Seven Years War (1756-63)
5:*102, 103, 104*
Severini, Gino *see Artists' Index*
Sèvres porcelain 5: 101, *101*
Boucher and 5:*78,* 81
Sforza, Bianca Maria, Duchess
of Milan 1:75, *78*
Sforza, Francisco, becomes
Duke of Milan 1:104, *104*
Sforza, Giovanni 2:37
Sforza, Ludovico, Duke of
Milan 1:*136;* 2:*14,* 15-16, 17,
18, 23, 41
Sforza Monument, The
(Leonardo) 2:15-16, 18
sfumato technique 2:29, 52
Shakespeare, William 5:38
Shakespeare and Company,
Paris 9:70, *70*
Sharkey's Club, New York
9:*134-5,* 135
Shaw, George Bernard 9:37
Shchukin, Sergei, and Matisse
8:15, 21
She-Goat, The (Picasso) 8:*50*
Shell Temple, Chatsworth,
Derbyshire 4:*70*
Shepherd Piping to a Shepherdess
(Boucher) 5:*108-9*
Sheridan, Richard Brinsley
5:73; 6:62, 104
Portrait of Mrs
(Gainsborough) 6:53, *62*
Sherwood Forest, England
6:*104,* 105
Shimeall, Revd Richard 7:39, 42
Shinn, Everett *see Artists' Index*
Shoshone Cliffs (Hopper) 9:*115*
Shostokovich, Matisse and
8:17
Shrovetide Revellers, The (Hals)
3:*50*
Shuffleton's Barber Shop
(Rockwell) 9:*116*
Siddons, Sarah
Portrait of (Gainsborough)
6:*63*

as the Tragic Muse (Reynolds)
6:19, *35,* 49
Sigismund I, Emperor 1:*40*
and Great Schism 1:42
Signac, Paul *see Artists'
Index*
'signature' 1:20
Signora Massimino (Boccioni)
8:*88*
silverpoint, use of 2:31, 32,
97; 3:*78*
Silvestre, Théophile, on Ingres
4:*114-15*
Simplon Tunnel opens (1906)
8:*138*
sin, Church teachings on
1:132-3
Singel Canal, Amersfoort
(drawing, Rembrandt)
3:*80-81*
Sirois: and Watteau 5:14-15, 16
Sirois and his Family (Watteau)
5:*14*
Sisley, Alfred *see Artists' Index*
Sistine Chapel, Rome 2:47, *48,*
50-51, 56-9, 60-63, 64-6, 77,
81, 85, 87; 3:*14;* 4:*36;* 6:*13*
inspiration for Reynolds
6:19, 35
ceiling of 2:47, *50-51, 56-9,*
64-5, 66-7, 85
copy of nude by Rubens
3:*14*
restoration of 2:67
Sistine Madonna, The (Raphael)
2:*94*
Sitting Bull, Chief 7:73
Sitwell Children, The (Copley)
9:*84*
Six, Portrait of Jan (Rembrandt)
3:*87*
detail 3:*87*
'six-footers' (by Constable) 6:80,
81
Sixtus IV, Pope 2:64
size, for mixing pigments 1:100
Skate, The (Chardin) 5:*44-5,* 46
Skiff, The (Renoir) 7:*123*
Slave Ship, The (Turner)
6:*114-15*
slave trade 6:130-2
slave traders 6:132
Sleeping Girl (Vermeer) 3:*116*
Sleeping Kitchen Maid (Maes)
5:*52*
Sleeping Woman (drawing,
Rembrandt) 3:*81*
Sloan, John *see Artists' Index*
Sluter, Claus *see Artists' Index*
Small Bather, The (Ingres) 4:*118*
smallpox 6:103
Smash the Hun (poster,
Hopper) 9:*109*
Smokers, The (Brouwer) 3:*140*

Smollett, Tobias 6:42
on Bath, England 6:70
Smyth, William, Bishop of
Lincoln 2:104
Snowstorm (Turner) 6:116, *117*
*Snowstorm; Hannibal Crossing
the Alps* (Turner) 6:*121*
Snowstorm; Mount Cenis
(Turner) 6:*111*
Snyders, Frans, and Rubens
3:19, 27
Société des Vingts (Les XX)
9:82
Société Nationale des Beaux
Arts, and Matisse 8:13
Society of Artists, The
and first public art exhibition
6:37
Gainsborough and 6:47
Society of Dilettanti, The 6:15,
37-8
by Reynolds 6:*15*
Sodoma, Il (Giovanni Antonio
Bazzi) 2:78
Soissons, Comte de 4:40
Soldier with a Laughing Girl
(Vermeer) 3:*121*
*Soldier Offering a Young Woman
Coins* (Terborch) 3:*133,* 134
Solus Lodge, Twickenham
6:*111*
Somerset House, London 6:*37,*
38, 39, 116
library ceiling (Reynolds)
6:*37*
Sophia Charlotte, Lady Sheffield
(Gainsborough) 6:*53*
Sorel, Agnes, by Fouquet
1:*106*
South Africa, 'diamond rush'
in (1867) 7:*42*
South of France
Camoin in 8:38
Cassatt in 9:49
Cézanne in 8:36-7
Chagall in 8:39
Cross in 8:37
Dufy in 8:39
Manguin in 8:38
Matisse and 8:*14,* 15, 17, 37,
38-9, *39*
Modigliani in 8:113, 117
Picasso in 8:39
Renoir in 8:37, *37*
Signac in 8:36, 37, *38*
South Sea Bubble (1720)
5:*40-43;* 6:*137;* 9:40-42, *41*
'Southern Outfall' 9:41
Soutine, Chaïm *see Artists'
Index*
Soviet Union
Bolsheviks in 9:105
Duma 8:*137,* 138
and Kellogg-Briand Pact

(1928) 9:136
general strike in (1905) 8:137-8
new era in 9:138
Stalinist purges 8:73-4
and World War I 9:105
see also Russia
Spain 2:132-8; 4:40-41, 42; 5:40, 42, 74, 136, 138; 6:103, 106, 137, 138
and colonial power 3:70
and Dutch trade 3:70
and First Coalition (1793) 4:104
invasion of France (1674) 3:71
in the Netherlands 3:44, 68-71
pact with France 6: 137-8
and the Quadruple Alliance 5:42
war with Chile (1866) 9:14
war with the Dutch (1585-1609) 3:44, 68-71
Spanish Civil War (1936-9) 8:48, *48, 49, 72-3, 74*
Spanish Guitarist, The (Manet) 3:53
Spengler, Oswald 9:106
sporting prints, English 7:66, *67*
Spring (Watteau) 5:13
Square Dining Room at Petworth (Turner) 6:110, *111*
squirrel, grey 7:74
Stag at Sharkey's (Bellows) 9:134-5
Stalin, Joseph 9:138
Standing Nude (Braque) 8:68
Stanley, H.M., finds Livingstone 7:137
Stanza d'Eliodoro (Raphael) 2:79, 92-3, 99
Stanza dell'Incendio (Raphael) 2:80, 81, 99
Stanza della Segnatura (Raphael) 2:79, 84, 90-91, 96-7, 98
States of Mind (Boccioni) 8:83
The Farewell 8:85, *94*
Those Who Go 8:95
steam, age of 6:133, *133*
steam engines 5:72
steamboats 6:105, 133
Steen, Jan *see Artists' Index*
Steeplechase Cracks (Herring) 7:66-7
Stein family
Gertrude on Paris 9:68, 71
and Matisse 8:15
and Picasso 8:46, 51
Stephanus Geraerts (Hals) 3:66
Steps, The (Renoir) 7:115
Sterne, Laurence 6:42
A Sentimental Journey through France and Italy by Mr Yorick

6:42
still-life 5:46
Still-Life with Oriental Rugs (Matisse) 8:24-5
Stock-Exchange (or Bourse), Amsterdam 3:100, 100-101
Stoffels, Hendrickje 3:80, 82, 83
Stolen Shirt, The (Fragonard) 5:115
Stolypin, Pyotr 8:138
Stonehenge (Constable) 6:97
'Storm and Stress' 5:73-4
Stormy Landscape (Rembrandt) 2:33
Stottard, William 9:17
Stour, River, England 6:86, 88, 90, 98, *98*
Stour Valley, England, scenes of (Constable) 6:82-3, *82-3*
Stourhead, England 4:70, *70*
Pantheon 4:*69*
Stowe, England 4:68, 69, 71
Strachey, Lytton 9:106
Stratford St Mary (sketch, Constable) 6:82
Strauss, Johann, the Younger 7:41
Stravinsky, Igor 8:42, *134*
in Paris 9:69
Street Enters the House, The (Boccioni) 8:82-3, 83-4
Street Scene with Snow (Henri) 9:132
Stresemann, Gustav 9:138
Stuart, Gilbert *see Artists' Index*
Stubbs, George *see Artists' Index*
Studio in the Batignolles Quarter (Fantin-Latour) 7:14
Study of an Old Man (Rembrandt) 3:77
Sudbury, Suffolk 6:45, 54, 55
Sueur, Eustache Le *see* Le Sueur, Eustache
Suez Canal
opening of (1869) 7:70, 73-4
Suffering Christ, The (Bellini) 2:140
Suffolk, Constable and 6: 98-101
Suffolk, Duke of
banished by Henry VI 1:105
execution of 1:105
Suffolk punch (horse) 6:98, *99*
Suisse, Charles 7:77
Suleiman the Magnificent 2:73
Sulking (Degas) 7:66-7
Summer (Poussin) 4:21, *34*
Sun Yat-sen, Dr 8:105
Sun Also Rises, The (Hemingway) 9:70
Sunday, Women Drying Their Hair (Sloan) 9:132-3

Sunday pastimes, in France 7:130-33, *131*
Sunlight in a Cafeteria (Hopper) 9:130
Surrealism, Picasso and 8:48, 52, 63
Susan on a Balcony Holding a Dog (Cassatt) 9:63
Suythof, Cornelius 3:83
Swan Lake (Tchaikovsky) 9:74
Sweden, war with Germany (1630) 3:41, 42; 4:41
Swinburne, Algernon Charles 9:16, *16*, 35
on *Little White Girl* (Whistler) 9:16
on *Ten O'Clock Lecture* (Whistler) 9:16
Swing, The (Cazes) 5:44
Swing, The (Fragonard) (1775) 5:122, 129
(1776-7) 5:111, *118-19, 121*
Swing, The (Renoir) 7:116
symbolism 3:50-51, 55, 59, 64, 114, 116, 118, 119, 134; 4:22, 23
in Bosch's works 1:114, 116
in *Hay Wain* 1:116
in Van Eyck's works 1:50-51, 56
in *The Arnolfini Wedding* 1:50, *60*
in *Ghent Altarpiece* 1:52, 53
in *The Madonna by the Fountain* 1:50
in *The Madonna in Her Chamber* 1:63
in *The Madonna with Chancellor Rolin* 1:61
in *The Mérode Altarpiece* 1:51
in *A Woman Weighing Pearls* 1:51
Symbolism (movement), Modigliani and 8:115
symbols, Dutch 3:71
in *Hals' work 3:50-51
'Symphonies' 9:19
Symphony in White, No. 1: The White Girl (Whistler) 9:22, *22-3, 24*
details 9:23
Symphony in White, No. 2: The White Girl (Whistler) 9:22, 23
Symphony in White, No. 3: (sketch, Whistler) 9:23
Syndics, The (Rembrandt) 3:98
Synthesis of Human Dynamism (Boccioni) 8:79

T

Tableau de Cébès, Le (Varin) 4:12-13

Tafur of Seville, on Bruges 1:71
Tahiti 6:40-41, *42*
Taj Mahal, India 3:74
'Talkies' 9:138
tapestries, by Rubens 3:17
see also Gobelins tapestry factory
'Ta-ra-ra-boom-de-ay!' (song) 7:106
Tarleton, Lieutenant-Colonel Sir Banastre 6:73
Portrait of (Reynolds) 6:19, *19*
Tarquin and Lucretia (Titian) 2:116-17
detail 2:*117*
preliminary drawing? 2:*116*
Tassi, Agostino 4:44, 49, 50
Tavors, Marquis of 5:*105*
Tchaikovsky, Peter
Nutcracker Suite 7:105
Swan Lake 9:74
Tcherincheva, Lubov 8:*135*
Technical Manifesto of Futurist Literature (Marinetti) 8:101
Technical Manifesto of Futurist Painters (Marinetti) 8:82
Telegraph, The (Ship) 6:76
telephone
first exchange 7:104-105
invention of 7:71
tempera 2:52
Poussin and 4:13
Tempest, The (Giorgione) 2:110
Temple Gold Medal 9:111
Temptation of St Anthony, The (Bosch) 1:121, *130-31*
details 1:*114-15*
sources 1:117, 130
Temptation of St Anthony (Ernst) 1:116
Ten O'Clock Lecture (Whistler) 9:16
Teniers, David *see Artists' Index*
Terborch, Gerard *see Artists' Index*
Terbruggen, Vermeer and 3:114
Terrace, The (Monet) 7:76-7
Terror during French Revolution 4:*137*
Tessin, C. G., Portrait of (Aved) 5:79
Teutsche Akademie 4:45
textiles, oriental 9:36
Thackeray, William 6:118
Thames, River
health hazard of 9:41
Turner and 6:108-109, 115
views along 6:*116*
Whistler and 9:13, 41
Thames near Walton Bridge, The (Turner) 6:114
Theatre Royal, Edinburgh 9:39
Theodore, Tsar 4:74, *74*

Theotocopoulus, Domenikos
see El Greco

Thicknesse, Philip, and
Gainsborough 6:45, 59
Portrait of Mrs
(Gainsborough) 6:59

Thief on the Cross (Campin)
1:141

Thins, Maria 3:109

Thirteen Colonies, revolt of
5:72-3, 72-3

Thirty Years War (1618-48)
3:39, 41; 4:41, 42

Thoré, Théophile 3:111, 112,
121

Thornhill, James 6:37

Three Bathers (Cézanne) 8:20

Three Crosses, The (etching,
Rembrandt) 3:86, 87

Three Dancers, The (Picasso)
8:48, 50-51

Three Graces, The 6:22

Three Graces, The (Rubens) 3:20

Three Ladies Adorning a Term of
Hymen (Reynolds) 6:22-3,
30-31

Three Resolutions, The (1629)
3:41

Three Trees, The (etching,
Rembrandt) 3:85

Ticonderoga 5:106

Tintern Abbey (Turner) 6:114

Tintoretto, Jacopo see Artists'
Index

Tissot, James see Artists' Index

Tite Street, Chelsea 9:14

Titian Vecellio see Artists' Index

Titus, Portrait of (Rembrandt)
3:82

Tivoli, Italy 4:45, 46; 5:110, 111,
120

Tobago, French capture of
(1781) 6:72, 72-3

Tobias and the Archangels (detail,
Botticini) 2:12

Toilette, La (Watteau) 5:17

Toklas, Alice B. 9:71

Tolstoy, Count Leo 9:40

Tom Sawyer (Twain) 7:72

tools of the artists' trade 1:102

topography 6:110, 114, 116-17

Torero and a Young Girl
(Cassatt) 9:45, 57

Torre de la Parada, Rubens
and 3:17

Torrigiano, Pietro see Artists'
Index

Torso Belvedere (sculpture) 2:51,
67

Tortoni's Restaurant, Paris
7:34, 35

Toscanelli, Paolo 2:13

Tour, Georges de La see La
Tour, Georges de

Tourneham, Le Normant de
5:100

Tower of London 6:130

Town Hall, Bruges 1:76-7
panels by Van der Weyden
1:76

Town Hall, Amsterdam 2:82,
82; 3:70

Townshend, Lord 'Turnip' 6:100

Townshend Acts (1768) 6:40, 41

Trafalgar, Battle of (1805) 6:116,
118, 131, 133, 133,
135, 138

Trajan's Column, Rome 2:101,
103; 4:18, 133

Transfiguration (Bellini) 2:140

Transfiguration (Raphael) 2:81,
83, 85, 95

Transport of the Body of St
Mark (Tintoretto) 2:141

Traviata, La (Verdi) 4:138; 7:37

Tréhot, Lise 7:109
and Renoir 7:109, 111

Trés Belles Heures de
Notre-Dame, Les (Limbourg
Brothers) 1:16

Trés Riches Heures du Duc de
Berry, Les (Limbourg
Brothers) 1:11, 16-17, 17,
18, 18, 19, 20,
calendar from 1:17, 18, 24-35
details from 'October' 1:22-3,
22-3
influence of Duc de Berry's
collection on 1:19

'Triangular Trade' (slave trade)
6:130-31

Trial of Moses, The (Giorgione)
2:140

Tribunal of the Uffizi, The
(Zoffany) 6:141

Tribute Money, The (detail,
Masaccio) 2:52

Trilby (du Maurier) 9:17

Triptych of the Virgin (Van der
Weyden) 1:80

Tristan and Isolde (Wagner) 9:42

Tristesse du Roi, La (Matisse)
8:34-5

Triumph of Galatea (Raphael)
2:79

Triumph of Pan, The (Poussin)
4:26

Triumph of Silenus (Poussin)
4:15

Triumph of Venus, The
(Boucher) 5:80, 88-9

Trocadero Palace, Paris 9:72,
72

Trotsky, Leon 9:136, 138

'Trotskyites' 8:73-4

Truman, Harry S. (USA
President) 8:42

Tub, The (Degas) 7:53

Tuileries Gardens, Paris 7:36

Tuileries Palace, Paris
ball at the 7:36-7
Court Banquet at 7:36

Tukashevsky, Marshal 8:74

tulips 3:103

Tull, Jethro 6:25

Tunis 2:133, 134

Turkey 4:74
and possible French
invasion 7:42
Sultan of 7:38-9

Turkish Bath, The (Ingres) 4:113,
117, 118-19, 129
changes in 4:118
details 4:118, 119
study for 4:119

Turkish Woman and her Slave
(Liotard) 5:68-9

Turner, Joseph Mallord
William see Artists' Index

Turner Bequest 6:113, 113, 139

Turenne, Portrait of the Comte de
(detail) David 4:83

Twain, Mark 7:72; 9:36

Twelve-Year Truce (1609-21)
3:16, 68, 69,132

Two Comedians (Hopper) 9:113

Two Dancers on Stage (Degas)
7:60

Two Kinds of Games (Steen)
3:108

Two Studies of Women (drawing,
Watteau) 5:18

Two Women in an Interior
(Matisse) 8:30

U

Uffizi Galleries, Florence 3:37

Ulyenburgh, Hendrik van 3:78

Ulysses (Joyce) 9:70

Ulrique, Louise 5:47

Umbrellas, The (Renoir) 7:128

Unique Form of Continuity in
Space (Boccioni) 8:79, 85

United Provinces 3:68-9, 100
allies of 3:73
in 1666 3:72-4
States General 3:71
war with England (1665-7)
3:72-3
war with Spain (1585-1609)
3:68-71
see also, Netherlands, the

United States see America

Universal Exhibition, Paris
(1867) 7:36, 40, 41
Delacroix and 4:113
Ingres and 4:113
royalty at 7:38-9

Uranus, discovery of (1781) 6:73

Urban VIII, Pope 2:71; 4:14, 15,
37, 38, 39, 54, 56

Urbino, Italy 2:76-7, 78

US Shipping Board, Hopper
and 9:109

Useless Resistance (Fragonard)
5:119

Utrecht, Holland 1:109
Caravaggisti in 3:53

Utrillo, Maurice see Artists'
Index

Uxmal, Mexico 4:135

V

vaccinations 6:103

Valenciennes, France 5:12, 14

Valhalla, The, Regensburg
4:136

Valley Farm, The (Constable)
6:81

Valparaiso (Whistler) 9:18-19

Valpinçon, Edouard 7:45
and Ingres 7:44

Valpinçon, Paul 7:48, 66
and family at the races
(Degas) 7:47

Valpinçon Bather, The (Ingres)
4:117, 121; 7:52

Van Eyck, Jan see Eyck, Jan van

Van der Weyden, Rogier see
Weyden, Rogier van der

Van Rijn, Rembrandt see
Rembrandt van Rijn

Vanderbilt Whitney, Gertrude
9:110

vanitas images 3:48, 51

varlet de chambre
Limbourgs as 1:14
Van Eyck as 1:44

Vanvitelli, Gaspar see Artists'
Index

Variations in Flesh Colour and
Green: The Balcony
(Whistler) 9:21

Varin, Quentin see Artists'
Index

varnishes
Gainsborough's 6:53
improvements in 1:50

Vasari, Giorgio 2:12, 13, 30,
32-3, 45, 50, 51, 64-5, 67, 80,
81, 82, 85, 87 108, 111,
114-15; 6:36

'Vasari of the North, The' (Van
Mander) 3:45

Vatican Palace, Rome 1:105;
2:47, 48, 56-7, 73, 78-81, 83-4,
90-93, 96-9, 102

see also Sistine Chapel
Vauxcelles, Louis
on artists 8:37-8
on Braque 8:71
Vecellio, Titian *see* Titian Vecellio
Veen, Otto van 3:13
Vega, Lope de 5:38
Velázquez, Diego Rodriquez de *see Artists' Index*
Velde, Willem van der, the Younger *see Artists' Index*
Venables, Robert 3:104, 106
Venice 2:104-106, *108-109, 118-19*; 6:*112*, 113, *115*, 117, *126*
Biennale 9:111
Venice, from the Canale della Giudecca (Turner) 6:*126*
Venice: Moonrise (Turner) 6:*115*
Venice Preserv'd (Otway) 4:*72-3*
Venus and Adonis (Lemoyne) 5:*76*
Venus Asleep (Boucher) 5:*117*
Venus of Urbino (Titian) 2:*126-7*; 7:*21*
Venne, Adriaen van der *see Artists' Index*
Verdi, Giuseppe 4:*138*
La Traviata 7:37
Verdonck, Rombout 3:12
Verhaecht, Tobias 3:13
Verlaine 8:45
Vermeer, Johannes (Jan) *see Artists' Index*
Veronese, Paolo *see Artists' Index*
Verrocchio, Andrea del *see Artists' Index*
Portrait of (di Credi) 2:*14*
Versailles, France 4:68, *68*, 74; 5:40, 82, 100, 101, *102, 112*, 116
Prussians at (1871) 7:135
Vespucci, Amerigo 1:*137*
Vesuvius, eruption of (1819) 6:112
Veth, Jan, on Vermeer 3:114
Vickers family, by Sargent 9:*79, 87*
Victoria, Queen of England 4:137, 138
attacks on 4:*128*; 7:*138*
as Empress of India 7:*73*, 74
and Napoleon III 7:40
and Palmerston 9:40
and Prince Albert 4:*138*
and the telephone 7:*104*
Vien, Joseph Marie *see Artists' Index*
View of La Crescenza (Claude) 4:*45*
View of Delft (detail, Vermeer) 3:*114, 123*

View of the Grande Galerie in the Louvre (Robert) 5:*81, 140*
View of Haarlem from Noorder Spaarne (Vroom) 3:*44-5*
View of Potrel Manor (Griffier) 5:*70*
View from the Luxembourg (David) 4:*79*
View of SS Trinità dei Monti (Claude) 4:*47*
Vigée-Lebrun, Elizabeth *see Artists' Index*
Villa Lante, Bagnaia 4:*44*
Villa Savoie, Poissy 9:*137*
Villeneuve, Admiral Pierre 6:135, 137, 138
Vincennes, Château de 1:*15*, 35
Vincenzo I, Duke of Mantua 3:14
Vinci, Leonardo da *see* Leonardo da Vinci
Vinci, Tuscany 2:12-13
violet paint, base material for 1:21
Virgil, Polydore 4:47, 50, 70
Virgin and Child, The 2:*85*
Virgin and Child, The (Geertgen tot Sint Jans) 1:141
Virgin and Child, The (Campin) 1:*78, 78*
Virgin and Child in a Niche (Van der Weyden) 1:78, 87
Virgin and Child with St Anne, The (Leonardo) 2:29
Virgin and Child with St Anne and John the Baptist, The (Leonardo) 2:26
Virgin in the Burning Bush (Froment) 1:140
Virgin of the Rocks, The (Leonardo) 2:32 (c. 1508), 2:15, 27
Visit to the Nursery, The (Fragonard) 5:*111*
Visitation, The (Rubens) 3:*22, 24*
Visscher, Nicholas
Allegory of Holland 3:*71*
Vlaminck, Maurice *see Artists' Index*
Vollard, Ambroise 8:39
and Picasso 8:51
Vollard Suite, The: No. 38 (Picasso) 8:*51*
Voltaire (François Marie Arouet) 5:*101*, 102, 103, 135
Voltel, Joost van der 3:102
Voragine, Jacobus de 1:117
Vow of Louis XIII, The (Ingres) 4:112
Vouet, Simon *see Artists' Index*
Vroom, Hendricksk *see Artists' Index*

W
Waddington, M. 7:72
Wagner, Richard, *Portrait of* (Renoir) 7:*112*
Walberswick, Cornwall 9:100
Waldensians 3:106
Wales, Edward, Prince of 7:*38-9*, 73-4, 138; 9:40-41
Wall Street Crash (1929) 9:71, *136-7*, 137
Wallenstein, Albert of, Duke of Friedland 3:41, *42*
Walpole, Horace 4:18, 70
Walpole, Robert 5:41
Wals, Gottfried 4:44, 45
Walter, Marie-Thérèse 8:47, 48
Portrait of (Picasso) 8:53, *53, 62*
war, glorification of 8:81, *81*
see also World War I
War (Rubens) 3:*69*
War and Peace (Tolstoy) 9:*40*
war artists 9:*104-105*
Sargent as 9:80, *80*, 81, 98-9
Warhol, Andy *see Artists' Index*
Washerwoman, The (Chardin) 5:*50-1*
Washington, George (President) 4:106; 5:73, *104*, 137, 138; 6:72, 74
Washington Square, New York 9:*112*
Waste Land, The (Eliot) 9:*70*
Water Urn, The (Chardin) 5:*50*
watercolour 6:116
Waterfall at Tivoli (Dughet) 4:*16, 141*
Waterlilies (Monet) 7:*96-7*
Waterloo, Battle of (1815) 4:106, 136; 6:101
Waterloo Bridge (Monet) 7:*81*
Watt, James 5:73
Watteau, Antoine *see Artists' Index*
Portrait of (Carriera) 5:*11*
weaving 6:98, 105
Webster, Captain 6:69
Wedekind, Frank 9:*138*
Well Of Moses (Sluter) 1:*37*
Wellington, Arthur, Duke of 6:103, *106*
Wellington, New Zealand 9:*42*
Wentworth, Thomas, Earl of Strafford 4:40, *42*
Werff, Adriaen van der *see Artists' Index*
Werve, Claus de *see Artists' Index*
West, Benjamin *see Artists' Index*
West India Company 3:101, 136, 137; 5:106; 6:131

West Point, Whistler at 9:18
Western Motel (Hopper) 9:*128-9*
Weyden, Corneille van der 1:79
Weyden, Goswijn van der 1:79
Weyden, van der (grandson) 1:79
Weyden, Pieter van der 1:79
Weyden, Rogier van der *see Artists' Index*
Whistlejacket (Stubbs) 6:*140*
Whistler, Anna Matilda 9:13
Whistler, Beatrix 9:15, *16-17*, 17
Whistler, Major George 9:12, *13*
Whistler, James Abbot McNeill *see Artists' Index*
Whitby, Yorkshire 9:100
White, Mme Henry, *Portrait of* (Sargent) 9:*78*
White Duck, The (Oudry) 5:*141*
White House, Chelsea, The (Girtin) 6:*140*
White House, Tite Street, London 9:14, 16, 79
white paint, base material for 1:21
Cassatt's use of 9:55
Ruben's use of 3:20
Whistler's use of 9:14
Whitney, Eli 4:106
Whitney Museum of American Art, and Hopper 9:110-11, 113
Whitney Studio Club, and Hopper 9:110
Whittle, Frank 8:74
Who Shall Deliver Me? (Khnopff) 8:*116*
'Wild Beasts, The' (Fauvists) 8:14, *14-15*, 22
Wild Poppies (Monet) 7:*88-9*
Wilde, Oscar 9:37
and Aesthetic Movement 9:*34*, 35-6
on himself 9:35
on Paris 9:68
as a sunflower (satirical cartoon) 9:*34*
trial of 9:37
and Whistler 9:*16*, 17, 36-7
Wildman, John 3:105
Wife, Portrait of his? (Van Eyck) 1:*46*
Wife, Portrait of his? (Van der Weyden) 1:*86*
Wilhelm I, Kaiser of Germany 7:135
Wilhelm II, Kaiser of Germany, abdication of 9:106
Wilkes, John 6:*41*
controversy over 6:40-41
Wilkie, Sir David 6:113

Willem van Heythuyzen (Hals) 3:*49*

William the Silent, Prince of Orange 2:136-7; 3:12

William II, Prince of Orange 3:71, 138

Willie Lott's cottage 6:*83, 86*

Wilson, Harold (British Prime Minister) 8:41

Wilson, Richard *see Artists' Index*

Wilson, Woodrow (USA President), and Fourteen Points 9:104

Wilton, Joseph 6:36

Wincklemann, Johann 4:76, 77, 84

Winter (engraving, Boucher) 5:*77*

Winter (Poussin) 4:21, *35*

Winter Garden, Paris 7:*36*

Winthrop, John 3:*40*

witches 3:73

Witches' Hammer 1:133, *135*

Witt, Jan de 3:71, 73-4

Witte, Count Sergie 8:*137*

Wolfe, Brigadier James 5:*105,* 106

Wolfenbüttel, Battle of (1641) 4:41

Wolff, Albert 7:47

Wolsey, Cardinal Thomas 2:74

Woman Bathing (Cassatt) 9:65

Woman with Blue Eyes (Matisse) 8:*19*

Woman in Blue Reading a Letter (Vermeer) 3:*109*

Woman Carrying a Child (drawing, Rembrandt) 3:*80*

Woman and Child Driving (Cassatt) 9:*60-61*

Woman in a Garden (Boccioni) 8:*82*

Woman and Goldfish (Matisse) 8:15, *28-9*

Woman at her Mirror (Cassatt) 9:*48-9*

Woman with Muff (Boucher) 5:*83*

Woman Reading a Book (Fragonard) 5:*127*

Woman Reading a Letter (Metsu) 3:*134*

Woman Sewing (Cassatt) 7:*48*

Woman Taking Tea (Chardin) 5:*45*

Woman Weighing Pearls, A (Vermeer) symbolism in 1:*51*

Woman's School of Design Henri and 9:132

Woman's Work (Sloan) 9:*134*

Women of Algiers (Delacroix) 8:*20*

Women in the Garden (Monet) 7:82, *82*

Women Ironing (Degas) 7:*63*

Women Picking Fruit (Cassatt) 9:*50-51*

Women Running on the Beach (Picasso) 8:*60-61*

Wood, Grant, *see Artists' Index*

Wood, John, on Bath 6:68

Woodcutter Courting a Milkmaid (Gainsborough) 6:*58*

word-pictures 8:*71*

'Words-in-Freedom' (Marinetti's use of language) 8:101-102

workshops 1:100-101; 2:12; 3:18

World, end of the 7:39

World War I
   last days of 9:105-106
   Sargent and 9:80, *80,* 81

World's Columbian Exposition Cassatt and 9:48

Worth, Charles 7:36-7

Wouk, Herman 8:42

Wren, Sir Christopher 4:74

Wright of Derby, Joseph *see Artists' Index*

Wyeth, Andrew *see Artists' Index*

Wynants, Johannes 6:45

Wyndham Lewis *see Artists' Index*

Wyndham Sisters, The (Sargent) 9:*95*

X

'X-films', introduced in Britain (1951) 8:42

Xaintrailles, Poton de 1:72

Y

yellow paint:
   base material for 1:*101*
   Rubens' use of 3:*20*
   Vermeer's use of 3:114

York, Duke of 4:105

Yorktown, Siege of (1781) 6:*72-3,* 74

Young Couples with Guitarist and Shepherd (Watteau) 5:*28*

Young Draughtsman, The (Chardin) 5:*59*

Young Englishman, The (Titian) 2:*128*

Young Girl (Cassatt) 9:*48*

Young Man, Portrait of (Van Eyck) 1:*59*

Young Plan (1929) 9:136
   Depression and 9:137

Young Woman, Portrait of a (Van der Weyden) 1:*86*

Young Woman with Blue Eyes (Manet) 7:*19*

Young Women on the Banks of the Seine (Courbet) 7:*117*

Young Spartans Exercising (Degas) 7:44-5, *50*

Ypres Salient at Night, The (Nash) 9:*104-5*

Z

Zampieri, Domenico *see* Domenichino

Zborowski, Leopold 8:*110, 111,* 112

Zelli's, Paris 9:69

Zoffany, Johann *see Artists' Index*

Zorndorf, Battle of (1758) 5:*102,* 105

Zuccati, Sebastiano 2:108

Zucchi, Antonio 6:16

A GLOSSARY IN PICTURES

Van Gogh's Palette

Although in nature there is an infinite number of colours, most artists choose quite a small range of shades to create their pictures. The set of colours used by the artist in any painting is called the artist's palette.

Van Gogh restricted his palette to a very few colours, but the effects he achieved were surprisingly varied. He particularly liked contrasting colours – brown and green, or blue and orange – which accentuate each other when placed together; they are known technically as complementary colours.

In *The Bridge at Langlois* Van Gogh used six basic colours to create a vivid scene. The orange banks and trees contrast with the blues of the river and the sky, while the grass is splashed with patches of dark brown. Only in the group of washerwomen, and the bridge with its horse and cart, does he extend his range by adding black and white.

Similarly, in *Starry Night* (1899), Van Gogh limited his palette to just four basic colours. The deep violet sky contrasts dramatically with the yellow stars and the moon. And against this brilliant background, the dark brown and green of the cypress tree add a sombre note of drama.

The Bridge at Langlois *1888*
21¼″ × 25½″ Kröller-Müller Museum, Otterlo

Fra Angelico's Gilding

Early Renaissance artists often used gold leaf to decorate altarpieces. This *Coronation of the Virgin* shows Fra Angelico's skill at using this material.

The gilding of a panel was done first so that the gold would not overlap onto the finished work. The areas to be gilded were covered with layers of bole, a form of red clay which gave body and richness to the gold. When the bole had been polished, the gold leaf was laid over it, pressed with cotton and burnished. The gold could then be tooled.

In this painting, Fra Angelico has incized the gold in the centre with very fine lines to catch the light and create the effect of shining rays. In the haloes, he has used compasses to trace patterns of concentric lines, and he has used tiny lumps of gesso (plaster of Paris) beneath the gold to make raised ornaments. The drapery of the male saints has been tooled with extreme delicacy to suggest brocade, while in the clothing of the female saints, the artist has painted lightly over the tooling to create the finest gold embroidery.

The Coronation of the Virgin *1434-35*
44" × 45" Uffizi, Florence

Giotto's Continuous Narrative

One of the most innovative features of Giotto's art was his use of a continuous narrative technique, which can be seen in this, one of the frescoes in the Arena Chapel.

The fresco contains two successive episodes in the Life of Christ – the Resurrection from the tomb and the discovery of the risen Christ by the Magdalen. Giotto has placed the figures parallel to the picture plane so that they appear to move across the picture space in a continuous procession from left to right, slowly unfolding the drama within – a movement accentuated by the gestures of the figures.

Giotto enhances the impression of continuous action by cutting off his figures at the edges of the picture. The angel on the left is partially hidden behind the decorative border of the fresco and the figure of Christ seems to be moving out of the picture into the next scene. The apparent continuity is also emphasized by the rocky slope in the background, which is a continuation of the background of the previous fresco – the scene of *The Lamentation* over the dead Christ.

The Resurrection and **Noli Me Tangere** *c.1303-06*
79¾″ × 72¾″ The Arena Chapel, Padua

Bellini's Sacra Conversazione

During the second half of the 15th century, artists in Italy began to develop a new form of altarpiece – the *sacra conversazione* or 'sacred conversation'. The term refers to a scene of the Madonna and Child with Saints, in which the figures are grouped together in a unified space. This new type of altarpiece gradually replaced the polyptych form, in which the figures are separated from each other by the frame of the painting, as in Van Eyck's *Ghent Altarpiece*, Van der Weyden's *Seven Sacraments Altarpiece* or Bellini's own *Frari Triptych*.

In the *Murano Altarpiece*, however, Bellini has adopted the form of the *sacra conversazione*. The Madonna and Child occupy the same space as the Saints and the kneeling Doge of Venice, Agostino Barbarigo. The figures are situated on a marble platform behind which stretches a continuous landscape.

The continuity of space in the *sacra conversazione* allowed the painter to develop a closer relationship between the figures who are usually united by their movements or gestures. Here, the kneeling Doge is 'protected' by the figure of St Mark standing behind him. His act of devotion is acknowledged by the Christ Child who raises his hand in blessing, while on the right the Doge's name-saint, Augustine, looks towards him and completes the balanced arrangement of the group. The unity of the figures is further emphasized by the red curtain which seems to form a frame around them.

In his *San Zaccaria Altarpiece* (1505), Bellini unites his figures under a large apse-like structure which creates an air of intimacy amongst the figures as they stand together in quiet, personal devotion.

The Murano Altarpiece *1488*
78½″ × 118″ San Pietro Martire, Murano

Leonardo's Underpainting

During the Renaissance, many altarpieces were painted on wooden panels. This was a complex process as the final colours were applied not to the bare wood but over layers of underpainting to give depth and solidity. First the panel would be covered with layers of gesso (plaster of Paris) which would then be scraped smooth. Onto this the artist would apply a layer of ground colour or underpaint.

Leonardo's *Adoration* is mostly at this stage of underpainting in yellow and brown. Over this he has drawn in the general design of the scene and the outlines of all the figures. Those in the background are only roughly sketched in, but those in the foreground are partially modelled in areas of black paint. When covered with the final layers of colour, these areas of black would appear as shadows on the figures' faces, or in the folds of their drapery.

Leonardo has also begun to add highlights to the picture. This is especially clear in the figure of the Christ Child and in the face of the old man to His left.

Scala

The Adoration of the Magi *1481-82*
96¾″ × 95½″ Uffizi, Florence

Botticelli's Classicism

During the Renaissance, artists and their patrons became very interested in classical themes. Many artists painted historical or mythological scenes based on accounts in classical literature. *The Calumny of Apelles* is based on a literary description of a lost work by the famous Greek painter Apelles and was probably painted for Botticelli's own satisfaction.

The work is described by the classical writer Lucian, in a dialogue on calumny. He tells how Apelles was falsely denounced as a traitor to his patron Ptolemy IV and took revenge by painting a picture illustrating the evils of slander.

Here, Botticelli recreates Apelles' work, following Lucian's description. On the right is an enthroned figure with ass's ears, who probably refers to Ptolemy. He listens to the words of two women who symbolize Ignorance and Suspicion. The innocent victim is dragged towards him by a beautiful woman who represents Calumny. On the left, the naked figure of Truth looks up to Heaven, pointing out the source of true knowledge. The scene takes place in a classical palace adorned with reliefs. Some of these are based on classical works, while others reproduce paintings by Botticelli.

The Calumny of Apelles *c.1496-7*
24½″ × 36″ Uffizi, Florence

Bronzino's Illusionism

During the Renaissance, artists often painted the ceilings of buildings in an illusionistic way. Here, for example, in the chapel of Eleonora of Toledo, Bronzino has created the illusion of an opening in the roof of the chapel through which we see the sky, filled with the figures of saints. The viewer is not intended to see the ceiling as a solid surface, but as a kind of open window, a portal through which a glimpse of the Divine world above can be gained.

Bronzino has made the illusion more complex by bridging the opening, or 'oculus', with a decorative cross. This decorative framework appears to belong to the 'real' architecture of the chapel, but the architectural surround is also a painted illusion. This type of painting was not only designed to display the artist's skill, but also to make the spectator feel closer to the realm of the Divine. Bronzino has exploited this idea very clearly in the figure of Saint Francis of Assisi, here seen in the top part of the ceiling. The Saint, who is shown receiving the Stigmata as a reward for the holiness of his life, looks upwards to the source of Divine Light, which appears to come from the area behind the medallion located in the centre of the oculus.

Ceiling of the Chapel of Eleonora of Toledo *1540-41*
Palazzo Vecchio, Florence

Watteau's Fête Galante

When Watteau presented *The Pilgrimage to the Island of Cythera* as his reception piece to the French Academy in 1717, the Academicians placed it in a category of its own, referring to it as a *fête galante*. With their gorgeous colouring, and featuring brilliantly-costumed figures engaged in leisurely outdoor pursuits such as listening to music or indulging in love games, the fêtes galantes show the influence of the Parisian fairs – and particularly of the performances of the Italian Comedy presented at them – which Watteau had often visited.

Appropriately, Watteau's fêtes galantes are all characterized by an air of performance, with the subjects seemingly acting out their own miniature dramas. Despite the theatricality of the pictures, however, Watteau's purpose was to portray a mood rather than a well-defined story. This mood was invariably a melancholy one. Love, health and happiness are pictured, but they are seen from a distance – as bounties which cannot be shared by the artist who depicts them. And many of his figures appear isolated, as in this picture, the *Récréation Galante:* none of the groups communicate with each other, and the figure on the left peers disdainfully at the artist.

Jorg P. Anders/Bildarchiv Preussischer Kulturbesitz

Récréation Galante *1717-18*
44″ × 64″ Berlin-Dahlem, Staatliche Museen

Boucher's Pastoral

Boucher's pastoral scenes, together with his erotic subjects, were his most popular works. Paintings of pastoral themes became fashionable in European art during the 16th and 17th centuries, and were largely derived from the traditions of pastoral poetry. They usually focus on simple activities placed in a rustic setting. In Boucher's painting a shepherdess feeds a shepherd with a grape, an action which, as the picture's title suggests, clearly has erotic overtones.

The painting is obviously not a realistic depiction of country life. The figures are elegantly dressed and beautifully groomed. Their clothes are spotlessly clean and show no traces of sweat or toil. The delightful sheep lie quietly at their feet, grouped harmoniously together, and the landscape is painted in a deliberately idealized manner.

This charming and sentimental vision reflects in part the attitudes of Boucher's 18th-century French patrons towards the countryside. As wealthy town-dwellers, they had little idea of the realities of rural life. To them, the country offered a pleasant retreat from the pressures of living in town, and the vision of a simpler, purer life.

Are They Thinking of Grapes? *1747*
30″ × 35″ Nationalmuseum, Stockholm

Gainsborough's Picturesque

In the middle of the 18th century, the market for landscape paintings in England was extremely small. Landscapes were generally considered to be uninteresting, particularly if they were taken directly from nature. Patrons preferred 'picturesque' landscapes in the style of the French painter, Claude (1600-82), who specialized in idyllic, highly contrived paintings of the Italian countryside.

In order to accommodate this taste, Gainsborough adopted the idiom of Claude, painting the English countryside in a deliberately picturesque way, as in the landscape shown here.

Although this may seem to epitomize the image of the English countryside, it is not actually a direct copy from nature but a carefully organized composition in which the landscape has been 'rearranged' to make it more pleasing. The trees have been deliberately placed to create a balanced composition, focusing around a framed tunnel through which we glimpse a hazy distance. This 'tunnel' of trees is marked by a gracefully winding path which leads the eye, 'guided' by strategically placed figures of peasants, to the horizon. The centre of the painting is marked by a beautifully shaped tree.

Cornard Wood *c.1748*
48″× 61″ National Gallery, London

Constable's Viewpoint

One of the most important decisions an artist makes is where to stand when painting or sketching. The choice of viewpoint – as it is known – is important, since it will have a profound effect on the impact of the finished picture.

Constable sometimes adopts a low viewpoint as in the painting shown here, in which distant objects are hazy and merge into the background. This involves the viewer with the foreground scene, and focuses attention on the main subject –

in this case the artist's father's boatyard. A low viewpoint can also be used to highlight the drama of the subject; in *Stonehenge* (1836), the large expanse of lowering sky provides a background of mystery for the ancient stones.

In contrast, a high viewpoint will give an overview, in which distant objects can be clearly seen and, in Constable's work, the viewer be invited to admire the Suffolk countryside that the artist loved so much.

Boatbuilding *1815*
20″× 24¼″ Victoria and Albert Museum, London

Millais' Props

As their titles indicate, many of Millais' pictures tell a story, and one of his favourite devices for communicating the narrative is the use of 'props' – distinctive objects or costumes which identify the characters and events. In *The Boyhood of Raleigh*, for example, the famous Elizabethan seaman is shown as a child, listening with a friend to a sailor's tale. Millais has to identify the characters and convey his theme.

He identifies the young Raleigh by dressing him in a richly embroidered green doublet and hose, with a feathered hat and shoes. His poorer companion is dressed simply in black. They sit enthralled by the story of the man in the foreground, who is clearly a sailor, since behind him lie an anchor and two exotic birds, brought back from foreign parts. As he relates his adventures he points out to sea, towards the lands Raleigh will later explore. A toy ship lying on the beach hints at the future.

Similarly, in *The Black Brunswicker* (1860), Millais depicts a soldier taking leave of his lover. The black uniform and the skull-and-crossbones on the soldier's hat identify him as a member of the German cavalry regiment which was based in England from 1809 to 1815. The picture on the wall, showing Napoleon on horseback, reminds us that the soldier is departing for Waterloo – perhaps to meet his death.

The Boyhood of Raleigh *1870*
47½″ × 56″ Tate Gallery, London

Turner's Composition

Arranging the objects or figures in a picture is one of the most fundamental steps in the artistic process. The composition, as it is known, must please the eye and make an effective whole. But it will also contribute to the emotional impact of the painting. A symmetrical, or balanced, composition is likely to seem calm, while an unbalanced scene can be disturbing.

In the picture shown here, Turner arranges the scene around a vertical column of light which runs through the middle of the picture. This shaft of light, together with the line of the ship's mast, divides the picture into two equal parts.

By dividing the picture in the centre Turner creates an effect of symmetry. The careful balance of shapes and the vertical line in the centre of the picture give the scene an air of tranquillity and calm. Turner also draws our attention to the moment of burial, for within the shaft of light at the very centre of the picture the dead man's coffin is lowered into the sea.

In *Calais Pier* (1803), Turner again gives his picture a central focus. The two ships passing each other beneath a break in the clouds draw our attention to the centre of the scene. Here, however, the composition is not symmetrical, for on the right Turner introduces the dark shape of the pier. The asymmetrical composition helps create the impression of a turbulent sea.

Peace: Burial at Sea *1842*
34¼″ × 34⅛″ Tate Gallery, London

Sargent's Watercolour

The medium of watercolour is particularly suited to capturing the effects of light. This is especially true of pure watercolour, in which the artist works by applying washes of colour to white or tinted paper. Because they are transparent, the washes allow the artist to reproduce the subtle variations in tone and colour of objects seen under different kinds of light. Watercolour thus had a special appeal for Sargent, who was particularly interested in the effects, in landscape, of both direct and reflected light. In this watercolour, Sargent recreates the whole range of light effects by using blue washes of widely differing intensities and tones. The part of the boat's hull to the left of the picture, which is placed in shadow, takes on the greenish blue of the water below, while the part which is in sunlight, towards the centre of the image, has a warmer, paler colour, with touches of mauve.

Sargent adds to the light effects by a judicious use of white. The furled sails of the boat, which are in full sunlight, have the pure white of the untouched paper. On the lower part of the boat, Sargent uses tiny strokes of more translucent white to suggest flashes of sunlight reflected off the water.

In a Levantine Port *c.1905-06*
11⅝″ × 17¾″ The Brooklyn Museum, New York

Seurat's Neo-Impressionism

Seurat devised Pointillism – or Divisionism, as the Neo-Impressionists preferred the technique to be called – according to strict scientific principles. The technique involved painting in tiny dots of colour and when, in May 1886, *La Grande Jatte* (Seurat's first major work employing the technique) was exhibited, the artist was hailed as offering the most significant way forward for Impressionism; it was after this exhibition that Seurat and his associates were named the Neo-Impressionists.

One of the key ideas of Divisionism was that of optical mixture. This involved placing unmixed dabs of colour side-by-side on the canvas, instead of pre-mixing them on the palette. The colours, Seurat held, would merge in the eye of the spectator without any loss of vibrancy, and the technique would not only enable the artist to achieve greater accuracy, but also to capture the shifting qualities of light and colour. The size of the dot was varied according to the size of the picture, and the distance from which the work was to be seen. In this picture – *Sunday, Port-en-Bressin* – Seurat utilized the technique to contrast the vibrancy of the natural light, both in the sky and as reflected in the water, with the subdued calm of the port itself.

Sunday, Port-en-Bressin *1888*
25½" × 32" Kröller-Müller Museum, Otterlo

Blake's Symbolism

Blake's pictures often have a moral purpose, which he conveys by a variety of symbolic devices. Here he depicts a battle between good and evil by showing two figures fighting for the body of a child. The angels have human forms, but are clearly imaginary, not real: they symbolize good and evil through the opposed qualities of beauty and ugliness, darkness and light and blindness and vision.

The Good Angel, on the right, is young and gentle, and his face is very beautiful. He stands at the edge of the purifying waters of the ocean, protecting the little child – a common symbol of innocence. In contrast, the Evil Angel is ugly and terrifying. His face is old and his eyes are blind, suggesting ignorance. His left foot is chained to the barren ground – in another reference to the ignorance, and limited power, of evil.

The background echoes the same moral conflict. The sun is rising on the horizon, bathing the Good Angel in life-giving light. The Evil Angel, however, is surrounded by flames, which symbolize the destructive fire of Hell. These flames shed no light, for above and below the fire everything is dark. Evil has cast its shadow across the earth.

The Good and Evil Angels *c.1795*
17½″ × 23″ Tate Gallery, London

Index of Artists

A

Abbey, Edwin Austin
  and Boston murals 9:103
  and Broadway 9:100, 101
  and Sargent 9:78
  O Mistress Mine 9:102
  She Stoops to Conquer 9:102
Aertsen, Peter
  *Christ in the House of Martha
  and Mary* 5:52
Aken, Jheronimous
  Anthonissen van
  see Bosch, Hieronymus
'American Hogarth, The' *see*
  Sloan, John
Audran, Claude III 5:*13*
  and Rococo 5:14
  and Watteau 5:13-14
  engraving after Watteau's
  Island of Cythera 5:*22*
Audubon, John James 9:140
Aved, Jacques
  and Chardin 5:47, *47*
  portrait of C. G. Tessin 5:*79*

B

Baburen, Dirck van
  and Vermeer 3:114
  The Procuress 3:*111*, 112, 114,
  125
Balla, Giacomo 8:77, 140
  and Boccioni 8:76-7
  and Divisionism 8:83
  and Marchesa Casati 8:*103*
  subjects 8:77
  technique 8:77
  Girl Running on a Balcony
  8:*100, 140*

Bassano, Jacopo 5:15
  caricature of Titian 2:*112*
  Christ and the Money-Lenders
  (detail) 2:*112*
Bazille, Frédéric 7:140
Bellini, Gentile 2:108, 140
Bellini, Giovanni
  death of 2:110
  Madonnas 2:85, *85*; 6:*26*
  and Titian 2:108-109, *114*
  The Agony in the Garden 4:*53*
  Doge Loredano 2:*140*
  Madonna of the Meadow 2:*85*
  Pietà 2:*140*
  St Jerome 2:*140*
  The Suffering Christ 2:*140*
  The Transfiguration 2:*140*
Bellini, Jacopo 2:140
Bellows, George 9:108, 134-5
  favourite subjects 9:134-5
  Stag at Sharkey's 9:*134-5*
Benton, Thomas Hart 9:140
Berckhyde, Job
  The Baker 3:134, *135*
Bernini, Gian Lorenzo 4:*36*
  in France 4:18
  on Poussin's work 4:18
  and Queen Christina of
  Sweden 3:138
  Rome at the time of 4:36-9
  Apollo and Daphne 4:*38*
  Baldacchino 2:*71*; 4:*37*
  The Piazza Navona 4:36-7, *38*
  St Peter's Square 2:*68, 69*; 4:*37*
  Sant 'Andrea al Quirinale 4:*39*
Bingham, George Caleb 9:140
Blake, William, and Reynolds
  6:18, 39
Boccioni, Umberto 8:*75, 78, 80,
  81*
  artistic studies 8:76

character 8:77
and Divisionism 8:83
early life 8:76
financial problems 8:77
finding an identity 8:77
and Futurists 8:79
  first painting 8:79-80, 83
gallery guide 8:139
importance of Cubism to 8:85
influence of Balla 8:77
influence of Braque 8:80
influence of Picasso 8:80
influence of Previati 8:83
key dates 8:77
and light effects 8:83
on 'lines of force' 8:84
and Modigliani 8:109
and movement 8:81, *81*, 82-3,
  84, 97
on his paintings 8:83
in Paris 8:77-8
photograph of (1912?) 8:*8*
in Rome 8:76
and Salon d'Automne 8:80
and sculpture 8:79, 85
sketching 8:*86*
trademarks 8:85
on war 8:81
war service 8:78, 80, *80*
The Charge of the Lancers 8:*81*
The City Rises 8:84, 86, *86-7,
  92-3*
  colour studies for 8:*87*
  detail 8:*86*
design for Italian Automobile
  Club 8:*77*
Development of a Bottle in Space
  (sculpture) 8:*83*, 85
Dynamism of a Cyclist 8:*83*
Dynamism of a Human Body
  8:*97, 98*

Elasticity 8:*8*
The Laugh 8:*84*
  detail 8:*84*
Modern Idol 8:*83, 96*
The Morning 8:*90*
Portrait of Ferruccio Busoni 8:*99*
portrait of his mother 8:*76*
Riot in the Galleria 8:*83, 91*
self-portrait 8:*89*
Signora Busoni 8:*80-81*
Signora Massimino 8:*88*
States of Mind (series) 8:*83*
  The Farewell 8:*85, 94*
  Those Who Go 8:*95*
The Street Enters the House
  8:*82-3, 83-4*
Synthesis of Human Dynamism
  (sculpture) 8:*79*
*Unique Forms of Continuity in
  Space* 8:*79*, 85
Woman in a Garden 8:*82*
Boldoni, Giovanni
  Pansies 8:*85*
Bonnard, Pierre 8:45
  Nude in the Bath 7:*52*
Borromini, Francesco 4:37, 42
  S. Carlo alle Quattro Fontane
  4:*42*
  S. Ivo alla Sapienza 4:37
Bosch, Hieronymus 1:*107, 109*
  3:133
  and Adamites 1:109
  and attainment of paradise
  1:117
  and Brethren of the
  Common Life 1:109
  and Brotherhood of Our Lady
  1:110-11
  chronology of work 1:121
  connections with Cathedral of
  St John 1:108

death notices 1:111
draughtsmanship 1:114
early life 1:108
early work 1:*120-21*, 121
gallery guide 8:139
and Hellfire doctrine 1:135
influence of religious works
    1:114
in Italy? 1:*111*
key dates 1:109
landscapes 1:117
later works 1:117
marriage 1:110
master of the grotesque 1:114,
    114-15
monsters 1:*114-15*, 116-17
popularity of work in Spain
    1:117
quality of early works 1:114,
    116
'reality' of paintings 1:112
religious standpoint 1:132
skill in other art forms 1:111
style 1:113
subject-matter 1:112-13
symbolism 1:114, 116
techniques 1:113-14, 121
themes used by
    contemporaries 1:112
trademarks 1:*117*
The Adoration of the Magi 1:*122*
Christ Carrying the Cross
    1:*112-13*
Christ Child 1:*113*, 114
The Conjuror 1:*120-21*
The Crowning with Thorns
    1:121, *129*
The Cure of Folly 1:*112*, 114
Ecce Homo 1:*123*
The Garden of Earthly Delights
    1:109, 117, 121, *126-7*
    details 1:*118-19*
Hay Wain 1:121, *124-5*
    symbolism of 1:116
The Last Judgement 1:111
    details 1:*114-115*
reverse of *Ascent to Calvary*
    1:113
St Christopher 1:*113*
*St John the Baptist in the
    Wilderness* 1:121, *128*
    sources for 1:117
Self-portrait? (drawing)
    1:*107*
The Seven Deadly Sins 1:*112*
The Temptation of St Anthony
    1:121, *130-31*
    details 1:*114-15*
    sources for 1:117
Botticelli, Sandro
    Pietà 1:*85*
Botticini, Francesco
    Tobias and the Archangels
        (detail) 2:*12*

Boucher, François
    attitude to nature 5:85
    and Cars 5:76, 77
    chief model 5:78, *78-9*
    commissions: first royal 5:78
    criticism of work 5:81
    and David 4:76; 5:80-81
    decorative works 5:*78*, 78-9,
        82-4, 109
    domestic life 5:78
    early life 5:76
    eclipse of popularity 5:82
    and engraving 5:76-7, *77*
    and the exotic 5:83-4
    and Fontainebleau 5:80-81
    and Fragonard 5:109
    gallery guide 5:139
    and Gobelins tapestry factory
        5:81, 83
    and grisaille 5:84
    influence of Bloemaert 5:83
    influence of Dutch art on 5:83
    influence of Lemoyne 5:76
    influence on Renoir 7:109
    influence of Watteau on 5:76,
        83
    key dates 5:76
    life 5:76-81, 102, 108, 109, 110,
        114, 117
    and Madame de Pompadour
        5:78, 79-80, 81, 84, 96, 98, 102
    and Paris Salon 5:79, 85
    patronage 5:78, 79, 80
    and Prix de Rome 5:77, *77*
    pupils 5:80-81; 6:46
    and Sèvres porcelain factory
        5:78, 81
    siting of paintings 5:82-3
    style 5:117
        sources of 5:83
    subjects 5:84-5
    success 5:79
    and the theatre 5:84
    trademarks 5:85
    travels in Italy 5:77, *77*
    and Watteau 5:77
    working methods 5:82-5
The Bridge 5:*94*
Le Déjeuner 5:*90*
Diana After Bathing 5:*84*, 85;
    7:*117*
*Half-naked Woman Bending
    Over* (sketch) 5:*83*
*Landscape with Figures
    Gathering Cherries* 5:82
Landscape with Watermill 5:*82-3*
Madame de Pompadour
    (1758) 5:*98*
    (1759) 5:*99*
Madamoiselle O'Murphy 5:*86-7*,
    92-3, 134
    details 5:*86*, *87*
    early sketch 5:*87*
The Mill 5:*95*

La Modiste 5:*91*
The Odalisque 5:*87*
*Portrait of the Duc de
    Montpensier* 5:*83*
Portrait of Madame Baudouin
    5:*80*
Portrait of Madame Boucher 5:*79*
Rinaldo and Armida 5:*78-9*
The Rising of the Sun 5:84, *96*
Salle du Conseil
    (Fontainebleau) 5:*80-81*
Self-portrait 5:*77*
The Setting of the Sun 5:84, *97*
Shepherd Piping to a Shepherdess
    5:*108-109*
The Triumph of Venus 5:80, *88-9*
Venus Asleep 5:*117*
Winter (engraving) 5:*77*
Woman with Muff 5:*83*
Boudin, Eugène 7:76, 140
    and painting out of doors
        (plein-air) 7:82
Bourdon, Sébastien 4:140
Bouts, Dirck
    and Van der Weyden 1:140
    *The Altarpiece of the
        Sacrament* 1:140
    The Justice of Emperor Otto 1:140
Bramante, Donato d'Angelo
    and rebuilding of St Peter's,
        Rome 2:47, 68-72, 80,
        101-102
    St Peter's 2:68, *69*, 70
    Santa Maria delle Grazie,
        Milan, cupola 2:41
    The Tempietto 2:68
Brancusi, Constantin 8:110, 140
    Modigliani and 8:110, 115
    in Paris 9:69
Brant, Sebastian
    theme for Bosch's work 1:113
    The Ship of Fools 1:113
Braque, Georges 8:140
    Boccioni and 8:80
    and Cézanne 8:69
    and collage 8:71
    and Cubism 8:68-9, 71
    and *Les Demoiselles d'Avignon*
        8:47
    in Paris 9:69
    and Picasso 8:46, 68-9
    studio 8:68
    subjects 8:69
    and World War I 8:47
    The Musician's Table 8:*68-9*
    Standing Nude 8:68
Bronzino, Agnolo
    Eleanora of Toledo and her Son
        4:*117*
Brouwer, Adriaen 3:140
    Hals and 3:47
    themes 3:133
    The Pancake Baker 3:*133*
    The Smokers 3:140

Bruegel, Jan
    and Rubens 3:18
Bruegel, Pieter, the Elder
    and genre painting 3:133, 134
Buonarotti, Michelangelo *see*
    Michelangelo Buonarotti
Burne-Jones, Sir Edward 9:20
    The Garden of the Hesperides
        9:*20*
Buytewech, Willem
    Merry Company in the Open Air
        3:*132*

C

Caillebotte, Gustave 7:140
Calder, Alexander 9:140
Campin, Robert 1:46
    influence on Van der Weyden
        1:78, *78*
    as Master of Flémalle 1:51, *51*
    type of work 1:49
    Van der Weyden as
        apprentice 1:75, 76
    workshop of 1:*101*
    The Descent from the Cross 1:78
    Mérode Altarpiece 1:*51*, 141
    The Nativity 1:101, *102*
    The Virgin and Child 1:*78*
    School of:
        St Joseph 3:*116*
Canaletto, Antonio
    *The Thames from Somerset
        House* 6:*116*
Carline, Sidney
    *The Destruction of the Turkish
        Transport* 9:*105*
Carolus-Duran 9:*77*
    influence of Velázquez 9:82
    and Manet 9:82
    and Sargent 9:82
Carpaccio, Vittore
    *Miracle of the Reliquary of the
        True Cross* 1:*111*
Carracci, Annibale
    and Bolognese Academy 6:36
    contemporaries 3:14
    and landscape 4:49
    pupil of 4:*41*
    and Rome 3:14
Carravaggio, Michelangelo
    Merisi da 4:76
    contemporaries 3:14
    David and 4:76
    genre style 3:53
    Honthorst and 3:114
    Rembrandt and 3:84
    and Rome 3:14
    use of light/shade 3:40
Carriera, Rosalba
    Portrait of Watteau 5:*11*
Cassatt, Mary 7:47, 140
    brushwork 9:52

commission for World's
    Columbian Exposition 9:48
and Courbet 9:45, 46
draughtsmanship 9:51
and drypoint etching 9:53
Dutch and American
    influence 9:54
early academic training 9:44
early life 9:44
etching of, by Degas 9:47
exhibitions: one-woman 9:48,
    49
    with the Impressionists
        9:46, 74
final years 9:49
gallery guide 9:139
influence of Japanese prints
    9:48
influence of the Renaissance
    masters 9:44, 44-5
influence of Rubens 9:45
influence of Velázquez 9:45,
    52
interest in line 9:53
key dates 9:44
large canvases 9:48
linguistic skills 9:44
and Madonna and Child 9:45,
    51
and Manet 9:45, 46
models 9:48, 50
and Monet's The Boating Party
    9:48-9
in Paris 9:44-8, 68
    subject-matter in 9:46-7
and Paris Salon 9:45
and pastels 9:49, 51, 52
    technique with 9:53
and printing 9:48
    techniques with 9:53
and Realism 9:45
relationship with Degas
    9:45-6, 47, 51
    collaboration with 9:46
    influence of 9:52-3
    portrait by 9:45
in her seventies 9:49
in the South of France 9:49
studies in Italy 9:44-5
subject matter 9:45, 50
    mothers and children 9:47,
        49
trademarks 9:52
use of colour 9:52, 53
use of blue and white 9:55
visits America 9:49
visits Antwerp 9:45
visits Egypt 9:49
visits Madrid 9:45
and Whistler 9:74
working methods 9:52
The Bath 9:52
    detail 9:52-3
The Blue Room 9:46, 53, 58-9

The Boating Party 9:48, 53, 66-7
The Cup of Tea 9:55
Emmie and her Child 9:51
The Fitting 9:64
Kneeling in an Armchair 9:51
Lady at a Tea Table 9:53, 54-5,
    62
    details 9:55
The Letter 9:49
The Little Sisters 6:20, 21; 9:10
Lydia Crocheting in the Garden
    at Marly 9:46, 47
Lydia Leaning on her Arms
    Seated in a Loge 9:50
Lydia and her Mother at Tea 9:54
'Modern Women' 9:48
    Young Girls Pursuing Fame
        9:48-9
    Young Women Plucking the
        Fruits of Knowledge and
        Science 9:48
On the Balcony during the
    Carnival 9:56
portrait of her sister 9:46
Robert Kelso Cassatt 9:50
Self-portrait 7:48; 9:9, 43
Susan on a Balcony Holding a
    Dog 9:63
Torero and a Young Girl 9:45,
    57
Woman Bathing 9:65
Woman and Child Driving
    9:60-61
Woman at her Mirror 9:48-9
Women Picking Fruit 9:50-51
Women Sewing 7:48
Young Girl 9:48
Cazes, Pierre-Jacques
    and Chardin 5:44
    teaching methods 5:44, 50
    The Swing 5:44
Cézanne, Paul 4:21
    Braque and 8:69
    character 7:111
    death of 8:138
    last work 8:68
    Matisse and 8:20
    and Mediterranean light 8:36
    memorial exhibition 8:110
    Modigliani and 8:115
    on Monet 7:85
    and Salon des Refusés 7:15
    and the South of France
        8:36-7
    on sunlight 8:36
    Mont-Sainte Victoire 8:68
    Three Bathers 8:20
Chagall, Marc
    in South of France 8:39
Champaigne, Philippe de 4:13
    Portrait of Cardinal Richelieu
        3:39
Chardin, Jean-Baptiste-Siméon
    and the Academy 5:45-6, 50

made Councillor 5:47-8
apprenticeship 5:44
on his art 5:53
and Cazes 5:44, 50
and Cochin 5:48
contemporaries 5:46, 46
domestic life 5:46, 47, 49
early life 5:44
early training 5:50
and Exposition de la Jeunesse
    5:45
failing health 5:49
financial problems 5:45
and Fontainebleau 5:45 ,46
gallery guide 5:139
genre scenes 5:46-7, 50-52
influence of Aved 5:47, 47
key dates 5:44
and Louis XV 5:46-7, 48, 49,
    54
paintings: price of 5:48
    success of 5:47, 48
and the Paris Salon 5:47-8
and pastels 5:49
patrons 5:47
portrait (La Tour) 5:48
royal pension 5:46, 48
servants 5:68
still-lifes 5:46, 47, 50, 51, 53,
    55, 56-7, 64, 65, 66, 67
subjects 5:50-51
success: first 5:45
    with genre paintings 5:51-2
    late 5:49
technique, mastery of 5:52
trademarks 5:53
use of colour/tone 5:53
working methods 5:50-55
The Artist's Wife 5:47
Les Attributs des Arts 5:48-9
The Brioche 5:67
The Cellar Boy 5:68
The Cut Melon 5:65, 66
The Diligent Mother 5:54, 62
Flowers in a Vase 5:51
Girl Returning from Market
    5:50, 61
The Governess 5:60
Grapes and Pomegranates 5:66
The Jar of Apricots 5:63
The Jar of Olives 5:52-3
    detail 5:53
Kitchen Still-life with Cooking
    Pots and Eggs 5:56
Kitchen Still-life with Pestle and
    Mortar 5:57
Little Girl with a Shuttlecock
    5:58
Marguerite Pouget 5:47
Morning Toilet 5:51
Portrait of Aved 5:47
Saying Grace 5:54-5, 63
    details 5:55

Rotterdam version 5:54
    sketch of lost original 5:54
The Schoolmistress 5:50, 51
The Scullery Maid 3:117
Self-portrait (1771) 5:109,
    (1775) 5:43
The Skate 5:44-5, 46
The Washerwoman 5:50-51
The Water Urn 5:50
Woman Taking Tea 5:45
The Young Draughtsman 5:59
Charonton, Enguerrand see
    Quarton, Enguerrand
Chavannes, Puvis de
    Life of St Genevieve 9:74
Christus, Petrus
    finishes The Madonna
        with Jan Vos 1:47
    and Van Eyck 1:140
    A Carthusian Monk 1:140
    The Lamentation over Christ 1:140
    Nativity 1:140
    Weighing the Wedding Rings of a
        Bridal Couple 1:140
Claude Lorrain 6:77
    and aerial perspective 4:50
    apprenticeship 4:44, 44
    and assistants 4:44
    and Buen Retiro palace 4:45
    commissions 4:45
    compositional methods 4:48,
        50, 52, 53
    and Domenichino 4:41
    early life 4:44
    gallery guide 4:139
    influence of Carracci on 4:49
    key dates 4:44
    and landscape 4:45, 49, 48-50;
        6:84
        gardening 4:69-71
        monumental 4:52-3
    the Liber Veritatis 4:46, 49,
        50-51, 55
    and light 4:52
    and Metamorphoses (Ovid) 4:50
    patronage 4:46-7, 47
    and Poussin 4:45, 46, 52-3
    sketching trips 4:45, 46-7, 48
    subjects 4:46, 50
        for Colonna 4:47
    and Tassi 4:44, 49, 50
    trademarks 4:52
    travels in Italy 4:45-6
    Turner and 4:53; 6:110-11, 115
    working methods 4:16, 41, 45,
        46, 48-55
    Adoration of the Golden Calf
        4:51
    Ascanius Shooting the Stag of
        Silvia 4:47, 67
    Coast Scene with a Fight on a
        Bridge 4:51
    Coast View of Delos with Aeneas
        4:68-9, 70

The Embarkation of St Ursula 4:50, *51*, 54
The Enchanted Castle 4:47, 53, *65*
Landscape with a Goatherd 4:*48*, 50
Landscape with Egeria Mourning over Numa 4:66
Landscape with Hagar and the Angel 4:52-3; 6:77, 84
Landscape with the Landing of Aeneas at Pallanteum 4:46, 52
Landscape with the Marriage of Isaac and Rebekah 4:54, 62-3
Landscape with Narcissus and Echo 4:50, 58-9
Landscape with Psyche at the Palace of Cupid 4:53
Landscape with St George Killing the Dragon 4:50
Landscape with Samuel Anointing David 4:48-9
Pastoral Caprice with the Arch of Constantine 4:64
Pastoral Landscape (drawing) 4:49
Perseus and the Origin of Coral 4:50-51
Seaport with the Embarkation of the Queen of Sheba 4:50, 54-5, 60-61, 63
  details 4:54-5
  preliminary sketch 4:55
Seaport with the Landing of Cleopatra in Tarsus 4:57
Seaport with Setting Sun 4:56
Self-portrait, copy of engraving 4:*8*, 43
  sketch of the Campagna 4:45-6
View of La Crescenza 4:45
View of SS Trinità dei Monti 4:47
Cochin, Charles-Nicolas, the Elder 5:48
  engraving after Chardin's *Little Girl with Cherries* 5:48
Cochin, Charles-Nicolas, the Younger 5:*48*, 49
Codde, Pieter
  An Amsterdam Couple 3:101
Colombe, Jean
  finishes *Les Très Riches Heures du Duc de Berry* 1:*15*, 17, 18, 32, 34
Constable, John 4:48
  canal scenes 6:85
  classical references 6:21
  and Claude 4:*48*
  cloud studies 6:84, 85, *86*
  and Gainsborough 6:53, 55, 82, 84
  and George Beaumont 6:76-7, 112

influence of Claude on 6:77, 84
  gallery guide 6:139
  and John Fisher 6:78, 80, 92
  key dates 6:78
  life 6:76-81, 98-101
  and painting out of doors 7:82
  portrait of (Reinagle) 6:*75*
  rivalry with Turner 6:80, 81, 110, 112, 115
  and the Royal Academy 6:77, 78, 80-81, 82, 85
  on Rubens 3:21
  sketch of 6:*80*
  and Stour valley 6:82-3, *82-3*
  summer sketchbooks 6:83-5
  trademarks 6:85
  working methods 6:82-5
The Admiral's House 6:94
The Artist's Father 6:77
The Artist's Mother 6:77
Boatbuilding 6:84, *88*
Chain Pier, Brighton 6:96
The Cornfield 6:95
Dedham Lock and Mill 6:82-3
East Bergholt 6:83
East Bergholt House 6:76
Farmland views near East Bergholt 6:83
Flatford Mill 6:89
Golding Constable's Flower Garden (detail) 6:83
The Hay Wain 6:80, 83, *86-7*, 90-91
Landscape with a Goatherd (copy after Claude) 4:*48*
The Leaping Horse 6:85
The Lock 6:81
Man Carrying a Scythe (sketch) 6:*87*
The Millstream (sketch for) 6:83
Portrait of John Fisher 6:78
Salisbury Cathedral 6:92-3
Self-portrait 6:*8*, 75
Self-portrait (sketch) 6:77
Stonehenge 6:97
Stratford St Mary (sketch) 6:*82*
The Valley Farm 6:81
Conte, Jacopino del
  Portrait of Michelangelo 2:43
Cope, Charles West
  portrait sketch of Turner 6:*80*
Copley, John Singleton 9:140
  The Sitwell Children 9:84
Corot, Jean-Baptiste-Camile 7:140-41
Correggio, Antonio 6:29
  Cassatt and 9:*44*, 44-5
  Antiope 2:140
  The Assumption of the Virgin 2:140
  Jupiter and Io 2:*117*, 140
Cotman, John Sell 6:140

Greta Bridge 6:140
Courbet, Gustave 7:77
  Cassatt and 9:45, 46
  choice of subjects 7:114
  paints Joanna Heffernan 9:14
  Whistler and 9:12, 14
  Young Women on the Banks of the Seine 7:*117*
Cox, David 6:140
  Rhyl Sands 6:140
Coysevox, Antoine
  Louis XIV on Horseback (carved bas-relief) 5:*40*
Credi, Lorenzo di
  Portrait of Verrocchio 2:*14*
Crome, John ('Old Crome')
  and Norwich School 6:140
  Mousehold Heath 6:140
Cross, Henri-Edmond
  and Matisse 8:14
  in the South of France 8:37
  L'Air du Soir 8:*13*

D

David, Gerard 1:140
  Madonna with Three Female Saints 1:140
  Marriage at Cana 1:140
David, Jacques-Louis
  and the Academy 4:78
  and Antiquity 4:76, 77, 83, 85
  and Boucher 4:76; 5:80-81
  character 4:82
  commissions: Napoleonic 4:80
  death of 4:81
  domestic life 4:77
  early life 4:76
  exile 4:81, *81*
  and Fragonard 5:113
  and the French Revolution 4:77-8, *78*, 84, 85, 105
    activities 4:78
    paintings 4:78
    quality of work for 4:85
  gallery guide 4:139
  and Gros 4:80-81
  influence, early 4:77
  influence of Carravaggio 4:76
  influence of Delacroix 4:76
  influence of Desmaisons 4:*76*
  influence of Italy 4:76-7
  influence of Raphael 4:77
  and Ingres 4:109
  in Italy 4:76-7
  key dates 4:77
  and Napoleon 4:79, 80, 85, 98, 99
  paintings, organization of 4:83
  and Paris Salon 4:77
  and political propaganda 4:78

portrait by Langlois 4:*81*
  portraits 4:76, 80, 83, 85, 92, 97
  and Prix de Rome 4:76, 110
  pupils 4:77, 80, 81, *81*
  studio of 4:*108*
  style 4:77, 83-4
    early 4:76
    formulation of 4:83
  subjects 4:77, 84
  trademarks 4:85
  and Vien 4:76, 77, 82
  working methods 4:*82*, 82-5
  Antiochus and Stratonice 4:76, 82
  Belisarius Receiving Alms 4:84
  Brutus 4:84, *84-5*
  Comte de Turenne 4:83
  The Death of Marat 4:78, 84-5, *86-7*, 93
  The Death of Socrates 4:84, *90-91*
  Distribution of the Eagle Standards 4:80
  Intervention of the Sabine Women 4:83, *94-5*, 140
  Marie-Antoinette (sketch) 4:*79*
  The Marquise de Pastoret 4:92
  Mars and Minerva 4:76, *88*
  Mars and Venus 4:83, 85
  Napoleon Crossing the Alps 4:*80*, 98
  Napoleon Crowning Himself (sketch) 4:80
  Napoleon in his Study 4:99, 111
  Oath of the Horatii 4:77, 84, 89, 132
  Oath of the Jeu de Paume (sketch) 4:78, 82
  Lepelletier (copy) 4:87
  Portrait of Charlotte Pécoul 4:*39*
  Portrait of Desmaisons 4:76
  Portrait of Mme Récamier 4:76
  Portrait of the Comte de Turenne (detail) 4:*83*
  Le Sacre 4:80
    preliminary sketch 4:*80*
  Self-portrait 4:*9*, 75
  View from the Luxembourg 4:79
Degas, Edgar 7:15, 43, 49
  and Cassatt 7:47-9, *48*; 9:45-6, 47, 51
  comparisons 7:52
  composition of paintings 7:51, 52, 53
  death of 7:49
  description of 7:47
  draughtsmanship 7:50
  and drawing 7:50
  and the Dreyfus Case 7:49
  early life 7:44
  education 7:44
  etching of 7:47
  as exhibition organizer 7:47

eyesight 7:46, 48
family crisis 7:46-7
and finishing commissions
7:47
forces on his art 7:50
first teachers 7:44
gallery guide 7:139
and 'grand style' 7:45
'homes' in Paris 7:48, 48
Hopper and 9:108
and Impressionists 7:50
influence of Delacroix 7:45
influence of Ingres 7:44-5, 45,
50
influence of the Old Masters
7:44, 50
interest in horse racing 7:69
journey through Burgundy
7:49, 49
key dates 7:44
and Manet 7:45-6
in New Orleans 7:46
nudes 7:52, 52
outbursts against critics 7:50
and painting horses 7:45
portraits 7:45
and Paris Opéra 7:46, 47
and photography 7:49
and Renoir 7:109
repeated themes 7:52-3
reputation 7:47
and sculpture 7:48
sexuality of work 7:51-2
in siege of Paris 7:46
on significance of paintings
7:50
studio of 7:47, 48
style 7:47
subjects 7:51, 52
techniques 7:51, 53
temperament 9:46
trademarks 7:53
visits to Italy 7:44-5, 45
visit to Normandy 7:66
withdrawal from public life
7:48
on Wolff 7:47
and women 7:46
Absinthe 7:62
After the Bath 7:64
*Ballerina with a Bouquet,
Curtseying* 7:50-51
*Ballet Dancers in Butterfly
Costumes* 7:52-3
The Bellelli Family 7:44, 56
Combing the Hair 7:65
The Cotton Exchange 7:46
The Dancing Class 7:54, 61
details 7:54, 55
Four Dancers 7:51
*Jockeys before the Start, with
Flag-pole* 7:51
Little Dancer aged 14
(sculpture) 7:50

Mary Cassatt in the Louvre 9:47
Melancholy 7:45, 51
The Opéra Orchestra 7:45, 57
Paul Valpinçon at the Races 7:47
portrait of Mary Cassatt 9:45
Racehorses at Longchamp
7:58-9
Self-portrait 7:44; 9:47
Self-portrait aged 30 7:9, 43
sketch of Jules Perrot 7:55
Sulking 7:66-7
The Tub 7:53
Two Dancers on Stage 7:60
Women Ironing 7:63
Young Spartans Exercizing
7:44-5, 50
Delacroix, Eugène 4:81
Degas and 7:45
influence on Renoir 7:109
influence of Rubens on 3:21
and Ingres 4:112, 112
Picasso and 8:49
on Rembrandt 3:87
rivalry with Ingres 4:114
and Universal Exhibition
4:113
Massacre of Chois 4:112
Women of Algiers 8:20
Delaunay, Robert and Sonia
8:140
and Cubism 8:71
Demuth, Charles 9:140
Derain, André 8:46, 140
and Diaghilev 8:134
and Fauvism 8:14
and Matisse 8:22
and Salon d'Automne 8:15
in the South of France 8:38
Pool of London 8:14
Desportes, Alexandre-François
Dogs, Dead Game and Fruit 5:46
Deutsch, Niklaus Manuel
St Luke Painting the Virgin 1:102
Devis, Arthur
The James Family 5:52
Domenichino (Domenico
Zampieri) 4:37
Claude and 4:76
David and 4:76
landscapes 4:41
Poussin and 4:16, 41
*St John the Baptist with Sts
Andrew and Peter* 4:40-41
Donnatello 2:51, 52
St Mark 2:52
Dossi, Dosso 2:39
Bacchanal 2:38-9
Dou, Gerard (Gerrit) 3:78, 140
Anna and the Blind Tobit 3:140
Doyen, Gabriel-François
commission from Baron de
Saint-Julien 5:118, 119
Sainte Geneviève des Ardents
5:119

Drouais, François Hubert 5:140
*Portrait of Madame de
Pompadour* 5:103
Duchamp, Marcel 8:141
and Armory Show 9:111
and movement 8:85
Nude descending a Staircase
8:85
Dufy, Raoul 8:141
in the South of France 8:39
Dughet (Poussin), Gaspard 4:140
commissions from Colonna
4:47
Hoare and 4:70
and landscape painting 4:16,
16, 45-6
and Poussin 4:16
Waterfall at Tivoli 4:16, 140
Dürer, Albrecht 2:105
on *Ghent Altarpiece* 1:56
Dyck, Anthony Van 3:47; 6:20
and aristocratic portraits 9:84
commissions from Charles I
4:38
Gainsborough and 6:46-7
props 6:19, 25
Reynolds and 6:19, 25
Rubens and 3:18
treatment of sitters 3:50
Watteau and 5:17
Portrait of Charles I (detail) 3:16

E

Eakins, Thomas 9:140
'Eight, The' 9:113-14
and the Ashcan School 9:134
John Sloan and
El Greco (Domenikos
Theotocopoulos) 2:117, 140
The Agony in the Garden 2:140
The Assumption of the Virgin
2:140
El Espolio 2:141
The Opening of the Fifth Seal
2:140
Ernst, Max
Temptation of St Anthony 1:116
Eyck, Hubert van 1:46, 46
epitaph 1:46
and *Ghent Altarpiece* 1:46
grave 1:46
Eyck, Jan van 3:84
apprenticeship 1:44
and back view of figures 1:50
and backgrounds 1:49
breaks with tradition 1:49
in Bruges 1:68
comparison with Campin 1:49
contribution to portraiture
1:51, 51
death 1:47
diplomatic missions 1:45-8

early life 1:44
experiments with transparent
glazes 1:50
gallery guide 1:139
and *Ghent Altarpiece* 1:47
influence of 1:46
inscriptions in work 1:51
and invention of oil painting
1:43, 44,
key dates 1:45
and light 1:50, 51
marriage 1:47
meets Robert Campin 1:46
method of painting blue
1:102-103
method of perspective 1:50
methods of composition
1:49-50
paints for Nicholas Rolin 1:47
panels in *grisaille* 1:62
pension 1:47
refines composition 1:49-50
skill with oil paints 1:56
statues for Bruges City Hall
1:47
symbolism in work 1:50, 51,
56
technique 1:50
and texture 1:51
trademarks 1:51
types of paintings 1:56
varlet de chambre 1:44
works for aristocratic patrons
1:49-50
works for Philip the Good
1:44, 45, 48
*The Angel and the Virgin of the
Annunciation* 1:62
The Arnolfini Wedding 1:50, 56,
60
Baudouin de Lannoy 1:56, 64
Cardinal Albergati 1:56, 58
Ghent Altarpiece 1:52-5, 56-7
Giovanni Arnolfini 1:49
Jodocus Vyd 1:53
The Madonna by the Fountain
1:50
The Madonna in a Church 1:48
The Madonna in Her Chamber
1:63
*The Madonna with Canon van
der Paele* 1:56, 66-7
*The Madonna with Chancellor
Rolin* 1:56, 61
The Madonna with Jan Vos 1:47
portrait of Isabella of Portugal
1:47
Portrait of Jan de Leeuw 1:65
portrait of his wife? 1:46
Portrait of a Young Man 1:59
St Barbara 1:49
*St Francis Receiving the
Stigmata* 1:48-9
Self-portrait 1:43

F

Fabriano, Gentile da
The Adoration of the Magi 1:*76-7*
Fabritius, Carel 3:109, 110
and optical experimentation 3:109
and Vermeer 3:109
Goldfinch 3:*110*
Self-portrait 3:*110*
Fantin-Latour, Henri
Studio in the Batignolles Quarter 7:*14*
Flémalle, Master of *see* Campin, Robert
Fontainebleau, School of 4:12
Diana the Huntress 5:*85*
Fouquet, Jean 1:140
portrait of Agnes Sorel 1:*106*
Melun Diptych 1:140
Pietà 1:140
Fragonard, Jean-Honoré
apprenticeship 5:108-109
and Boucher 5:108, 109, 112, 114, 117
and Chardin 5:108
classifying 5:114
commissions 5:111, *111*
museums 5:113
royal 5:112, *112*
and David 5:113
domestic life 5:*111*, 112
early life 5:106-107
and Ecole des Elèves Protégés 5:109
erotic appeal 5:115
fancy portraits 5:112, 114, 116
'figures de fantasie' 5:*116*
gallery guide 5:139
influence of Italian masters 5:*109*
influence on Renoir 7:109
key dates 5:108
and Marguerite Gérard 5:112, 113
and Old Masters 5:109
output 5:115-16
and Paris Salon 5:111, 112
patronage 5:110, *112*
and Prix de Rome 5:109, *109*
in Rome 5:109-10
trademarks 5:116
working methods 5:114-17, 132
speed of 5:116
style 5:114-15, 116-17
out of fashion 5:113
subjects 5:111, 112, 114, 116-17, 132
travels in Italy 5:112
versatility 5:114
The Actor 5:*116*
The Bathers 5:*122*
Bed with Cupids (sketch) 5:*117*

Blind Man's Buff 5:112, *128*
The Bolt 5:113, *130-31*
Boy Dressed as a Pierrot 5:*115*
Coresus Sacrificing Himself to Save Callirhoé 5:*110*, 111
Fête at Rambouillet 5:*114-15*, 118
The Gardener 5:*114*
The Gardens of the Villa d'Este 5:*110*, 120
Girl Making her Dog Dance on her Bed 5:*123*
Inspiration 5:*110*, 116
The Longed-For Moment 5:112, *114*, 115
The Love Letter 5:*126*
Portrait of Marguerite Gérard (sketch) 5:*113*
Portrait of Sophie Guimard 5:*111*
Pursuit of Love 5:112, 114, *124-5*
The Reader 5:*115*
Resistance 5:*119*
Self-portrait? 5:*107*
The Stolen Shirt 5:*115*
The Swing (1775) 5:112, *129*
(1776-7) 5:*111*, 118-19, *121*
The Useless Resistance 5:*119*
The Visit to the Nursery 5:*111*
Woman Reading a Book 5:112, *127*
Frith, W. P. 7:68-9
Derby Day 7:*68*, 68-9
Froment, Nicholas 1:140
Lazarus Triptych 1:140
Virgin in the Burning Bush 1:140

G

Gaddi, Taddeo
The Presentation of the Virgin 1:*17*
Gainsborough, Thomas 5:21
apprenticeship 6:14-15
in Bath 6:*46*, 46, 47
commissions 6:46
exhibits in London 6:47
fancy pictures 6:49, 53, 64
gallery guide 6:139
influence of Dutch painting on 6:45, 49, 50
influence of Gravelot on 6:44-5, 46, 51
influence of Murillo on 6:49
influence of Rubens on 6:47, 51, 53, 66
influence of Van Dyck on 6:46-7
interest in landscape 6:45-6, 47, 50-51, 66
key dates 6:45
life 6:20, 29, 37, 39, 44-9, *45*, 68, 71
and portrait painting 6:45-6, 47

and Reynolds 6:20, 48, 49, 51-2, 53, 61
and the Royal Academy 6:47, 48, 49
success in London 6:48-9
technique 6:52-3
trademarks 6:53
use of lay figures 6:46, 51
use of light 6:48, 50-52
working methods 6:50-53
The Artist's Daughters 6:46
The Blue Boy 6:*47*, 61
The Charterhouse 6:44, 45
Cornard Wood 6:8, 84
The Cottage Girl with Dog and Pitcher 6:*64*
The Duke of Bedford 6:47
The Gainsborough Family 6:44
The Harvest Wagon 6:52
detail 6:*53*
Heneage Lloyd and his Sister 6:50-51
A Lady Walking to the Right (sketch) 6:*50*
The Mall 6:51
Mary, Countess Howe 6:60
The Market Cart 6:66, *67*
Moonlight Landscape with Figure at the Door of a Cottage 6:50
The Morning Walk 6:65
Mrs and Mrs Andrews 6:46, 54-5, 56-7, 65
Mrs Philip Thicknesse 6:59
Mrs Richard Brinsley Sheridan 6:53, 62
Mrs Sarah Siddons 6:63
A Music Party (sketch) 6:47
The Painter's Daughters Chasing a Butterfly 6:51
Peasants Smoking at a Cottage Door 6:67
Pomeranian Dogs 6:47
Portrait of Garrick 6:48
Self-portrait 6:8, 43
(1787) 6:*49*
Sophia Charlotte, Lady Sheffield 6:53
Woodcutter Courting a Milkmaid 6:58
Gauguin, Paul
on colour 8:20
Matisse and 8:20
Geertgen tot Sint Jans 1:140-41
Nativity at Night 1:141
Virgin and Child 1:141
Gellée, Claude *see* Claude Lorrain
Gérard, Baron François-Pascal 4:140
Cupid and Psyche 4:140
Portrait of Madame Récamier 4:140

Gérard, Marguerite 5:*113*
and Fragonard 5:113
Sad Tidings 5:113
Portrait of (sketch, Fragonard) 5:*113*
Géricault, Théodore 4:81
Ghirlandaio, Domenico
and Michelangelo 2:44, 52
Birth of John the Baptist 2:44
Gillot, Claude 5:*13*, 15
and etching 5:15
and Watteau 5:12-13, *13*, 14-15, *15*, 16-17
The Quarrel of the Cabmen 5:14
Gillray, James
Edward Jenner Giving the First Vaccinations 6:*103*
Giorgione da Castelfranco 2:109, 110, 116; 5:21
legend of 2:110
Fête Champetre 5:*21*, 28
The Madonna and Child 2:140
The Tempest 2:110
The Trial of Moses 2:140
Giotto di Bondone
Mattisse and 8:17
Girodet de Roucy-Trioson, Anne-Louis
and David 4:140
Danäe 4:140
Endymion 4:140
Entombment of Atala 4:140
Girtin, Thomas
and Turner 6:140
The White House, Chelsea 6:140
Glackens, William James
and the Ashcan School 9:132
works rejected 9:133
Hammerstein's Roof Garden 9:*133*
Gleyre, Charles 7:78-9, 141; 9:12
art school of 7:109
artists in studio of 7:109
and Renoir 7:109, 114
and painting out of doors 7:109
Goes, Hugo van der 1:141
The Adoration of the Shepherds 1:141
The Death of the Virgin 1:141
The Montforte Altarpiece 1:141
Portinari Altarpiece 1:141
(detail) 1:*103*
Gogh, Vincent van 8:*36-7*
on colour 8:36
on Hals 3:52, 53
influence on Fauves 8:14
on light 8:36
Gonzalès, Eva 7:141
Gorky, Arshile 9:140
Gossaert, Jan
method of painting red 1:*102*, 103
Goya, Francisco de, Hopper and 9:108

Grandma Moses *see* Robertson, Mary Anne
Gravelot, Hubert 6:51
  influence on Gainsborough 6:44-5, 46-7
  The Judicious Lover 6:46, *47*
Greco, El *see* El Greco
Greuze, Jean-Baptiste 5:140
  Fragonard and 5:*130*
  and moralistic paintings 5:*113*, 140
  The Broken Pitcher 5:140
  The Father of the Family Reading the Bible 5:140
Gris, Juan 8:46, 141
  and World War I 8:*71*
  Landscape of Céret 8:70
Gros, Baron Antoine-Jean
  and David 4:77, 80, *81*, 140
  Napoleon and 4:80, 140
  Battle of Eylau (detail) 4:*81*
  The Plague at Jaffa 4:140
  Self-portrait 4:*80*
Guardi, Francesco
  San Giorgio Maggiore 4:*106*
Guérin, Pierre-Narcisse 4:140-41
  Hippolytus and Phaedra 4:141
  The Return of Marcus Sextus 4:*84*, 141
Guillaumin, Armand 7:141

H
Hals, Dirck 3:44, *46*, 47
  Merry Company in a Renaissance Hall 3:*46*, 110
Hals, Frans
  and assistants 3:47
  brushwork 3:48, 49, 50, 52, 53
  character 3:46
  and characterization 3:52
  commissions: refuses to complete 3:46
    militia companies' 3:52
  comparison with Van Dyck 3:50
  compositional schemes 3:50
  domestic life 3:44, 45, 46, 47
  earliest known paintings 3:45
  financial problems 3:45, 46, 47
  gallery guide 3:139
  and Guild of St Luke 3:44-5, 47
  Halsmuseum 3:*46*
  influence on Manet 3:53
  influence on Van Gogh 3:52, 53
  and Italian art 3:52
  key dates 3:44
  and Leyster 3:47
  Luks and 9:134
  and militia companies 3:45-6
  pupils 3:47
  spontaneity of work 3:48-50

studio 3:47
  surviving portraits 3:48
  symbols and emblems 3:*50-51*
  technical variations 3:50, 51
  and texture 3:*54*
  trademarks 3:52
  use of black 3:52
  working methods 3:46, 48-53, 86
  Banquet of the Officers of the St George Civic Guard 3:45, 52
  Banquet of the Officers of the St Hadrian Civic Guard 3:60-61
  Boy with a Flute 3:52-3
    detail 3:*53*
  Family Group 3:52, 65
  Family Group in a Landscape 3:*64*, 65
  Gipsy Girl 3:62
  Isaac Massa 3:55
  Isabella Coymans 3:52, 67
  Lady Governors of the Old Men's Home at Haarlem 3:86
  Laughing Boy 3:48, *49*
  The Laughing Cavalier (detail) 3:*50*, 51, 57
    detail 3:50, *51*
  Malle Babbe 3:49, 63
  Married Couple in a Garden 3:*54-5*, 58-9
  The Merry Drinker 3:48
  Nurse and Child 3:56
  Portrait of a Seated Woman 3:48, *49*
  The Prodigal Son in a Tavern 3:*51*
  The Regentesses 3:47, 49, 50, 86
  Self-portrait? 3:9, 43
  The Shrovetide Revellers 3:50
  Stephanus Geraerdts 3:66
  Willem van Heythuyzen 3:49
Hayman, Francis 6:37, 54
  influence on Gainsborough 6:45
  Margaret Tyers and her Husband 6:54
Haytley, Edward
  The Brockman Family at Beachborough Manor 4:70-71
Henri, Robert 9:*109*
  aims in art 9:133
  and the Ashcan School 9:132-5
  and Exhibition of Independent Artists 9:135
  and Hopper 9:108, *108-109*
  studies in Europe 9:132
  Street Scene with Snow 9:132
Herring, J. F.
  Gladiateur 7:69
  Over the Fences 7:67
  Steeplechase Cracks 7:66-7
Hogarth, William 6:29, *41*, 136
  Wilkes and Liberty 6:41

Holst, Bartholomeus van der
  The Company of Captain Roelof Bicker 3:88-9
  The Company of the St George Civic Guard 3:70-71
Homer, Winslow 9:140
Honthorst, Gerrit van 3:140
  and Caravaggio 3:53, 140
  and Charles I 3:140
  Vermeer and 3:114
  The Merry Fiddler 3:53
Hooch, Pieter de 3:135, 140
  and Amsterdam 3:*103*
  and genre painting 3:135
  and Vermeer 3:140
  Courtyard in Delft 3:*134*
Hopper, Edward 9:*107*
  acquires a dealer 9:110
  aims in art 9:114, 117
  and Armory Show 9:111
  and the Ashcan School 9:135
  attack on abstract art 9:112-13
  bequeaths paintings 9:113
  birthplace 9:*108*
    brushwork 9:114
  and Cape Cod 9:111, 112, *112-13*
  commercial career 9:108, 109, 110
    designs 9:109, *110-11*
  commitment to representational art 9:112
  develops style 9:110
  early life 9:108
  and the environment 9:115
  exhibitions 9:109
    first one-man 9:110
    retrospective 9:110-11
  favourite subjects 9:114
  finances 9:109
  first art school 9:108
  gallery guide 9:139
  in Henri's classes 9:108, *108-109*
  influence of the Impressionists 9:109, 114, 115-16
  influence of Realist painters 9:108
  interests 9:111-12
    etching 9:114
    play of light 9:116
  key dates 9:109
  last picture 9:113
  marriage 9:110, *111*
  paintings sold to Brooklyn Museum 9:110
  prizes and honours 9:*110*, 111
  progress 9:109-110
  record of paintings 9:*112*
  recurrent themes 9:116-17
  on Sloan 9:134
  speed of working 9:113
  studio 9:109, 111, *113*
  typical subjects 9:111

trademarks 9:*116*
  use of colour 9:114
  use of space 9:117
  use of viewing angles 9:116
  and Venice Biennale 9:111
  visits Paris 9:108-109
  watercolour: importance of 9:114-15
    successful 9:110
  and Whitney Museum of American Art 9:110, 113
  working methods 9:117
  Automat 9:121
  Early Sunday Morning 9:110, *112-13*
  Eleven a.m. 9:120
  Evening Wind (etching) 9:115
  Gas 9:124-5
  High Road 9:112-13
  House by the Railroad 9:114
  Lighthouse at Two Lights 9:114-15
  Nighthawks 9:118-19, 126-7
    details 9:*118*, *119*
    preliminary sketches 9:119
  Office at Night 9:116-17
    detail 9:*117*
  portrait of his mother 9:*108*
  Second-storey Sunlight 9:*131*
  Self-portrait 9:9, *107*
  Shoshone Cliffs 9:*115*
  Smash the Hun (poster) 9:109
  Sunlight in a Cafeteria 9:*130*
  Two Comedians 9:113
  Western Motel 9:128-9
Hudson, Thomas 6:12, 13, 18
  John Percival Egmont 6:12

I
Ingres, Jean-Auguste-Dominique
  and the Academy 4:112
  and anatomy (distorting) 4:*116*, 116-17
  commissions 4:110, 112-13
  and costume prints 4:*119*
  criticism of work 4:110, 111-12
  and David 4:108, 109, 114, 132
  domestic life 4:*110*, 111
  early life 4:108
  and Ecole des Beaux-Arts 4:109, 113
  in Florence 4:113
  gallery guide 4:139
  influence of Greek art on 4:116, *116*, 117
  influence of Raphael on 4:109, 111, 112, 114, 117
  key dates 4:108
  and Légion d'Honneur 4:112, 113
  Matisse and 8:*20*

and Napoleon 4:110-11, 121
in old age 4:113
and Old Masters 4:111, 114
and Paris Salon 4:113
and portrait painting 4:110,
114, 114
and Prix de Rome 4:109,
109-110
prizes 4:109
rivalry with Delacroix 4:112,
112, 113, 114
scholarship 4:111
search for perfection 4:115
trademarks 4:116
and Universal Exhibition
4:112, 113
use of distortion 4:111-12, 116,
122-3
work in Rome 4:111, 115
working methods 4:114-17
The Ambassadors of Agamemnon
in the Tent of Achilles 4:109,
110
Antiochus and Stratonice 4:93,
114-15
The Apotheosis of Homer 4:112
The Apotheosis of Napoleon
(sketch) 4:131
The Comtesse d'Haussonville
4:128
costume prints 4:119
The Death of Leonardo 2:19
The Dream of Ossian 4:111, 114
The Forestier Family (sketch)
4:109
La Grande Odalisque 4:111, 112,
114, 116, 117, 122-3; 8:20
Julie Forestier 4:109
Jupiter and Thetis 4:111, 116
detail 4:116
Madame de Senonnes 4:124
Mademoiselle Rivière 4:114
Martyrdom of St Symphorian
4:113
Monsieur Bertin 4:125
Napoleon as Emperor 4:110, 130
Napoleon as First Consul 4:110,
120
nude studies 4:115, 115-16
Odalisque with Slave 4:126-7
portrait drawings 4:115
Portrait of Delphine Ramel 4:113
Queen Caroline Murat 4:111,
111
Raphael and La Fornarina 2:80
Roger Freeing Angelica 4:8-9,
111
studies for 4:115, 115
Self-portrait 4:8, 107, 118
The Small Bather 4:8, 118
Turkish Bath 4:113, 117, 118-19,
129
changes in 4:118
details 4:118, 119

study for 4:119
The Valpinçon Bather 4:117, 118,
121
The Vow of Louis XIII 4:112

J

Jongkind, Johan Barthold 7:141
Jordaens, Jacob 3:140-41

K

Kauffmann, Angelica 6:16, 17
and the Royal Academy 6:39
Self-portrait 6:16
Sculpture 6:17
Keyser, Thomas de 3:86
The Anatomy Lesson of Dr
Sebastian Egbertsz 3:86
Constantijn Huygens and his
Secretary 3:39
Khnopff, Fernand
and Symbolism 8:116
Who Shall Deliver Me? 8:116

L

La Hyre, Laurent de 4:141
Allegory of Grammar 4:141
The Birth of Bacchus 4:141
La Tour, Georges de
Magdalen with a Lamp 3:40
La Tour, Maurice Quentin de
5:140
Portrait of Chardin 5:48
Portrait of Madame de
Pompadour 5:100, 140
Lancret, Nicolas 5:16, 140
Langlois
portrait of David 4:81
Lastman, Pieter
pupils 3:77, 78
Rembrandt and 3:77, 84
Juno Discovering Jupiter with Io
3:77
Lawrence, Sir Thomas 6:140-41
The Countess of Bressingham
9:84
Portrait of Wellington 6:106
Le Sueur, Eustache 4:141
Life of St Bruno 4:141
Lebrun, Charles
and French Academy 4:141
and Poussin 4:21
Hercules and the Horses of
Diomedes 4:141
Léger, Fernand 8:141
and Cubism 8:71
Lemoyne, François 5:76, 79, 83,
140
Apotheosis of Hercules 5:140

The Bather 5:140
Venus and Adonis 5:76
Leonardo da Vinci
anatomical studies 2:16, 17, 19,
30,31
apprenticeship 2:12
and The Baptism of Christ 2:12,
13
and the Borgias 2:18, 36
botanical drawings 2:17
commission for the church of
San Francesco Grande 2:15
death of 2:19, 19, 111
drapery studies 2:30
draughtsmanship 2:32-3
drawings 2:16-17, 30, 30, 31,
31, 32, 34, 34-5, 35, 77
and Duke Ludovico Sforza of
Milan 2:15-16
early life 2:12
as engineer 2:15, 16, 17, 18
first dated work 2:13
flying machines 2:16
gallery guide 2:139
and the Great Horse 2:15-16
ideal architecture 2:17
intellectual pursuits 2:15
key dates 2:12
last commission 2:19
Leonardo museums 2:12, 19
life 2:11-19, 36, 39, 41, 79
in Milan 2:15-16, 17, 18, 36
as military engineer 2:15, 17,
18-19
and oil painting 2:31-2
as painter-philosopher 2:31-2
on painting 2:31
proportions of the human
figure 2:16
and Raphael 2:83-4
sexuality 2:14-15, 16, 19
'sfumato' 2:29
trademarks 2:33
travels in Italy 2:18
Treatise on Painting 2:16, 19, 33
and Verrocchio 2:12-13, 15
working methods 2:30-35, 52,
83
The Adoration of the Magi 2:14
study for 2:32
The Annunciation 2:20-21
drapery study for 2:30
Arno Landscape 2:13
The Baptism of Christ (detail) 2:13
Battle of Anghiari 3:27
(copy) 2:18, 30, 32, 77
Ginevra de' Benci 2:22
Horse and Rider (bronze) 2:30
Lady with an Ermine 2:23
The Last Supper 2:16, 18, 24-5,
32, 34-5
details 2:35
Mona Lisa 2:18, 24
stolen 8:106

An Old Man and a Youth 2:15
portrait of? 2:12
Portrait of a Musician 2:31
St James (study) 2:34
St Jerome 2:31
Self-portrait, aged about 60 2:8,
11
Self-portrait? (1513) 2:19
The Sforza Monument 2:15-16,
18
The Virgin and Child with St
Anne 2:29
The Virgin and Child with St
Anne and John the Baptist 2:26
The Virgin of the Rocks: (c.1483)
2:32 (c.1508) 2:15, 27
Lewis, P. Wyndham
Portrait of Ezra Pound 9:68
Leyster, Judith 3:46, 47
Boy Playing a Flute 3:47
Self-portrait 3:46, 47
Lichtenstein, Roy 9:140
Lievens, Jan 3:78, 79
The Raising of Lazarus 3:78
Self-portrait 3:78
Limbourg, Herman de 1:11
apprentice in Paris 1:12-13
in Brussels jail 1:13, 13
portrait? 1:13
Limbourg, Jean de 1:11
apprentice in Paris 1:12-13
in Brussels jail 1:13, 13
portrait? 1:13
returns to Paris 1:13
Limbourg, Paul de 1:11
elopement 1:14
murals in Château de Bicêtre
1:14, 18
portrait? 1:13
returns to Paris 1:13
visits Italy 1:14, 19
Limbourg brothers
Bible for Philip the Bold 1:13,
19
deaths of 1:17
gallery guide 1:139
glorification of patron 1:21
influences on 1:16-17, 19
key dates 1:12
method of working 1:21
and other art forms 1:18-19
pay from Philip the Bold 1:13
presents to/from the Duc de
Berry 1:16, 18-19
style in Très Riches Heures 1:17
trademarks 1:20
use of camera obscura 1:19
varlets de chambre 1:14
working methods 1:19-21
Les Très Belles Heures de Notre-
Dame 1:16
Les Très Riches Heures du Duc de
Berry 1:9, 11, 16-17, 18, 18,
19, 20

calendar from 1:17, 18, 22-3, 22-3, 24-35
Liotard, Jean-Etienne
La Chocolatière 5:71
A French Woman and her Maid 5:68-9
Lipchitz, Jacques
by Modigliani 8:*118, 119, 123*
on Modigliani 8:116-17
and sculpture 8:118, *118*
The Guitar Player 8:118
Loo, Carle van 5:77, 81, 140-41
The Artist at Work 5:81
Denis Diderot 5:81
The Hunt Luncheon 5:69
Lorenzetti, Ambrogio
frescoes in Palazzo Pubblico 1:16
Good Government in the Countryside 1:16-17
Good Government in the Town (detail) 4:*20*
Loutherbourg, Philippe James de 6:48, 51, 141
Coalbrookdale by Night 6:141
Luks, George
early career 9:134
and Henri 9:132
influence of Hals 9:134
work rejected 9:133
The Miner 9:135

M

Maes, Nicholas 3:141
Saying Grace 3:*133*, 134
The Sleeping Kitchen Maid 5:52
Malouel, Jean 1:12
court painter in Burgundy 1:12
work in Dijon 1:37
work for Isabella of Bavaria 1:12
Manet, Edouard 3:53, 7:*11*, 12, 77
and American Civil War 7:*15*
apprenticeship 7:12
approach to painting 7:18
and Berthe Morisot 7:17, *17*
and café society 7:15, 34
career 7:12-14
Carolus-Duran and 9:82
and Cassatt 9:45, 46
categorizing 7:18
comparisons 7:21
'court' of 7:15
death of 7:17
and Degas 7:45-6
description of 7:13
duel with journalist 7:16
and Durand-Ruel 7:16
early life 7:12
and execution of Emperor Maximilian of Mexico 7:41

first teacher 7:12
and flower painting 7:*19*
as a founder of modern art 7:21
in Franco-Prussian War 7:16
gallery guide 3:139
and Hals 3:53
Hopper and 9:108
illness 7:16-17
and Impressionists 7:18, 20
influence of fellow painters 7:16
influence of Japanese prints 7:20, 21, *21*
influence of Old Masters 7:18, 20, 23
influence of Veláquez on 7:15, 20, *78*
and Isabelle Lemonnier 7:16
key dates 7:12
and Koëlla 7:13, *13*
and Légion d'Honneur 7:17, *17*
man-about-town 7:15-16
models 7:20-21, *22-3*
and Monet 7:14, 16
and non-conformists 7:15
painting out of doors (*plein-air*) 7:16, 20
and pastels 7:16, 19, *19*
as printmaker 7:*18*, 19, 20
private exhibitions 7:14, 15-16
public hostility to 7:16
range of paintings 7:19
and Renoir 7:16, 109
and the Salon 7:14, 15, 16
first submission to 7:14
and Salon des Refusés 7:14-15
and sketching 7:19-20
social life 7:15
struggle for effect 7:20
in studio of couture 7:12-13
subjects 7:18, 20
and Suzanne Leenhoff 7:13, *13*
tomb of 7:17
trademarks 7:20
travels on the Continent 7:14, 20
visit to Italy 7:13-14
visit to Spain 7:15
The Absinthe Drinker 7:14, *18*
Argenteuil 7:9
At Père Lathuille's 7:32
The Balcony 7:17, *31*
A Bar at the Folies-Bergère 7:21, *33*
Berthe Morisot with a Bunch of Violets 7:17, 140
Boating 7:20-21
The Cats' Rendezvous 7:18
Concert in the Tuileries Gardens 7:12-13, 14, 37
The Dead Toreador 7:18-19

The Execution of Maximilian 7:29
The Fifer 7:20, *78*
The Luncheon on the Grass 7:15, 19, 20, 24-5; 8:49
M. and Mme Auguste Manet 7:13
Olympia 7:15, 20, 21, *22-3, 26-7*; 8:*20*; 9:82
details 7:22
sketch for 7:23
Pinks and Clematis 7:19
Portrait of Emile Zola 7:20-21, *30*
Self-portrait 7:9, 11
The Spanish Guitarist 3:53
Venus of Urbino (copy after Titian) 7:23
Villa at Rueil 7:16
Young Woman with Blue Eyes 7:19
Mander, Karel van 1:113-14; 3:44, 45, 46
Mantegna, Andrea 4:15, 20
The Agony in the Garden 2:33, 140
The Dead Christ 2:140
The Judgement of Solomon 2:140
Judith 2:140
Lodovico Gonzaga and his Family 2:140
Parnassus 4:20
Marinetti, Filippo Tommaso 8:78, *78, 80*
aims 8:100, 102
and Futurism 8:78-9, 100
on 'superman' 8:85
influence of Marchesa Casati 8:*103*
on movement 8:82
and new language 8:101-102
on war 8:103
Masaccio 2:51, 52, 66
The Tribute Money (detail) 2:52
Matisse, Henri 8:*12, 13*, 46
and Armory Show 9:111, *111*
on art 8:18
beginnings of success 8:13
and Bouguereau 8:12
characterization of 8:17
Chevalier de Légion d'Honneur 8:17
on colour 8:19, 20
death of 8:17
and Derain 8:22
designs for Ballets Russes 8:17
and Diaghilev 8:134
early drawing classes 8:12
early influences 8:13
early life 8:12
early subjects 8:13, 18
early works 8:13
and etching 8:15
and Exposition Universalle 8:14
expressing his ideal 8:18
family 8:13, 14
and Fauvism 8:17, 19

first works 8:14-15
gallery guide 8:139
and *gouache découpée* 8:*16-17*, 20, *34-5*
on himself 8:17
illustrates Mallarmé poems 8:17
and Impressionism 8:13-14
influence of Cézanne 8:20
influence of Coptic fabrics 8:*15*
influence of Cross 8:14
influence of Gauguin 8:20
influence of Ingres 8:20
influence of Japanese prints 8:19
influence of the Mediterranean 8:14, 15
influence of Moreau 8:12
influence of Old Masters 8:17
influence of Signac 8:14
key dates 8:13
last years 8:16-17
and light 8:15, *16, 30*
and line drawing 8:*19*
marriage 8:14
models 8:14, 16, 17, 18, *18*
murals for Barnes Foundation 8:17
odalisques 8:15, 20
official recognition 8:17
on painting 8:12, 18
in Paris 8:13, 14-15; 9:69
patrons 8:15
Picasso and 8:52
and primitive art 8:52
and Salon d'Automne 8:15, 37
and sculpture 8:18, *26*
influence on 8:20
serious illness 8:16, 17
Shchukin commission 8:15, 21, *21*
simplification of work 8:20, 21, *21*
and Société des Beaux-Arts 8:13
in South of France 8:14, 38
as stage painter/designer 8:14, 17
and Stein family 8:15
'sublimated voluptuousness' 8:18
favourite themes 8:22, *28*, 37
recurring themes 8:24
trademarks 8:21
and Turner 8:14
use of brushwork 8:19
use of colour 8:14, 18-19
visits Collioure 8:*14-15*
visits Corsica 8:*12*, 14
visits Germany 8:15
visits London 8:14
visits North Africa 8:*14-15*, 15, 20
visits Russia 8:15

visits Spain 8:15
visits Tahiti and America 8:17
and World War I 8:15, 17
The Blue Window 8:20, *27*
Chapel of the Rosary 8:16, *16*, 17
    technique for windows 8:*16*
Dance 8:15, 20, 21, *21*
The Dining Table 8:13
The Egyptian Curtain 8:20, *33*
Goldfish and Sculpture 8:*26*
The Green Stripe see Madame Matisse
Jazz 8:19
Luxe, Calme et Volupté 8:13, 14, 18, *18*
Madame Matisse 8:*23*
Odalisque with Red Bloomers 8:*31*
The Open Window 8:15, 19
Open Window, Collioure 8:*22*
Red Interior, Still-Life on a Blue Table 8:*32*
The Red Studio 9:*111*
Le Rouge et le Noir 8:17
Self-portrait (drawing) 8:*11*
Still-life with Oriental Rugs 8:*24-5*
La Tristesse du Roi 8:*34-5*
Two Women in an Interior 8:*30*
Woman and Goldfish 8:*28-9*
Woman with Blue Eyes 8:19
Memling, Hans
    influence of Van der Weyden on 1:79, *79*, 102, 141
    The Donne Triptych 1:*79*
Mengs, Anton Raphael 4:77
    Giacomo Casanova 5:*132*
Mercier, Philippe
    Frederick, Prince of Wales, and his Sisters 6:*52*
Metsu, Gabriel 3:141
    The Breakfast 3:*21*
    The Music Lesson 3:141
    The Sick Child 3:141
    Woman Reading a Letter 3:*134*
Michelangelo, the new *see* Bernini, Gian Lorenzo
Michelangelo Buonarotti 2:47, 49, *49*
    and anatomy 2:45
    apprenticeship 2:44-5, 52
    architecture 2:49, 53, 70-71
    character 2:48-9
    and classical art 2:46, 51, 52
    commission from Pope Julius II 2:46-7, *47*
    David and 4:76
    early life 2:44
    emotional expression 2:51-2
    gallery guide 2:139
    and Ghirlandaio 2:44, 52
    and Julius II 2:46-7, 49, 64, *67*
    key dates 2:45

life 2:43-9, 73-4, 79, 81, 101, 115-16
and the Medicis 2:44-5, 46, 48
Picasso and 2:47
portrait (del Conte) 2:*8, 43*
poses 2:52-3
Reynolds and 6:12, 13, 16, 19, 35, 49
on sculpture 2:53
sexuality 2:48
on Titian 2:115
trademarks 2:53
travels in Italy 2:46
and Vittoria Colonna 2:48, *48-9*
working methods 2:50-53, 64-7, 115-16
The Awakening Slave 2:*51*
Bacchus 2:46
The Battle of Cascina 2:*18*
    preliminary studies 2:*50*
The Battle of the Centaurs 2:*45*
Capitol (design for) 2:*49*
The Creation of Adam 6:*83*
David 2:46, 52, *55*, 77
The Doni Tondo 2:*50*
The Dying Slave 2:*53*
The Fate of Tityus 2:*48*
The Last Judgement 2:48, 51, 60-63
Laurentian Library 2:*51*, 52, 73-4
Medici Tombs 2:48, *51*, 52
nude (Rubens' copy after) 3:*14*
Pietà: Duomo 2:*49*
    St Peter's 2:46, *54*; 4:*87*
Self-portrait, aged 70 (drawing) 8:*8*
Sistine Ceiling 2:47, 48, *50-51*, 52, *56-9, 64-7*, 97
    details 2:*64-5, 66-7*
    plan 2:*65*
Sleeping Cupid (sculpture) 2:46
Taddei Tondo 2:*52*
Tomb of Julius II 2:46, *47*, 51
Mignard, Pierre 4:141
    Marquise de Seignelay 4:*141*
Millet, Frank 9:100
    and Broadway 9:100-103
    and Sargent 9:79
    caricature of 9:*87*
    Between Two Fires 9:*100-101*
Miro, Joan
    and Diaghilev 8:134
Modigliani, Amedeo 8:*8, 107, 108, 112-13*
    aide-memoires 8:116-17
    apprenticeship 8:111
    artist friends 8:109
    and Beatrice Hastings 8:111-12
    on his character 8:110
    contribution to modern art 8:117
    and Cubism 8:110
    death of 8:113
    descriptions of 8:111

early life 8:108-109
early studies 8:109
first one-man show 8:112-13
gallery guide 8:139
and Guillaume 8:112
health 8:109
influence of Brancusi 8:115
influence of Cézanne 8:113, 115
influence of Symbolism 8:115
first landscape 8:113
key dates 8:109
models 8:117
    style when painting 8:116
old-fashioned style 8:110
in Paris 8:109-12, *111*; 9:69
patrons 8:110
photograph of 8:*8*
and poetry 8:109
and Salon d'Automne 8:112
and sculpture 8:110, 111, *111*, 115-16
    effect of on painting 8:115-16
    first 8:115
and sitters 8:116
and *Stile Liberty* 8:115
style of nudes 8:116
subjects 8:114, 117
superstitions 8:113
temple to humanity 8:115
trademarks 8:*116-17*
unreasonable behaviour 8:110
use of line 8:116
visits Italy 8:109
visits South of France 8:113, 117
working methods 8:116-17
and World War I 8:112
and Zborowski 8:112
The Bride and Groom 8:*122*
Caryatids 8:*111*, 115
The Equestrienne 8:*120*
Gypsy Woman with Baby 8:*117*
    detail 8:*116-17*
Landscape at Cagnes 8:*115*
The Little Girl in Blue 8:*129*
The Little Peasant 8:*128*
Portrait of Frank Burty Haviland 8:*121*
Portrait of Jeanne Hébuterne 8:*112, 130-1*
Portrait of Jacques Lipchitz and his Wife 8:*118-19, 123*
    preliminary drawings 8:*119*
Reclining Nude 7:*21*; 8:*124-5*
A Seated Man Leaning on a Table 8:*126-7*
Seated Nude 8:*114*
Self-portrait 8:*114*
Moitte, Pierre Etienne
    The Kitchenmaid 5:*69*
Monet, Claude 5:21; 7:14, *14*, 15, *75, 76*, 109

aims of 7:83
and Alice Hoschedé 7:79
in Argenteuil 7:79
in the Army 7:77-8
at Atelier Suisse 7:77
brushwork 7:84, *85*
comparisons 7:*84*
death of 7:81
and Durand-Ruel 7:79, *79, 80*
early life 7:76-7
in England 7:79
exhibitions of work by 7:80
eye operation 7:81
financial problems 7:78-9
and Forest of Fontainebleau 7:*131*
gallery guide 7:139
and gardening 7:80, *98, 98-101, 101*
in Giverny 7:79-80, *81*
and Gleyre 7:78, 109
growing reputation 7:80
on *The Haystacks* 7:84
and independent exhibition 7:47
influence of Boudin 7:76
influence of Jongkind 7:78
key dates 7:77
on landscape painting 7:77
later subjects 7:80
and light 7:80
in London 7:80, *81*
in Norway 7:80
on painting 7:85
painting at speed 7:84-5
painting out of doors (*plein-air*) 7:80, 83-4, 115-16
paintings presented to nation 7:81
in Paris 7:77-8
and Renoir 7:9, 109-110, 114-15
and Sargent 9:82, 83-4
    portrait by 9:*84-5*
scale of works 7:81
'series' pictures 7:83, *83*, 84, 85
and studio work 7:85
style 7:115-16
techniques 7:84
trademarks 7:84-5
travels 7:80
in Venice 7:*80*
and waterlilies 7:80, *82*, 101
and Whistler 9:16
The Boating Party 9:*48-9*
Boulevard des Capucines 7:*90*
The Bridge at Argenteuil 7:*91*
Camille on her Deathbed 7:*83*
Gare St Lazare 7:*92*
The Haystacks 7:80, *83*
Impression: Sunrise 7:*78-9*
Lady with a Parasol 7:*83*
Poplars 7:*94*
Regatta at Argenteuil 7:*84-5*

Rouen Cathedral series 7:86-7
  detail 7:87
  studio for 7:86, 87
Rouen Cathedral in Full Sunlight
  7:86, 95
  detail 7:87
The Rue Montorgeuil Decked
  with Flags 7:93
Self-portrait 7:75
The Terrace 7:76-7
The Thames below Westminster
  6:116
Waterlilies series 7:84, 85, 96-7
Waterloo Bridge 7:81
Wild Poppies 7:88-9
Women in the Garden 7:82
Moore, Albert
  use of colour themes 9:20, 20
  Dreamers 9:20
Mor, Anthonis
  replaces a Van der Weyden
    painting 1:80
Morisot, Berthe 7:141; 9:47
  and Manet 7:17, 17, 20, 140
  The Cradle 9:53
Moulins, Master of 1:141
  Annunciation 1:141
  Nativity with Cardinal Jean Rolin
    1:141
Murillo, Bartolomé Estebán 6:49
  The Birth of the Virgin 3:106
Mytens, Daniel
  Charles I and Henrietta Maria
    Departing for the Chase 3:41

N

Nash, Paul
  The Ypres Salient at Night
    9:104-105
Natoire, Jean-Marc 5:141

O

O'Keefe, Georgia 9:141
Oudry, Jean-Baptist 5:141
  Boucher and 5:78, 81, 85
  and Gobelins tapestry factory
    5:78, 81
  The Dead Wolf 5:46
  The White Duck 5:141

P

Parmigianino, Francesco
  Cassatt and 9:44-5
  Madonna with the Long Neck
    8:116
Pasture, Rogier de la see
  Weyden, Rogier van der
Patenier, Joachim 1:141

Rest on the Flight into Egypt
  1:141
St Christopher 1:141
Pater, Jean-Baptiste 5:16, 141
Penni, Gianfrancesco
  finishes Vatican apartments
    2:81
Perugino, Pietro 2:141
  commission from the Vatican
    2:78
  Raphael and 2:76-7, 77, 83, 86
  Collegio del Cambio frescoes
    2:76
  The Donation of the Keys 2:77, 83
  St Sebastian 2:141
Picasso, Pablo Ruiz 8:8, 43, 44,
  45, 46, 47, 49
  academic work 8:45, 51
  on art 8:50, 51
  and avant-garde style 8:45
  and Balzac's Chef d'Oeuvre
    inconnu 8:48
  'Blue' period 8:45-6
    subjects 8:46
  Boccioni and 8:80
  and Braque 8:47, 68-9
  and ceramics 8:52
  on children's drawing 8:49
  and Cocteau 8:46, 47
  collages 8:52, 71
  complicated relationships
    8:48-9
  and composition 8:52
  and contemporary poets 8:45
  and Cubism 8:46, 52
    aims of 8:69
    Analytical 8:71
    first sculpture 8:71
    Synthetic 8:71
  and Diaghilev 8:46, 47, 134
  Director of the Prado 8:49
  and distortion 8:53, 66-7
  'drawing in space' 8:52
  early life 8:44
  early training 8:44
  encouragement of parents
    8:44
  end of poverty 8:46
  as engraver 8:48
  on enthusiasm 8:52
  final years 8:49
  and form 8:52
  gallery guide 8:139
  Government commission
    8:49
  greatest inspiration 8:52
  and human condition 8:48
  human 'monsters' 8:48
  importance of colour 8:52
  influence of Humbert 8:47
  and Jacob 8:45
  key dates 8:45
  'la vie snob' 8:47
  and line 8:52

  and linocutting 8:52
  and Manet 8:49
  and Matisse 8:52
  media 8:50
  'Negro' period 8:52
  and new developments 8:47-8
  and Old Masters 8:47
  on his art 8:50
  and Ovid's Metamorphoses 8:48
  paints Gertrude Stein 8:49
  in Paris 8:45, 45, 46, 50; 9:69
  photograph (1963) 8:8
  and 'reality' in art 8:50-51, 52
  'Rose' period 8:46
    subjects 8:46
  and sculpture 8:49, 52
  in South of France 8:39
  and Spanish Civil War 8:48, 49
  speed of working 8:50
  stimulating environment for
    8:45
  styles 8:45-6, 52
  on subjects 8:52
  and Surrealism 8:48, 63
  trademarks 8:53
  use of model 8:51
  and Velázquez 8:49
  visits Rome 8:46, 47
  visual memory 8:52
  working methods 8:52
  and World War I 8:47
  The Acrobat's Family with a
    Monkey 8:55
  Bottle of Vieux Marc, Guitar, and
    Newspaper 8:58-9
  Déjeuner sur l'Herbe 8:49
  Les Demoiselles d'Avignon
    8:46-7, 56-7, 68
    inspiration for 8:52
  The Dream 8:63
  The Dream and Lie of Franco
    (leaflet) 8:48
  Les Femmes d'Algers 8:49
  Girl in a Chemise 8:54
  Guernica 8:48, 49, 64-5
  Guitar (sculpture) 8:52
  Joie de Vivre paintings 8:49
  Las Meninas (series) 8:49
  Nude in a Red Armchair 8:62
  Parade (drop curtain) 8:46
  portrait of his mother 8:44
  Reclining Nude with Necklace
    8:66-7
  Seated Woman 8:53, 53
  The She-Goat (sculpture) 8:50
  The Three Dancers 8:48, 50-51
  The Vollard Suite: No 38 8:51
  Women Running on the Beach
    8:60-61
Pietro da Cortona
  Boucher and 5:77
  Fragonard and 5:110
  ceiling of the Barberini Palace,
    Rome 5:109

Pinturicchio, Bernardino
  The Disputation of St Catherine
    2:36
  Portrait of Alexander VI 2:37
Piombo, Sebastiano del
  Portrait of Vittoria Calonna 2:49
Pissarro, Camille 7:77, 117, 141
  and independent exhibitions
    7:47
  and the Louvre 7:117
  The Boulevard Montmartre 7:84
  La Place du Théâtre Francais 7:140
Pissarro, Lucien 7:141
Pollock, Jackson 9:141
Post, Franz
  A Dutch Colony in Brazil 3:136-7
Poussin, Gaspard see Dughet,
  Gaspard
Poussin, Nicolas 6:22, 23
  and antiquity 4:13, 14, 15, 17,
    18-21, 22, 24
  apprenticeship 4:12
  and Cassiano del Pozzo
    4:14-15, 17
  Classicism of 4:17
  commissions 4:14-15, 16-17
    first major public 4:15
  and Domenichino 4:16, 41
  domestic life 4:15-16
  early life 4:12
  gallery guide 4:139
  and Gaspard Dughet 4:16
  influence of Aldobrandini and
    Ludovisi collections 4:16
  influence of Raphael 4:17, 22
  influence of Titian 4:16, 18
  key dates 4:13
  and landscape 4:17
  and Metamorphoses 4:13, 14
  at Palais de Luxembourg 4:13
  in Paris 4:12, 16-17
  patronage 4:14, 15, 15, 17
  in Rome 4:14, 17
  scale of works 4:15
  style, development of 4:18
  subjects 4:17, 19, 21
  on his success 4:20
  tempera paintings 4:13
  and the theatre 4:20-21
  trademarks 4:21
  travels 4:12-13
  working methods 4:18-23, 52-3
  The Adoration of the Golden Calf
    4:27
  Apollo and Daphne 4:17
  Bacchanalian Revel before a Term
    of Pan 4:20-21
  Blind Orion Searching for the
    Rising Sun 4:32
  Confirmation 4:28
  Dance to the Music of Time 6:22,
    23
  The Death of Germanicus 4:15,
    24-5, 84

INDEX OF ARTISTS

drawings from Trajan's Column 4:*18*
Et in Arcadia Ego 4:16, *18-19*
Extreme Unction 4:*15*
(1644) 4:*29*
The Funeral of Phocion 4:*32*
Holy Family on the Steps 4:*22-3, 30-31*
Holy Family with Six Putti 4:*19*
Landscape with a Man Killed by a Snake 4:*19*
the 'Marino' drawings 4:*13*, 14
The Martyrdom of St Erasmus 4:14, *14*, 15, *18*
Self-portrait 4:*9, 11, 46*, (drawing) 4:*14*
Summer 4:21, *34*
The Triumph of Pan 4:*26*
Triumph of Silenus 4:*15*
Winter 4:21, *35*
Prud'hon, Pierre-Paul 4:*141*
Justice and Divine Vengeance Pursuing Crime 1:141

Q

Quarton, Enguerrand 1:141
The Coronation of the Virgin 1:141

R

Raeburn, Sir Henry
The Paterson Children 6:*21*
Ramsay, Allan 6:141
Raphael Sanzio 4:91; 6:15
and Ancient Rome 2:82, 100-103
as archaeologist 2:*103*
architecture 2:79-80, 81
burial place 2:81, *81*
cartoons, 'Auxiliary' 2:*83*
and Chigi 2:79
frescoes for 2:79
criticism of 2:81
J. L. David and 4:77
death of 2:111
development of style 2:82-3
earliest commissions 2:77
earliest work? 2:*77*
early life 2:76
in Florence 2:77-9
gallery guide 2:139
hallmark of art 2:84-5
income of 2:80
influence of Leonardo 2:76, 83, 84, 88
influence of Michelangelo 2:84, 85
Ingres and 4:111, *112*, 114, 115
and Pope Julius II 2:78, 79, 80, 98, 101
key dates 2:76
and La Fornarina 2:80-81
last major work 2:81
and Pope Leo X 2:81
life 2:14, 69, 76-81, 100-103, 104
Madonnas 2:77, 83
marriage proposal 2:80-81
papal architect 2:79-80
papal commissions 2:77-8
and Perugino 2:76-7, 78, 83, 86
Picasso and 8:47
Poussin and 4:13, 17
preliminary drawings 2:84
range of work 2:82, 83-4
Renoir and 7:112
on restoration of Rome 2:103
Reynolds and 6:12, 13
in Rome 2:77-9
tapestry cartoons 2:81, *83*
trademarks 2:84
and Vatican apartments 2:79-80
working methods 2:82-5, 96-9
The Betrothal of the Virgin 2:*86*
Disputà 2:84, *98*
details 2:*98*
preliminary drawings 2:*98*
The Entombment 2:*89*
The Fire in the Borgo 2:*99*
detail 2:*99*
The Horses of Monte Cavallo 2:*103*
The Judgement of Paris 2:*78*
Loggia of Cupid and Psyche 2:*81*
Madonna del Granduca 2:*84*
detail 2:*85*
Madonna della Sedia 2:*9*, 80, *82*; 4:*117*
Madonna of the Fish 4:*22*
The Madonna of the Goldfinch 2:*84, 88*
The Mass of Bolsena 2:*99*
detail 2:*99*
The Miraculous Draught of Fishes (cartoon) 2:*83*
Parnassus 2:*98*
Portrait of Agnolo Doni 2:*87*
Portrait of Castiglioni 2:*78*
Portrait of Julius II 2:*79*
Portrait of Leo X and Two Cardinals 2:*80*
The St Cecilia Altarpiece 2:*83*
St Michael and the Dragon 2:*82*
School of Athens 2:79, 84, *90-91, 96-7*, 98
Self-portrait 2:*8, 75*
drawing 2:*76*
The Sistine Madonna 2:*94*
Stanza d'Eliodoro 2:79, *92-3, 99*
Stanza dell' Incendio 2:80, 81, *99*
Stanza della Segnatura 2:79, 84, *90-91, 96-7, 98*
Transfiguration 2:81, *83*
Triumph of Galatea 2:*8*, 79
Ray, Man 9:*141*
Reinagle, Ramsay 6:77
Portrait of Constable 6:*75*
Rembrandt van Rijn
and Amsterdam Town Hall 3:82
original plan 3:*82*
apprenticeship 3:77
attitudes towards 3:87
and ben Israel 3:105
brushwork 3:84-5
commissions 3:80
first 3:79
domestic life 3:80
drawings 3:*80-81*, 84, 85, 86
early life 3:76-7
early work 3:84
as employee 3:83
etchings 3:80, 84, 85, *85*, 86, 87
final years 3:83
financial problems 3:82-3
gallery guide 3:139
graphic work 3:*80-81*
greatness 3:86-7
and *impasto* 3:85
key dates 3:76
and Lastman 3:77, *77*, 84
late works 3:83
and Lievens 3:78, 79
mistresses 3:80-82
Netherlandish influence 3:84-7
as portrait painter 3:79, 82
pupils 5:52, 80
first 3:78
self-portraits 3:*83*, 86, *90, 97*
subjects 3:84
change in 3:80
trademarks 3:87
Turner and 6:115
use of paint 3:84, 85, 86
working methods 3:84-9
The Anatomy Lesson of Dr Tulp 3:*79, 84*
Aristotle Contemplating a Bust of Homer 3:*94*
Bathsheba 3:*95*
Belshazzar's Feast 3:*84-85*
The Entombment of Christ 3:*85*
The Jewish Bride 3:*99*
The Night Watch 3:*88-9, 92-3*
details 3:*88, 89*
watercolour copy 3:*89*
The Oath of Julius Civilis 3:*82*
The Omval 3:*81*
The Polish Rider 3:84
Portrait of Agatha Bas 3:*85*
Portrait of the Artist's Mother 3:*76*
Portrait of Jan Six 3:*87*
detail 3:*87*
Portrait of Saskia 3:78, *79*
Portrait of Titus 3:*82*
Saskia as Flora 3:*91*
Self-portrait (1658) 3:*97*
aged 23 3:*77*
aged 34 (detail) 3:*9, 75*
aged 63 3:*83*
Self-portrait with Saskia 3:*90*
Singel Canal, Armersfoort 3:*80-81*
Sleeping Woman 3:*81*
Stormy Landscape 2:*33*
Studies of Heads and Figures 3:*81*
Study of an Old Man 3:*77*
Study of a Pig 3:*80*
The Syndics 3:*98*
The Three Crosses 3:*85*
The Three Trees 3:*85*
Woman Carrying a Child Downstairs 3:*80*
René Master 1:141
Le Cuer d'Amour Espris 1:141
Reni, Guido 4:76; 6:13
and Rubens 3:20-21
Renoir, Pierre-Auguste 3:21; 7:*14*, 15, *107, 108, 112-13*
American enthusiasm for 7:112
apprenticeship 7:108-109
and Argenteuil 7:79
on art 7:114
biography of 7:*113*
character 7:111
choice of subjects 7:114, 116
commission from Lascaux 7:112, *112*
and the Commune 7:110, 137
comparisons 7:*117, 117*
and Courbet 7:114
crisis in painting 7:112
dependence on commissions 7:111
early life 7:108
exhibits with Impressionists 7:116
family life 7:112, *112*
favourite paintings 7:*117*
and fellow students 7:114
financial problems 7:110, 111
flower paintings 7:*115*, 117
and Forest of Fontainebleau 7:*108*, 109, 131
gallery guide 7:139
on Gleyre 7:78
in Gleyre's studio 7:109, 114
'harsh' style 7:112, *114*, 117
illnesses 7:112-13
and independent exhibition 7:47
influence of Old Masters 7:*111*, 112, 117
influence of Rubens 3:21
key dates 7:108
on *The Lacemaker* 3:130

last home 7:113, *113*
and light 7:116
and 'the machine' 7:109
marriage 7:111-12
model mistresses 7:109, *109*
models 7:112, *112*, 116
and Monet 7:109-110, 115
on the nude 7:111, 117, *129*
on painting 7:113
painting out of doors (*plein-air*)
 7:115-16
in Paris 7:108
patrons 7:110, *111*
preparatory drawings *7:115*
and the Salon 7:111, 114, 117
and sculpture 7:113, 117
in South of France 7:113; 8:36
 37, 39
and still-lifes *7:118*
studios 7:110-111, *112*, 113
style 7:109-112, *112*, 115-16,
 117
success as portrait painter
 7:110, 114
trademarks 7:116
travels *7:111, 112, 112*
use of colour 7:114-15, 117
 blue 7:116
visit to Algeria *7:111*, 112
visits to the Louvre 7:109, 117
After the Bath 7:129
The Bathers 7:114
 method for painting 7:117
Dance in the Town 7:127
Dance in the Country (detail)
 7:111
The First Night Out 7:122
Fruits of the Midi 7:126
La Grenouillère 7:120, 125
La Loge 7:121
*The Luncheon of the Boating
 Party 7:111-12, 118-19*
 details *7:118, 119*
 friends in *7:119*
*Madame Charpentier and her
 Children 7:110*
*Madame Monet and her Son Jean
 7:77*
Monet at 35 7:9
Moss Roses 7:115
Mother Anthony's Inn 7:109
Le Moulin de la Galette 7:114-15,
 116-17
The Odalisque 7:109
Pont Neuf 7:84
Richard Wagner 7:112
Self-portrait 7:107
The Skiff 7:123
The Steps 7:115
The Swing 7:116
 detail *7:116*
The Umbrellas 7:128
Venus Victrix (sculpture) *7:115*
Victor Chocquet 7:114

Reynolds, Sir Joshua
and Angelica Kauffmann 6:16
and Annibale Carracci's work
 6:13
apprenticeship 6:12-13
approach to painting 6:18-19
and Boucher 5:85
and classical art 6:13, 14-15, 16,
 18-19, 21, 22-3, 24, 25
the *Discourses* 6:14, *15*, 16, 17,
 22, 39
gallery guide 6:139
influence of Michelangelo on
 6:12, 13, 19, 35, 48
influence of Rubens on 6:17,
 20
influence on Gainsborough
 6:52
influence on portrait painting
 6:18
key dates 6:13
King's principal painter 6:16
life 6:12-17, 36-9, 48, 51-2, 53,
 61
and the Literary Club 6:14, 15
organization of studio 6:21
on Poussin 4:18-19
and Raphael's works 6:13
in Rome 6:13
and the Royal Academy 6:14,
 15, 16, 17, 18, 36-9, 48
on Rubens 3:18
technique 6:20-21
and Thomas Hudson 6:12-13,
 18
trademarks 6:21
use of drapery painters 6:21
visits to Holland and Flanders
 6:17
on Watteau 5:21
working methods 6:18-21
The Brummell Children 6:33
ceiling in Somerset House 6:37
*Commodore Keppel 6:14, 19, 24,
 25*
*Count Ugolino and his Children
 6:17*
The Death of Dido 6:17, 18-19
*The Family of George, 4th Duke of
 Marlborough 6:18*
*Garrick between Tragedy and
 Comedy 6:28-9*
*Georgiana, Countess Spencer,
 and her Daughter 6:26*
*Georgiana, Duchess of
 Devonshire, and her Daughter
 6:20-21*
Heads of Angels 6:19
The Infant Academy 6:39
James, 7th Earl of Lauderdale 6:25
Lady Betty Hamilton 6:18
Lady Caroline Scott 6:32
*Lavinia, Countess Spencer 6:20,
 21*

*Lieutenant-Colonel Sir Banastre
 Tarleton 6:19, 19*
Lord Heathfield 6:13, 13
Mrs Joseph Hamar 6:13, 13
Nelly O'Brien 6:27
Oliver Goldsmith (copy) *6:14*
Portrait of George III 6:36
Samuel Johnson 6:15
*Sarah Siddons as the Tragic Muse
 6:19, 35, 49*
Self-portrait 6:11
*Self-portrait as Doctor of Civil
 Law 6:16, 17*
Self-portrait as Rembrandt 6:9, 48
The Society of Dilettanti 6:15, 15
*Three Ladies Decorating a Term of
 Hymen 6:22-3, 30-31*
Rijn, Rembrandt van *see*
 Rembrandt van Rijn
Robert, Hubert 5:110, 120, 141
*A Servant Reading to his Master
 5:71*
*View of the Grande Galerie in the
 Louvre 5:81, 140*
Robertson, Mary Anne
 (Grandma Moses) 9:141
Rockwell, Norman 9:141
Shuffleton's Barber Shop 9:116
Rodin, Auguste
 on Sargent 9:79
Rohan Hours, Master of the
 1:141
Rohan Hours (detail) *1:140*
Rolla, Henry
Gervex 5:117
Romney, George 6:141
Rossellino, Antonio
*Laughing Madonna and Child
 2:85*
Rothko, Mark 9:141
Rowlandson, Thomas
The Comforts of Bath 6:69
Exhibition Day 6:38
Rubens, Peter Paul
apprenticeship 3:13
on his art 3:18
and art collection, Mantua
 3:14
and assistants 3:17, 19-20
book illustrations 3:17, 18
Cassatt and 9:45
and Charles I 3:16, *16*, 17, 40
and Classical art 3:14, 20, 23
commissions 3:14, 16-17, *17*, 19
Constable on 3:21
diplomatic missions 3:14-15,
 17
early life 3:12, *12*
in England 3:16, *17*
family life 3:15-16, 17, 21
and fêtes galantes 5:21
Gainsborough and 6:47, 53, 66
gallery guide 3:139
and 'Grand Manner' 3:15

growing reputation 3:15
and Infanta Isabella 3:17
influence of Elsheimer 3:14
influence on other painters
 3:21
in Italy 3:14-15, 20
and Jan Brueghel 3:18
key dates 3:12
linguistic skills 3:17
as page to Countess of
 Lalaing 3:13
paintings: list of 3:19
 number of 3:18
patron, first 3:14
political career 3:13, 14, 15, 16,
 17
pupil, first 3:14
in retirement 3:17
Reynolds and 6:17, 20
in Rome 3:14, 15
on second marriage 3:17
studio 3:16, 18
style, formation of 3:20
trademarks 3:20
use of paint 3:20, *20*
use of panels 3:20
and Van Dyck 3:16, 18
and Van Noort 3:13
Watteau and 5:14, 17, 18
working methods 3:18-23
Allegory of War 3:69
*Autumn Landscape with a View of
 Het Steen 3:32*
*Banqueting House, Whitehall
 3:16, 17, 40*
Blessings of Peace 3:40
'Costume Book' 3:13
Le Chapeau de Paille 3:29
*Chiesa Nuova Altarpiece 3:14,
 15*
copy of Leonardo's *Battle of
 Anghiari 2:18*
costume studies 3:13
*The Descent from the Cross 3:15,
 20, 22-3, 24-5*
 details 3:22-3
 modello for 3:22
drawing after Michelangelo
 nude 3:14
Duke of Lerma 3:13
The Effects of War 3:69
The Fall of the Damned 3:19
The Feast of Venus 3:34-5
The Garden of Love 5:21
Head of a Child 3:28
*Hippopotamus and Crocodile
 Hunt 3:26-7*
*History of the Emperor
 Constantine 3:17*
*Jesuit Church ceiling,
 Antwerp 3:16, 17*
*Landscape with a Shepherd and
 his Flock 3:33*
Laocoön (drawing) *3:23*

Leda 3:18
Marie de' Medici cycle 3:17, 30, 31, 36-9
The Nymphs of Diana Surprised by Satyrs 5:84-5
Portrait of the Archduke Albert 3:15
Portrait of the Infanta Isabella 3:15
Portrait of Isabella Brant 3:14
Portrait of a Little Boy 3:21
Portrait of Paracelsus 2:73
The Presentation in the Temple 3:23, 25
The Prodigal Son 3:18-19
The Raising of the Cross 3:15,20, 22
Romulus and Remus and the She-Wolf 3:8
Rubens and Isabella Brandt in a Honeysuckle Bower 3:18
St George and the Dragon 3:19
Santa Maria, Vallicella, altarpiece 3:15
Self-portrait 3:9, 11
Self-portrait with Friends 3:13
Self-portrait with Hélène Fourment 3:16-17
The Three Graces 3:20
Torre de la Parada paintings 3:17
Venus and Adonis 6:17
The Visitation 3:22, 24
Ruisdael, Jacob van 6:45, 84
Landscape with Ruin 6:84
Ryder, Albert Pinkham 9:141

S

Saenredam, Pieter 3:141
Church Interior, Haarlem 3:47
Sanders, John
The Royal Academicians 6:37
Sanzio, Raphael *see* Raphael Sanzio
Sargent, John Singer 9:75, 76
in America 9:78, 79
apprenticeship 9:77
and Broadway 9:79, 100-103
brushwork 9:84, 85
early landscapes 9:82
early life 9:76
early sketchbooks 9:76
education 9:76
and effects of light on colour 9:79
in England 9:79
friendship with Monet 9:82, 83-4
gallery guide 9:139
influence of Carolus-Duran 9:82
influence of Hals 9:82

influence of Impressionists 9:82
influence of Monet 9:85
influence of Reynolds 9:79
influence of Velázquez 9:78
and Isabella Gardner 9:79
key dates 9:77
and Marquand 9:79
new subjects 9:84-5
one-man exhibition 9:79
painting holidays 9:78, 80-81, *81*
in Paris 9:77, 79
and Paris Salon 9:82, *88*
pattern of life 9:80-81
plein-air works 9:78, 79, 82, 85
method of working 9:82-3
portrait painting 9:78, 79-80
style of early 9:82
technique 9:85
preparation for sketching 9:83
range of work 9:82
and Royal Academy 9:79, 94
and Société des Vingts 9:82
travel sketches 9:76-7
travels 9:78, 80, 82
visits Normandy 9:83-4
visits North Africa 9:78, 79
as war artist 9:80, *80*, 81, *98-9*
'at work' 9:87
work in England 9:82-4
Bedouins 9:80
Breakfast in the Loggia 9:83
The Brook 9:83
Carnation, Lily, Lily, Rose 9:86, 91, 100, 103
details 9:86-7
preliminary sketches 9:86
Claude Monet at the Edge of a Wood 9:84-5
The Daughters of Edward D. Boit 9:78, *90*
Ellen Terry as Lady Macbeth 9:93
Garden Study of the Vickers Children 9:87
Gassed 9:98-9
In a Levantine Port 9:8
The Interior of a Hospital Tent 9:80
El Jaleo 9:78, *88-9*
Lady Agnew 9:79, *94*
Lady with the Rose 9:81, *82-3*
Madame X (Madame Pierre Gautreau) 9:78, *92*
Mountain Stream 9:97
murals for Boston Public Library 9:79-80, *81*, 84-5, 103
murals for Museum of Fine Art, Boston 9:79-80, 84-5, 103
research expeditions for 9:80, *80*
The Oyster Gatherers at Cancale 9:82

Pagan Deities: Astarte and Neith 9:81
Pomegranates 9:96
portrait of Carolus-Duran 9:77, 78
Self-portrait 9:9, 75
Severini, Gino 8:141
Shinn, Everett 9:133
and Henri 9:132
works rejected 9:133
Signac, Paul
and Matisse 8:14
in South of France 8:36, 37
Sisley, Alfred 7:78, 141
and Argenteuil 7:79
and Gleyre 7:109
by Monet 7:*109*
Sloan, John 9:132, 134
Night Windows 9:134
Sunday, Women Drying Their Hair 9:132-3
Woman's Work 9:134
Sluter, Claus
work in Dijon 1:37
tomb of Philip the Bold 1:37, *37*
Well of Moses 1:37
Snyders, Frans 3:141
and Rubens 3:19, 141
Soutine, Chaim 8:141
Steen, Jan 3:141
subjects 3:134, 141
The Doctor's Visit 3:134
Two Kinds of Games 3:108
Stuart, Gilbert 9:141
Stubbs, George 6:141
Anatomy of a Horse 6:141
Whistlejacket 6:*140*

T

Teniers, David 3:141; 5:16
Terborch, Gerard 3:141
Lady at her Toilet 3:135
Parental Admonition 3:141
Soldier Offering a Young Woman Coins 3:133, 134
Theotocopoulus, Domenikos *see* El Greco
Tintoretto, Jacopo 2;113, 117, 141; 3:20
The Discovery of the Body of St Mark 2:141
The Liberation of Arsinoe 2:141
St Mark Freeing a Christian Slave 2:141
Transport of the Body of St Mark 2:141
Tissot, James
Henley Regatta 3:134-5
Titian Vecellio
and Alfonso d'Este 2:109, 110-111, 114, 125
apprenticeship 2:108-109

assistants 2:117
atmosphere in paintings 2:116
and Bellini 2:108-109, 110, 114
brushwork 2:114-16
caricature by Bassano 2:*112*
and Charles V 2:110, 111, 112, 129, 132, 133, 134, 135
commissions 2:*109*, 117
early work 2:109
gallery guide 2:139
and Giorgione 2:109, 110, 116
key dates 2:108
last years 2:113
and Leo X 2:109-110
life 2:108-13, 134, 135
and Michelangelo 2:115
official painter to the Republic (Venice) 2:110
paintings for Camerino d'Alabastra 2:110-111
patrons 2:109-110, 111-12
and Philip II of Spain 2:111-12, 113, 114, 130, 135
'poesie' 2:130-31
Poussin and 4:16, 18
private life 2:112
Renoir and 7:112
Spanish royal family and 3:15
tondo 2:50, 82
trademarks 2:116
travels in Germany 2:111
working methods 2:114-17
workshop production 2:116-17
The Andrians 2:111, *114-15*
The Assumption of the Virgin 2:109, 110, 116, *124*
original setting 2:109
Bacchus and Ariadne 2:111, *125*
The Battle of Spoleto 2:114
Charles V on Horseback 2:129, 135
Danaë 2:130
Death of St Peter Martyr (copy) 2:111, 116
Empress Isabella 2:133
The Entombment 2:115
La Gloria 2:125
The Jealous Husband 2:109
Man with a Blue Sleeve 2:121
Noli Me Tangere 2:120
The Pesaro Madonna 2:10
Pietà 2:113, 116
Portrait of Aretino 2:113
Portrait of Charles V 2:132-3
Portrait of Federico Gonzaga 2:110
Portrait of Paul III and his Grandsons 2:111
Portrait of Philip II in Armour 2:114, *135*
Portrait of Ranuccio Farnese 2:114
The Rape of Europa 2:131
Sacred and Profane Love 2:110,

118-19, 122-3
St Mary Magdalen 2:*115, 116*
Salome 2:*112*
Self-portrait 2:*9, 107*
Tarquin and Lucretia 2:*116-17*
Venus of Urbino 2:*126-7; 7:21*
The Young Englishman 2:*128*
Torrigiano, Pietro 2:*45*
  and Michelangelo 2:*45*
Troy, François de 5:*141*
  The Garter 5:*134-5*
  The Hunt Breakfast 5:*141*
  A Lunch of Oysters 5:*70*
Turner, Joseph Mallord
  William 5:*21*
  caricature of 6:*117*
  character 6:*109*
  choice of viewpoint 6:*116*
  and Claude 4:*53*
  description of 6:*109*
  erotic sketches 6:*112, 113*
  in France 6:*111*
  gallery guide 6:*139*
  influence of Claude on
    6:*110-111, 115*
  in Italy 6:*112-13, 115, 117, 126*
  key dates 6:*108*
  life 6:*80, 81, 107-113, 130, 132,
    133, 136*
  and Lord Egremont 6:*110, 113*
  Matisse and 8:*14*
  and the picturesque 6:*114-15*
  rivalry with Constable 6:*80,
    81, 110, 112, 115*
  and River Thames 6:*107-108,
    115, 132*
  and the Royal Academy 6:*80,
    109, 110, 111, 113*
  and Ruskin 6:*112, 113, 117*
  secret life of 6:*112*
  in Switzerland 6:*111-12*
  technique in oils 6:*116*
  'topographical' watercolours
    6:*110, 111, 114, 116*
  trademarks 6:*117*
  travels 6:*110, 110*
  working methods 6:*114-17*
  *Calais Pier; an English Packet
    Arriving* 6:*120*
  Dawn after the Wreck 6:*128*
  Dido Building Carthage 4:*53*
  The Fighting Temeraire 6:*113,
    118-19, 124-5*
  Fishermen at Sea 6:*110*
  Glacier Valley of Chamonix 6:*115*
  HMS Victory (sketch) 6:*112,
    115-16*
  Norham Castle: Sunrise 6:*122-3*
  The Parting of Hero and Leander
    6:*115*
  Peace, Burial at Sea 6:*113*
  Rain, Steam and Speed 6:*113,
    117, 129*
  Rockets and Blue Lights 6:*127*

Self-portrait 6:*9, 107*
The Slave Ship 6:*114-15*
Snowstorm 6:*116, 117*
*Snowstorm: Hannibal Crossing
  the Alps* 6:*121*
Snowstorm; Mount Cenis 6:*111*
*The Square Dining Room at
  Petworth* 6:*110, 111*
The Thames near Walton Bridge
  6:*114*
Tintern Abbey 6:*114*
Venice from the Giudecca 6:*126*
Venice: Moonrise 6:*115*

U

Utrillo, Maurice 8:*109*
  Le Lapin Agile 8:*108-109*

V

Van der Weyden, Rogier *see*
  Weyden, Rogier van der
Van Eyck, Jan *see* Eyck, Jan van
Van Rijn, Rembrandt
    Harmenzoon *see*
    Rembrandt van Rijn
Vanvitelli, Gaspar
  The Ponte Sisto, Rome 6:*12-13*
Varin, Quentin
  Poussin and 4:*12*
  Le Tableau de Cébès 4:*12 13*
Vecellio, Titian *see* Titian Vecellio
Velázquez, Diego Rodriquez de
    Silva 3:*53*
  Carolus-Duran and 9:*82*
  Cassatt and 9:*45, 52*
  Hopper and 9:*108*
  Picasso and 8:*49*
  Renoir and 7:*112*
  Rubens and 3:*17*
  Sargent and 9:*78, 90*
Velde, Willem van der, the
    Younger 3:*141*
Venne, Adriaen van der
  Fishing for Souls 3:*68*
  The Harbour at Middleburg 3:*69*
Vermeer, Johannes (Jan)
  approach to subject-matter
    3:*113, 114, 116, 117, 120,
    124, 129, 130, 135*
  and Bramer 3:*109*
  brushwork 3:*114*
  and the *camera obscura*
    3:*114-15, 116, 117*
  colour harmonies 3:*114*
  commissions 3:*114*
  dated paintings 3:*112*
  domestic scenes 3:*112-13*
  earliest surviving work 3:*112*
  early influences 3:*108, 114*
  early life 3:*108*

and Fabritius 3:*109, 110*
financial problems 3:*110, 111*
forgeries 3:*111*
gallery guide 3:*139*
key dates 3:*109*
and light 3:*114*
number of paintings 3:*112*
and optical experimentation
  3:*109, 116-17*
and painters' guild 3:*110*
patrons 3:*111*
portrait of? 3:*9, 107*
rediscovery of 3:*111*
subjects 3:*112*
technique 3:*114*
trademarks 3:*117*
working methods 3:*114-15,
  118-19, 135*
Allegory of Faith 3:*109-110, 114,
  118*
The Artist's Studio 3:*114,
  118-19, 126*
The Astronomer 3:*112, 129*
The Concert 3:*125*
*Christ in the House of Mary and
  Martha* 3:*112, 112*
Diana and her Companions 3:*112*
The Geographer 3:*112, 128*
The Glass of Wine 3:*120*
The Guitar Player 3:*131*
The Lacemaker 3:*114, 130*
*Lady Reading a Letter at an Open
  Window* 3:*10*
Lady Seated at the Virginals
  3:*113*
Lady Standing at the Virginals
  3:*117*
The Little Street 3:*122*
The Love Letter 3:*127*
The Milkmaid 3:*114, 115*
The Music Lesson 3:*124*
The Pearl Earring 3:*113*
The Pearl Necklace 3:*113*
The Procuress 3:*112, 128*
Sleeping Girl 3:*116*
Soldier with a Laughing Girl
  3:*121*
View of Delft (detail) 3:*114, 123*
Woman in Blue Reading a Letter
  3:*109*
A Woman Weighing Pearls 1:*47*
Woman with a Balance 3:*114*
Veronese, Paolo 2:*113; 5:15*
  The Rape of Europa 2:*117*
Verrocchio, Andrea del 2:*14, 14*
  and Leonardo 2:*12-13*
  Portrait of (di Credi) 2:*14*
  Baptism of Christ 2:*13*
  Bust of Lorenzo de' Medici 2:*45*
  The Colleoni Monument 1:*14*
  David (detail) 2:*14*
Vien, Joseph Marie 4:*76, 77, 82,
  141*
  Apotheosis of Winckelmann 4:*141*

Cupid Seller 4:*141*
Greek Girl at the Bath 4:*141*
Merchant of Loves 4:*77*
Vigée-Lebrun, Elizabeth
  *Mme Vigée-Lebrun and her
    Daughter* 9:*53*
Vinci, Leonardo da *see* Leonardo
  da Vinci
Visscher, Nicholas
  Allegory of Holland 3:*71*
Vlaminck, Maurice 8:*46, 141*
  and Salon d'Automne 8:*15*
Vouet, Simon 4:*141*
  Allegory of Wealth 4:*141*
Vroom, Hendricksk
  *View of Haarlem from Noorder
    Spaarne* 3:*44-5*

W

Warhol, Andy 9:*141*
Watteau, Antoine
  and the Academy 5:*14-15, 16,
    22, 27*
  apprenticeship 5:*12*
  Boucher copies of 5:*77*
  commissions, specific 5:*13, 14*
  compositional methods 5:*18,
    19, 20, 22, 23*
    technical problems of 5:*18,
      20*
  deterioration of canvases 5:*21*
  early works 5:*12*
  in England 5:*15*
  and the *fête galante* 5:*12, 15, 16,
    17-18, 20, 21, 22*
  gallery guide 5:*139*
  and Gillot 5:*12-13, 14, 15, 15,
    16-17*
  illness 5:*13*
  and imperfection 5:*20-21*
  influence of Audran 5:*13-14*
  influence of Flemish art 5:*16*
  influence of Rubens 3:*21; 5:14,
    17, 18*
  influence on Renoir 7:*109*
  key dates 5:*13*
  main followers 5:*16*
  mood in paintings 5:*18*
  and Old Masters 5:*17*
  and Paris Opéra 5:*12*
  personality 5:*13*
  and Prix de Rome 5:*14*
  pupil 5:*14*
  style 5:*16-17*
  subjects 5:*14, 16-17*
  and the theatre 5:*12-13, 15,
    16-17, 17, 18, 19, 30-33,
    36, 39*
  trademarks 5:*20*
  travels 5:*15*
  use of colour 5:*17*
  use of oils 5:*21*

use of paint 5:20-21
working methods 5:16-21
Actors of the Comédie Française
5:30
Actors of the Comédie Italienne
5:31
The Cajoler 5:17
The Country Dance 5:16
*Dancing Couple, Bagpiper and
Eight Other Figures* 5:29
drawings 5:18-19
decorative panels 5:17
L'Enseigne de Gersaint 5:14, 15,
16, 18, 34-5
Fête in a Park 5:20-21
Les Fêtes Venitiennes (detail)
5:15
La Gamme d'Amour 5:25
Gilles 5:33, 39
Iris 5:16
The Italian Comedians 5:39
Kneeling Man 5:19
Mezzetin 5:18, 32
Mezzetin with Guitar 5:19
The Music Party 5:17, 20
Old Savoyard 5:19
La Partie Quarrée 5:24
*Pilgrimage to the Island of
Cythera* 5:15, 16, 22-3, 26-7
Seasons 5:14
Spring 5:13
Seated Persian 5:18
Self-portrait 5:15
Sirois and his Family 5:14
studies of heads 5:18-19
La Toilette 5:17
Two Seated Women 5:18
*Young Couples with Guitarist
and Shepherd* 5:28
Werff, Adriaen van der
Self-portrait 3:21
Werve, Claus de
finishes tomb of Philip the
Bold 1:37
West, Benjamin 6:37, 38, 39;
9:141
Weyden, Rogier van der 1:75,
75, 77
apprentice to Campin 1:75, 76
attributable pictures 1:80
and Campin's work 1:102
choice of career 1:76
commissions 1:76
from Louvain Archers'
Guild 1:78-9
documented masterpieces
1:80-81, 82-3
and dramatic emotions 1:84-5,
85
expression of religious ideas
1:85
gallery guide 1:139
gifts to religious foundations
1:79

imitation of other art forms
1:81, *88-9*
influence on 1:78
influence on Memling 1:79, *79*,
102
key dates 1:77
moves to Brussels 1:76
naturalism in paintings 1:*82-3*
paintings in Spain 1:80
panels for Brussels Town Hall
1:76
and Philip the Good 1:*76, 77*
pilgrimage to Rome 1:79
portraits for Burgundian court
1:77
preliminary drawing for
portrait 1:*81*, 85
reputation in Italy 1:*78*, 79
social standing 1:79
techniques in religious
paintings 1:80-81, 83
trademarks 1:85
travels 1:79
working methods 1:85
altarpiece for Jean Chevrot *see*
Seven Sacraments Altarpiece
altarpiece for Louvain
Archers' Guild *see The*
Deposition
altarpiece for Nicholas Rolin
1:77, *77*
Braque Triptych 1:*84*
right wing 1:*80*
Columba Triptych 1:78, *94-5*
The Crucifixion 1:80, 81, *96*
The Deposition 1:78, 80-81,
90-91
details 1:*98-9*
Justice of Trajan and Herkinbald
1:76
detail *75*
The Last Judgement Altarpiece
1:*81*
detail 1:*10, 116*
The Miraflores Altarpiece 1:80,
88-9
Nativity Triptych 1:102
right wing 1:*81*
portrait of Charles the Bold
1:77
Portrait of a Lady 1:*97*
portrait of Philip the Good
1:76
portrait of his wife? 1:*86*
Portrait of a Young Woman
1:*86*
St Luke Drawing the Virgin 1:80
'Scupstoel' drawing 1:77
Self-portraits 1:77, *80*
The Seven Sacraments Altarpiece
1:78, *92-3*
Triptych of the Virgin 1:80
The Virgin and Child in a Niche
1:78, *87*

Whistler, James Abbot McNeill
7:15; 9:*11, 16-17*
aims 9:19
on art 9:20
artistic creed 9:19-20, 34
artistically confused 9:14-15,
37
bankruptcy 9:16
caricature by Beerbohm 9:*16*
Cassatt and 9:74
in Chile 9:14, *18-19*
and colour harmony 9:19
commissions 9:17
early life 9:12
and etching 9:17, *19*
favourite subjects 9:13, 41
in France 9:14
gallery guide 9:139
and Gleyre 9:12
'Harmonies' 9:19
on himself 9:12
illness 9:17
at Imperial Academy 9:12, 18
influence of Courbet 9:12, 14
influence of Japanese art 9:14
key dates 9:13
landscapes 9:21
later paintings 9:21
legal cases 9:*14-15*, 17, 73-4
and Leyland 9:15
life-style 9:16
and light and shade 9:19
in London 9:13-14
exhibition in 9:17
love of white and blue 9:14
and Mallarmé 9:16
marriage 9:17
and du Maurier 9:17
mistresses 9:13-14
models 9:13-14, 15
Nocturnes 9:15, 19
process of painting 9:20-21
and Oscar Wilde 9:*16*, 17, *36-7*
in Paris 9:12, 17
and Salon 9:78
and Salon des Refusés 7:15
patrons 9:15
and pattern/shapes 9:19
poet friends 9:16, *16*
portraits: preparing to paint
9:20
sold 9:17
starts to paint 9:15
techniques 9:20
titles 9:19
retrospective exhibition 9:17
and River Thames 9:13, 41
and Rossetti 9:14
and Royal Academy 9:13, 22
in Russia 9:12, *12-13*
seascapes 9:14, 21
'Symphonies' 9:19
trademarks 9:21
types of canvas used 9:21

unconventional training
9:18-20
use of colour themes 9:19
in Venice 9:16-17
visits North Africa 9:17
at West Point 9:12, *13*, 18
work attacked by Ruskin 9:14,
14-15
*Arrangement in Flesh Colour and
Black: Portrait of Théodore
Duret* 9:33
*Arrangement in Grey and Black:
Portrait of the Artist's Mother*
9:17, 20, *26-7*
At the Piano 9:13, 18
*Harmony in Pink and Grey:
Portrait of Lady Meux* 9:32
Joanna Heffernan (etching)
9:23
The Lange Leizen 9:18
Little Juniper Bud 9:19
*Nocturne in Black and Gold: The
Falling Rocket* 9:14, 15, *15-16*
*Nocturne in Grey and Gold:
Chelsea Show* 9:21, 29
*Nocturne: Grey and Gold –
Westminster Bridge* 9:28
The Peacock Room 9:15, *36*
Pink and Grey: Three Figures
9:*30-31*
Portrait of Thomas Carlyle
9:17
*La Princesse du Pays de la
Porcelaine* 9:25
Rotherhithe (etching) 9:19
Screen with Old Battersea Bridge
9:19
Self-portrait, aged 43 9:*9, 11*
*Symphony in White, No. 1: The
White Girl* 9:13-14, 22, *22-3,
24*
*Symphony in White, No 2: The
Little White Girl,* 9:14, 22, *23*
Symphony in White, No. 3
(sketch for) 9:*23*
Ten o'Clock Lecture 9:16
Valparaiso 9:*18-19*
*Variation in Flesh Colour and
Green: The Balcony* 9:21
Wilson, Richard 4:49; 6:37, 115,
141
Wood, Grant 9:141
Wright of Derby, Joseph 6:141
Wyeth, Andrew 9:141

Z

Zampieri, Domenico *see*
Domenichino
Zoffany, Johann 6:37, 141
*The Academicians of the Royal
Academy* 6:141
The Tribunal of the Uffizi 6:141

Index of Masterpieces

A

Absinthe (Degas) 7:62
Absinthe Drinker, The (Manet) 7:14, *18*
Academicians of the Royal Academy, The (Zoffany) 6:141
Acrobat's Family with a Monkey, The (Picasso) 8:55
Actor, The (Fragonard) 5:116
Actors of the Comédie Française (Watteau) 5:30
Actors of the Comédie Italienne (Watteau) 5:31
Admiral's House, The (Constable) 6:94
Adoration of the Golden Calf, (sketch, Claude) 4:51
Adoration of the Golden Calf, The (Poussin) 4:27
Adoration of the Magi, The (Fabriano) 1:76-7
Adoration of the Magi, The (Bosch) 1:122
Adoration of the Magi, The (Leonardo) 2:14
study for 2:32
Adoration of the Shepherds, The (Van der Goes) 1:141
After the Bath (Degas) 7:64
After the Bath (Renoir) 7:129
Agony in the Garden, The (Bellini) 53
Agony in the Garden, The (El Greco) 2:140
Agony in the Garden, The (Mantegna) 2:33
Air du Soir, L' (Cross) 8:13

Albergati, Cardinal Niccolò (Van Eyck) 1:56, *58*
Aldobrandini Marriage, The (Roman fresco) 4:22
Alexander Cassatt and his son Robert (Cassatt) 9:46
Allegory of Faith (Vermeer) 3:109-110, 114, *118*
Allegory of Grammar (La Hyre) 4:141
Allegory of Holland (Visscher) 3:71
Allegory of Wealth (Vouet) 4:141
Altarpiece of the Sacrament, The (Bouts) 1:140
Ambassadors of Agamemnon in the Tent of Achilles, The (Ingres) 4:109, 110
Amsterdam Couple, An (Codde) 3:101
Anatomy of a Horse (Stubbs) 6:141
Anatomy Lesson of Dr Sebastian Egbertsz, The (de Keyser) 3:86
Anatomy Lesson of Dr Tulp, The (Rembrandt) 3:79, 84, *84*
Andrians, The (Titian) 2:111, 114-15
Angel and the Virgin of the Annunciation, The (Van Eyck) 1:62
Anna and the Blind Tobit (Dou) 3:140
Annunciation, The (Leonardo) 2:20-21
drapery study for 2:30
Antiochus and Stratonice (David) 4:76, *82*
Antiope (Correggio) 2:140

Apollo and Daphne (sculpture, Bernini) 4:38
Apollo and Daphne (Poussin) 4:17
Apollo Belvedere 2:102 (sculpture) as inspiration for Reynolds 6:14, 19, 24, 38
Apotheosis of Hercules (Lemoyne) 5:140
Apotheosis of Homer, The (Ingres) 4:112
Apotheosis of Napoleon, The (sketch, Ingres) 4:131
Apotheosis of Winckelmann (Vien) 4:141
Argenteuil (Manet) 7:9
Aristotle Contemplating a Bust of Homer (Rembrandt) 3:94
Arno Landscape (Leonardo) 2:13
Arnolfini Wedding, The (Van Eyck) 1:60
feeling of space in 1:50
symbolism in 1:50, 60
Arrangement in Flesh Colour and Black: Portrait of Théodore Duret (Whistler) 9:33
Arrangement in Grey: Portrait of the Painter (Whistler) 9:11
Arrangement in Grey and Black: Portrait of the Artist's Mother (Whistler) 9:26-7
sale of 9:17
Artist at Work, The (Van Loo) 5:81
Artist's Daughters, The (Gainsborough) 6:46
Artist's Father, The (Constable) 6:77
Artist's Mother, The (Constable) 6:77

Artist's Studio, The (Vermeer) 3:114, *118-19*, 126
details 3:*118*, *119*
Artist's Wife, The (Chardin) 5:47
Ascanius Shooting the Stag of Silvia (Claude) 4:47, *67*
Ascent to Calvary (Bosch), reverse of 1:113
Assumption of the Virgin, The (Correggio) 2:140
Assumption of the Virgin, The (El Greco) 2:140
Assumption of the Virgin, The (Titian) 2:109, 110, 116, *124*
original setting for 2:109
Astronomer, The (Vermeer) 3:112, *129*
At Père Lathuille's (Manet) 7:32
At the Piano (Whistler) 9:13, *18*
Attributs des Arts, Les (Chardin) 5:48-9
Automat (Hopper) 9:121
Autumn Landscape with a View of Het Steen (Rubens) 3:32
Avignon Pietà, The 1:85
Awakening Slave, The (sculpture, Michelangelo) 2:51

B

Bacchanal (Dossi) 2:38-9
Bacchanalian Revel before a Term of Pan (Poussin) 4:20-21
detail 4:*21*
Bacchus (sculpture, Michelangelo) 2:46

Bacchus and Ariadne (Titian) 2:111, 125

Baker, The (Berckhyde) 3:134-5, 135

Balcony, The (Manet) 7:17, 31

Ballerina with a Bouquet, Curtseying (Degas) 7:50-51

Ballet Dancers in Butterfly Costumes (Degas) 7:52-3 detail 7:52

Banquet of the Officers of the St George Civic Guard Company (Hals) 3:45, 45, 52

Banquet of the Officers of the St Hadrian Civic Guard Company (Hals) 3:60-61

Baptism of Christ, The (detail, Leonardo) 2:13

Bar at the Folies-Bergère, A (Manet) 7:21, 33

Bath, The (Cassatt) 9:52 detail 9:52-3

Bather, The (Lemoyne) 5:140

Bathers, The (Fragonard) 5:122

Bathers, The (Renoir) 7:114, 117

Bathsheba (Rembrandt) 3:95

Battle of Anghiari, The (Leonardo) 2:30, 32, 77; 3:27 copy by Rubens 2:18

Battle of Cascina, The (Michelangelo) 2:18 preliminary study for 2:50

Battle of the Centaurs, The (Michelangelo) 2:45

Battle of Eylau (detail, Gros) 4:81

Battle of Spoleto, The (drawing, Titian) 2:114

Baudouin de Lannoy (Van Eyck) 1:56, 64

Bed with Cupids (sketch, Fragonard) 5:117

Bedford, Duke of (Gainsborough) 6:47

Bedouins (Sargent) 9:80

Belisarius Receiving Alms (David) 4:84

Bellelli Family, The (Degas) 7:44, 56

Belshazzar's Feast (Rembrandt) 3:84-5

Berthe Morisot with a Bunch of Violets (Manet) 7:17, 140

Betrothal of the Virgin, The (Raphael) 2:86

Between Two Fires (Millet) 9:100-101

Birth of Bacchus, The (La Hyre) 4:141

Birth of John the Baptist (Ghirlandaio) 2:44

Birth of the Virgin, The (Murillo) 3:106

Blessings of Peace (Rubens) 3:40

Blind Man's Buff (Fragonard) 5:112, 128

Blind Orion Searching for the Rising Sun (Poussin) 4:33

Blue Boy, The (Gainsborough) 6:47, 61

Blue Room, The (Cassatt) 9:46, 53, 58-9

Blue Window, The (Matisse) 8:20, 27

Boatbuilding (Constable) 6:84, 88

Boating (Manet) 7:20-21

Boating Party, The (Cassatt) 9:48, 53, 66-7

Boating Party, The (Monet), Cassatt and 9:48-9

Bolt, The (Fragonard) 5:113, 130-31

Bonaparte as First Consul (Ingres) 4:120

Bottle of Vieux Marc, Guitar, Glass and Newspaper (Picasso) 8:58-9

Boulevard des Capucines (Monet) 7:90

Boulevard Montmartre, The (Pissarro) 7:84

Boy Dressed as a Pierrot (Fragonard) 5:115

Boy Playing a Flute (Leyster) 3:47

Boy with a Flute (Hals) 3:52 detail 3:53

Braque Triptych, The (Van der Weyden) 1:84 right wing 1:80 use of landscape in 1:84

Breakfast, The (Metsu) 3:21

Breakfast in the Loggia (Sargent) 9:83

Bride and Groom, The (Modigliani) 8:122

Bridge, The (Boucher) 5:94

Bridge at Argenteuil, The (Monet) 7:91

Brioche, The (Chardin) 5:67

Brockman Family and Friends in the Rotunda at Beachborough Manor, The (Haytley) 4:70-71

Broken Pitcher, The (Greuze) 5:140

Brook, The (Sargent) 9:83

Brummell Children, The (Reynolds) 6:33

Brutus Receiving the Bodies of His Sons (David) 4:84-5 detail 4:85 at the Salon 4:78

C

Cajoler, The (Watteau) 5:17

Calais Pier (Turner) 6:120

calligrammes (Apollinaire) 7:71

Camille on her Deathbed (Monet) 7:83

Campagna (sketch, Claude) 4:46-7

Carnation, Lily, Lily, Rose (Sargent) 9:86, 91, 100, 103 details 86-7 preliminary sketches 86

Carthusian Monk, A (Christus) 1:140

Caryatids (Modigliani) 8:111, 115

Cats' Rendezvous, The (Manet) 7:18

Cellar Boy, The (Chardin) 5:68

Céret, Landscape of (Gris) 8:70

Chain Pier, Brighton (Constable) 6:96

Chapeau de Paille, Le (Rubens) 3:29

Charge of the Lancers, The (Boccioni) 8:81

Charles I and Henrietta Maria Departing for the Chase (Mytens) 3:41

Charles V on Horseback (Titian) 2:129, 135

Charterhouse, The (Gainsborough) 6:44, 45

Chocolatière, La (Liotard) 5:71

Christ Carrying the Cross (Bosch) 1:113

Christ Child (Bosch) 1:113, 114

Christ and the Money-Lenders (Bassano), detail 2:112

Christ in the House of Martha and Mary (Aertsen) 5:52

Christ in the House of Mary and Martha (Vermeer) 3:112, 112

Church Interior, Haarlem (Saenredam) 3:47

City Rises, The (Boccioni) 8:84, 86, 86-7, 92-3 colour studies 8:87 detail 8:86

Claude Monet Painting at the Edge of a Wood (Sargent) 9:84-5 detail 85

Coalbrookdale by Night (Loutherbourg) 6:141

Coast Scene with a Fight on a Bridge (sketch, Claude) 4:51

Coast View of Delos with Aeneas (Claude) 4:68-9

Columba Triptych, The (Van der Weyden) 1:78, 94-5

Combing the Hair (Degas) 7:65

Company of Captain Roelof Bicker, The (Van der Holst) 3:88-9

Company of the St George Civic Guard, The (Van der Holst) 3:70-71

Comte de Turenne (David) 4:83

Comtesse d'Haussonville, The (Ingres) 4:128

Concert, The (Vermeer) 3:125

Concert in the Tuileries Gardens (Manet) 7:14

Confirmation (Poussin) 4:28

Conjurer, The (Bosch) 1:120-21

Constantijn Huygens and his Secretary (de Keyser) 3:79

Coresus Sacrificing Himself to Save Callirhoé (Fragonard) 5:110, 111

Cornard Wood (Gainsborough) 6:8, 84

Cornfield, The (Constable) 6:95

Coronation of the Virgin, The (Quarton) 1:141

Cottage Girl with Dog and Pitcher, The (Gainsborough) 6:64

Cotton Exchange, The (Degas) 7:46

Count Ugolino and his Children (Reynolds) 6:17

Countess of Bressingham, The (Lawrence) 9:84

Country Dance, The (Watteau) 5:16

Courtyard in Delft (de Hooch) 3:135

Courtyard Scene (de Hooch) 3:103

Cradle, The (Morisot) 9:53
Creation of Adam (Michelangelo) 6:13
Crowning with Thorns, The (Bosch) 1:121, 129
Crucifixion, The (Van der Weyden) 1:80, 96
use of landscape in 1:84
technique in 1:81
Cuer d'Amour Espris, Le (René Master) 1:141
Cup of Tea, The (Cassatt) 9:55
Cupid and Psyche (Gérard) 4:140
Cupid and Psyche (Natoire) 5:141
Cupid Seller (Vien) 4:141
Cure of Folly, The (Bosch) 1:112
symbolism in 1:114
Cut Melon, The (Chardin) 5:65, 66

D

Danaë (Girodet de Roucy-Trioson) 4:140
Danaë (Titian) 2:115, 130
Dance (Matisse) 8:15, 20, 21, 21
Dance in the Country (detail, Renoir) 7:111
Dance in the Town (Renoir) 7:127
Dance to the Music of Time (Poussin) 6:22, 23
Dancers at the Ball (Severini) 8:103
Dancing Class, The (Degas) 7:54, 60
details 7:54
perspective of 55
Dancing Couple, Bagpiper and Eight Other Figures (Watteau) 5:29
Daughters of Edward D. Boit, The (Sargent) 9:78, 90
David (sculpture, Michelangelo) 2:46, 52, 55, 77
Dawn after the Wreck (Turner) 6:128
Dead Christ, The (Mantegna) 2:140
Dead Toreador, The (Manet) 7:18-19
Dead Wolf, The (Oudry) 5:46
Death of Dido, The (Reynolds) 6:17, 18-19

Death of Germanicus, The (Poussin) 4:15, 24-5, 84
Death of Leonardo, The (Ingres) 2:19
Death of Marat, The (David) 4:84, 86-7, 93
details 4:86, 87
Death of St Peter Martyr (copy, Titian) 2:111, 116
Death of Socrates, The (David) 4:84, 90-91
Death of the Virgin, The (Van der Goes) 1:141
Dedham Lock and Mill (Constable) 6:82-3
Déjeuner, Le (Boucher) 5:90
Déjeuner sur l'Herbe (Manet) see Luncheon on the Grass, The
Déjeuner sur l'Herbe (series, Picasso) 8:49
Demoiselles d'Avignon, Les (Picasso) 8:46-7, 52, 56-7, 68
Denis Diderot (Van Loo) 5:81
Deposition, The (Van der Weyden) 1:78, 80-81, 90-91
details 1:90-91
levels of reality 1:80-81
Derby Day (Frith) 7:68, 68-9
Descent from the Cross, The (Campin) 1:78
Descent from the Cross, The (Rubens) 3:15, 22-3, 24-5
details 3:22-3
modello 3:22
Destruction of the Turkish Transport (Carline) 9:105
Development of a Bottle in Space (sculpture, Boccioni) 8:83, 85
Diana and her Companions (Vermeer) 3:112
Diana after Bathing (Boucher) 5:84; 7:117
detail 5:85
Diana the Huntress (School of Fontainebleau) 5:85
Dido Building Carthage (Turner) 4:53
Diligent, Mother, The (Chardin) 5:54, 62
Dining Table, The (Matisse) 8:13
Discovery of the Body of St Mark (Tintoretto) 2:141
Disputà, The (Raphael) 2:84, 98
details 2:98

preliminary study 2:98
Disputation of St Catherine, The (Pinturicchio) 2:36
Distribution of the Eagle Standards (David) 4:80
Doctor's Visit, The (Steen) 3:134
Doge Loredano (Bellini) 2:140
Dogs, Dead Game and Fruit (Desportes) 5:46
Donation of the Keys, The (Perugino) 2:77, 83
Dondi Tondo, The (sculpture, Michelangelo) 2:50
Donne Triptych, The (Memlinc) 1:79
Dream, The (Picasso) 8:63
Dream of Ossian (Ingres) 4:111, 114
Dreamers (Moore) 9:20
Duke of Lerma (Rubens) 3:13
Dutch Colony in Brazil, A (Post) 3:136-7
Dying Slave, The (sculpture, Michelangelo) 2:53
Dynamism of a Cyclist (Boccioni) 8:83
Dynamism of a Human Body (Boccioni) 8:97, 98

E

Early Sunday Morning (Hopper) 9:110, 122-3
East Bergholt House (Constable) 6:76
Ecce Homo (Bosch) 1:123
Edward Jenner giving the first vaccinations (satirical cartoon, Gillray) 6:103
Effects of War, The (Rubens) 3:69
Egyptian Curtain, The (Matisse) 8:20, 33
Elasticity (Boccioni) 8:8
Eleanora of Toledo and her Son (Bronzino) 4:117
Eleven a.m. (Hopper) 9:120
Ellen Terry as Lady Macbeth (Sargent) 9:93
Embarkation of St Ursula (sketch, Claude) 4:50, 51, 54
Emmie and her Child (Cassatt) 9:51
Enchanted Castle, The (Claude) 4:53, 65
Endymion (Girodet de Roucy-Trioson) 4:140

Enseigne de Gersaint, L' (Watteau) 5:14, 18, 34-5
Entombment, The (Raphael) 2:89
Entombment, The (Titian) 2:115
Entombment of Atala (Girodet de Roucy-Trioson) 4:140
Entombment of Christ, The (oil sketch, Rembrandt) 3:85
Equestrienne, The (Modigliani) 8:120
Espolio, El (El Greco) 2:141
Et in Arcadia Ego (Poussin) 4:16, 18-19
Evening Wind (Hopper) 9:115
Execution of Maximilian, The (Manet) 7:29
Extreme Unction (Poussin) 4:15, (1644) 4:29

F

Fall of the Damned, The (Rubens) 3:19
Family Group (Hals) 3:52
Family Group in a Landscape (Hals) 3:64, 65
Family of George, 4th Duke of Marlborough, The (Reynolds) 6:18
Farmland Views near East Bergholt (Constable) 6:83
Farnese Hercules, The 6:38
Fate of Tityus, The (Michelangelo) 2:48
Father of the Family Reading from the Bible, The (Greuze) 5:140
Feast of Venus, The (Rubens) 3:34-5
Femmes d'Algers, Les (Delacroix) 8:49
series by Picasso 8:49
Fête Champetre (Giorgione) 5:21, 28
Fête in a Park (Watteau) 4:20-21
Fête at Rambouillet, The (Fragonard) 5:114-15, 118
Fêtes Venitiennes, Les (detail, Watteau) 5:15
Fifer, The (Manet) 7:20, 78
Fighting Temeraire, The (Turner) 6:113, 118-19, 124-5
Fire in the Borgo, The (Raphael) 2:99
detail 2:99

First Cloud, The (Orchardson) 9:116

First Night Out, The (Renoir) 7:122

Fishermen at Sea (Turner) 6:110

Fishing for Souls (Van der Venne) 3:68

Fitting, The (Cassatt) 9:64

Flatford Mill (Constable) 6:89

Floating Studio (Monet) 7:78

Flowers in a Vase (Chardin) 5:51

Forestier Family, The (sketch, Ingres) 4:109

Four Dancers (Degas) 7:51

Frederick, Prince of Wales and his Sisters (Mercier) 6:52

French Woman and her Maid, A (Liotard) 5:68-9

Fruits of the Midi (Renoir) 7:126

Funeral of Phocion, The (Poussin) 4:32

G

Gainsborough Family, The (Gainsborough) 6:44

Gamme d'Amour, La (Watteau) 5:25

Garden of Earthly Delights, The (Bosch) 1:117, 121, 126-7
details 1:118-19
meaning of 109

Garden of Love (Rubens) 5:21

Garden of the Hesperides, The (Burne-Jones) 9:20

Garden Study of the Vickers Children (Sargent) 9:87

Gardener, The (Fragonard) 5:114

Gardens of the Villa d'Este, The (Fragonard) 5:110, 120

Gare St-Lazare (Monet) 7:92

Garrick Between Tragedy and Comedy (Reynolds) 6:28-9

Garter, The (de Troy) 5:134-5

Gas (Hopper) 9:124-5

Gassed (Sargent) 9:98-9

Geographer, The (Vermeer) 3:112, 128

Georgiana, Countess Spencer, and her Daughter (Reynolds) 6:26

Georgiana, Duchess of Devonshire,

and her Daughter (Reynolds) 6:20-21

Gervex (Rolla) 5:117

Ghent Altarpiece (Van Eyck) 1:46, 49
details 1:52-5
exterior paintings 1:52-3
history 1:56
interior paintings 1:54-7

Giacomo Casanova (Mengs) 5:132

Gilles (Watteau) 5:33, 39

Ginevra de' Benci (Leonardo) 2:22

Giovanni Arnolfini and his Wife (Van Eyck) see *Arnolfini Wedding, The*

Gypsy Girl (Hals) 3:62

Girl in a Chemise (Picasso) 8:54

Girl Making her Dog Dance on her Bed (Fragonard) 5:123

Girl Returning from Market (Chardin) 5:61

Girl Running on a Balcony (Balla) 8:100, 140

Glacier Valley of Chamonix (Turner) 6:115

Gladiateur (Herring) 7:69

Glass of Wine, The (Vermeer) 3:120

Gloria, La (Titian) 2:135

Goldfinch (Fabritius) 3:110

Goldfish and Sculpture (Matisse) 8:26

Golding Constable's Flower Garden (detail, Constable) 6:83

Good Government in the Countryside (Lorenzetti) 1:16-17

Good Government in the Town (detail, Lorenzetti) 4:20

Governess, The (Chardin) 5:60

Grande Odalisque, The (Ingres) 4:111, 112, 114, 116, 117, 122-3; 8:20

Grapes and Pomegranates (Chardin) 5:66

Greek Girl at the Bath (Vien) 4:141

Grenouillère, La (Renoir) 7:120, 125

Greta Bridge (Cotman) 6:140

Guernica (Picasso) 8:48, 49, 64-5

Guitar (sculpture, Picasso) 8:52

Guitar Player, The (sculpture, Lipchitz) 8:118

Guitar Player, The (Vermeer) 3:131

Gypsy Woman with Baby (Modigliani) 8:117
detail 8:116-17

H

Half-naked Woman Bending Over (sketch, Boucher) 5:83

Hammerstein's Roof Garden (Glackens) 9:133

Harbour at Middleburg, The (Van der Venne) 3:69

Harmony in Pink and Grey: Portrait of Lady Meux (Whistler) 9:32

Harvest Wagon, The (Gainsborough) 6:52-3

Hay Wain, The (Bosch) 1:121, 124-5
derivation of theme 1:125
symbolism in 1:116

Hay Wain, The (Constable) 6:80, 81, 83, 86-7, 90-91

Haystacks, The (Monet) 7:83

Head of a Child (Rubens) 3:28

Heads (drawing, Watteau) 5:18-19

Heads and Figures (studies, Rembrandt) 3:81

Heneage Lloyd and his Sister (Gainsborough) 6:50-51

Henley Regatta (Tissot) 4:124-5

Hercules and the Horses of Diomedes (Lebrun) 4:141

High Road (Hopper) 9:112-13

Hippolytus and Phaedra (Guérin) 4:141

Hippopotamus and Crocodile Hunt (Rubens) 3:26-7

History of the Emperor Constantine (tapestries, Rubens) 3:17

Holy Family on the Steps, The (Poussin) 4:22-3, 30-31
details 4:23
geometrical structure 4:23
preparatory drawing 2:43

Holy Family with Six Putti (Poussin) 4:19

Horse and Rider (bronze, Leonardo) 2:30

Horses of Monte Cavallo, The (drawing, Raphael)

2:103

Hours of the Duchess of Burgundy 1:21

House by the Railroad (Hopper) 9:114

Hunt Breakfast, The (de Troy) 5:141

Hunt Luncheon, The (Van Loo) 5:69

I

Impression: Sunrise (Monet) 7:78-9

In a Levantine Port (Sargent) 9:8

Infant Academy, The (Reynolds) 5:39

Infanta Isabella (Rubens) 3:15

Inspiration (Fragonard) 5:110

Interior of a Hospital Tent, The (Sargent) 9:80

Intervention of the Sabine Women, The (David) 4:80, 83, 94-5
preliminary sketch 4:83

Iris (Watteau) 5:16

Isaac Massa (Hals) 3:55

Isabella Coymans (Hals) 3:52, 67

Italian Comedians, The (Watteau) 5:39

J

Jaleo, El (Sargent) 9:78, 88-9

James, 7th Earl of Lauderdale (Reynolds) 6:25

Jan de Leeuw, Portrait of (Van Eyck) 1:65

Jar of Apricots, The (Chardin) 5:64

Jar of Olives, The (Chardin) 5:52-3
detail 5:53

Jazz (Matisse) 8:19

Jealous Husband, The (Titian) 2:109

Jesuit Church ceiling, Antwerp (Rubens) 3:16, 17

Jewish Bride, The (Rembrandt) 3:99

Jockeys before the Start, with Flag-pole (Degas) 7:51

Joie de Vivre (series, Picasso) 8:49

Judgement of Paris, The
  (engraving after Raimondi)
  2:78
Judgement of Paris, The (Raphael)
  2:78
Judgement of Solomon, The
  (Mantegna) 2:140
Judith (Mantegna) 2:140
Julie Forestier (drawing, Ingres)
  4:109
Juno Discovering Jupiter with Io
  (Lastman) 3:77
Jupiter and Io (Correggio)
  2:117
Jupiter and Thetis (Ingres) 4:111,
  116
  detail 4:116
Justice and Divine Vengeance
  Pursuing Crime (Prud'hon)
  4:141
Justice of Emperor Otto, The
  (Bouts) 1:140
Justice of Trajan and Herkinbald
  (detail, tapestry) 1:75

K

Kitchen Objects (Chardin) 5:55
Kitchen Still-Life with Cooking Pots
  and Eggs (Chardin) 5:56
Kitchen Still-Life with Pestle and
  Mortar (Chardin) 5:57
Kitchenmaid, The (Moitte)
  5:69
Kneeling in an Armchair (Cassatt)
  9:51
Kneeling Man (drawing,
  Watteau) 5:19

L

Lacemaker, The (Vermeer) 3:114,
  130
Lady Agnew (Sargent) 9:79,
  94
Lady Betty Hamilton (Reynolds)
  6:18
Lady Caroline Scott (Reynolds)
  6:32
Lady Governors of the Old Men's
  Home at Haarlem (Hals)
  3:86
Lady Reading a Letter at an Open
  Window (Vermeer)
  3:10
Lady Seated at the Virginals

(Vermeer) 3:113
Lady Standing at the Virginals
  (Vermeer) 3:117
Lady at a Tea Table (Cassatt) 9:53,
  54-5,62
  details 9:55
Lady at her Toilet (Terborch)
  3:135
Lady Walking to the Right, A
  (sketch, Gainsborough)
  6:50
Lady with a Parasol (Monet)
  7:83
Lady with an Ermine (Leonardo)
  2:23
Lady with the Rose (Sargent) 9:81,
  82-3
Lamentation over Christ, The
  (Christus) 1:140
Landscape with Ascanius Shooting
  the Stag of Silvia (Claude)
  4:67
Landscape at Cagnes (Modigliani)
  8:115
Landscape with Figures Gathering
  Cherries (Boucher)
  5:52
Landscape with a Goatherd (copy
  after Claude by Constable)
  4:48, 50
Landscape with Hagar and the
  Angel (Claude) 4:52-3
Landscape with the Landing of
  Aeneas at Pallanteum (Claude)
  4:46, 52
Landscape with Man Killed by a
  Snake (Poussin) 4:19
Landscape with the Marriage of
  Isaac and Rebekah (Claude)
  4:54, 62-3
Landscape with Narcissus and Echo
  (Claude) 4:58-9
Landscape with the Nymph Egeria
  Mourning over Numa (Claude)
  4:66
Landscape with Psyche at the Palace
  of Cupid (Claude)
  4:53
Landscape with Samuel
  Anointing David (Claude)
  4:48-9
Landscape with a Shepherd and his
  Flock (Rubens) 3:33
Landscape with St George Killing
  the Dragon (sketch, Claude)
  4:50
Landscape with Watermill
  (Boucher) 5:82-3
Lange Leizen, The (Whistler)
  9:18
Laocoön, The (Greek sculpture)
  2:46, 47, 103; 3:23
  drawing by Rubens 3:23
Lapin Agile, Le (Utrillo) 8:108-109

Last Judgement, The (Bosch) 1:111
  details 1:114-15
Last Judgement, The
  (Michelangelo) 2:48, 51,
  60-63
Last Judgement Altarpiece, The
  (Van der Weyden) 1:77, 81
  detail 1:116
  emotion in 1:84-5
  exterior wing 1:77
Last Supper, The (Leonardo) 2:16,
  18, 24-5, 32, 34-5
  details 2:35
  restoration of 2:34
Laugh, The (Boccioni) 8:84
  detail 8:84
Laughing Boy (Hals) 3:48, 49
Laughing Cavalier, The (Hals)
  3:50, 51
  detail 3:50, 51, 57
Laughing Madonna and Child
  (sculpture, Rossellino) 2:85
Lavinia, Countess Spencer
  (Reynolds) 6:20, 21
Lazarus Triptych (Froment) 1:140
Leaping Horse, The (Constable)
  6:85
Leda (Rubens) 3:18
Lepelltier (David) 4:86-7
Letter, The (Cassatt) 9:49
Liber Veritatis (Claude) 4:46, 49,
  50-51, 55
Liberation of Arsinoe, The
  (Tintoretto) 2:141
Life of St Bruno (Le Sueur)
  4:141
Life of St Genevieve (Chavannes)
  9:74
Lighthouse at Two Lights
  (Hopper) 9:114-15
Little Girl in Blue, The
  (Modigliani) 8:129
Little Girl with Cherries (Chardin)
  engraving after by Cochin
  5:48
Little Girl with a Shuttlecock
  (Chardin) 5:58
Little Juniper Bud (Whistler) 9:19
Little Peasant, The (Modigliani)
  8:128
Little Sisters, The (Cassatt)
  6:20, 22; 9:10
Little Street, The (Vermeer)
  3:122
Little White Girl, The (Whistler)
  9:23
Lock, The (Constable) 6:81
Lodovico Gonzago and his Family
  (Mantegna) 2:140
Loge, La (Renoir) 7:121
Longed-For Moment, The
  (Fragonard) 5:112, 114, 115
Lord Heathfield (Reynolds)
  6:34

Louis XIV on Horseback (relief
  carving, Coysevox) 5:40
Love Letter, The (Fragonard)
  5:126
Love Letter, The (Vermeer)
  3:127
Lucca Madonna see *Madonna in*
  Her Chamber, The
  (Van Eyck)
Lunch of Oysters, A (de Troy)
  5:70
Luncheon of the Boating Party
  (Renoir) 7:111-12,
  124-5
Luncheon on the Grass, The
  (Manet) 7:15, 19, 20, 24-5;
  8:49
Luxe, Calme et Volupté (Matisse)
  8:13, 14, 18, 18, 37
Lydia Crocheting in the Garden at
  Marly (Cassatt) 9:46, 47
Lydia Leaning on her Arms Seated
  in a Loge (Cassatt)
  9:50
Lydia and her Mother at Tea
  (Cassatt) 9:54

M

Madame Charpentier and her
  Children (Renoir)
  7:110
Madame Matisse (Matisse)
  8:23
Madame Monet and her son Jean
  (Renoir) 7:77
Madame de Pompadour (Boucher),
  (1758) 5:98
  (1759) 5:99
Madame de Senonnes (Ingres)
  4:124
Mme Vigée-Lebrun and her
  Daughter (Vigée-Lebrun)
  9:53
Madame X (Madame Pierre
  Gautreau) (Sargent) 9:78, 92
Mademoiselle O'Murphy
  (Boucher) 5:86-7, 92-3
  details 5:86, 87
  early sketch for 5:87
Mademoiselle Rivière (Ingres)
  4:114
Madonna and Child, The
  (Giorgione) 2:140
Madonna del Granduca (Raphael)
  2:84
  detail 2:85
Madonna with Canon van der
  Paele, The (Van Eyck) 1:49,
  66-7

Madonna in Her Chamber, The (Van Eyck) 1:*63*

Madonna with Chancellor Rolin, The (Van Eyck) 1:*61*
back views in 1:*50*

Madonna in a Church, The (Van Eyck) 1:*48*

Madonna of the Fish (Raphael) 4:*22*

Madonna by the Fountain, The (Van Eyck) 1:*50*

Madonna of the Goldfinch, The (Raphael) 2:*88*
drawing for 2:*84*

Madonna with Jan Vos, The (Van Eyck) 1:*47*
Petrus Christus and 1:*47*

Madonna with the Long neck (Parmigianino) 8:*116*

Madonna of the Meadow (Bellini) 2:*85*

Madonna della Sedia (Madonna of the Chair) (Raphael) 2:*80, 82*; 4:*117*

Madonna with Three Female Saints (David) 1:*140*

Magdalen with a Lamp (La Tour) 3:*40*

Maid with a Milkjug (Vermeer) 3:*114, 115*
detail 3:*115*

Malle Babbe (Hals) 3:*49, 63*

Man Carrying a Scythe (sketch, Constable) 6:*87*

Man with a Blue Sleeve (Titian) 2:*121*

Man with a Red Turban (Van Eyck) 1:*47*

Margaret Tyers and her Husband (Hayman) 6:*54*

Margaret van Eyck, Portrait of (Van Eyck) 5:*46*

Marguerite Pouget (pastels, Chardin) 5:*47*

Marie-Antoinette (sketch, David) 4:*79*

Marie de' Medici cycle (Rubens) 3:*17, 30, 31, 36-9*

'Marino' drawings (Poussin) 4:*13*

Market Cart, The (Gainsborough) 6:*66*

Marquise de Pastoret, The (David) 4:*92*

Marriage at Cana (David, G.) 1:*140*

Married Couple in a Garden (Hals) 3:*54-5, 58-9*
detail 3:*54*

Mars and Minerva (David) 4:*76, 88*

Mars and Venus (David) 4:*83, 85*

Martyrdom of St Erasmus (Poussin) 4:*14, 15, 18*

Martyrdom of St Symphorian (Ingres) 4:*113*

Mary, Countess Howe (Gainsborough) 6:*60*

Mary Cassatt in the Louvre (etching, Degas) 9:*47*

Mass of Bolsena, The (Raphael) 2:*99*

Massacre of Chios (Delacroix) 4:*112*

Medici tombs (sculpture, Michelangelo) 2:*48, 51, 52*

Melancholy (Degas) 9:*45, 51*

Melun Diptych (Fouquet) 1:*140*

Meninas, Las (Picasso) 8:*49*

Meninas, Las (Velázquez) 8:*49*

Merchant of Loves (Vien) 4:*77*

Mérode Altarpiece (Master of Mérode) 1:*51, 51*
symbolism in 1:*51, 51*

Merry Company (Hals, D.) 3:*46, 110*

Merry Company in the Open Air (Buytewech) 3:*132*

Merry Drinker, The (Hals) 3:*48*

Merry Fiddler, The (Honthorst) 3:*53*

Mezzetin, The (Watteau) 5:*18, 19, 32*

Mill, The (Boucher) 5:*91*

Millstream, The (sketch, Constable) 6:*83*

Miner, The (Luks) 9:*135*

Miracle of the Reliquary of the True Cross (Carpaccio) 1:*111*

Miraculous Draught of Fishes, The (cartoon, Raphael) 2:*83*

Miraflores Triptych (Van der Weyden) 1:*80, 88-9*

Modern Idol (Boccioni) 8:*83, 96*

'Modern Woman' (Cassatt) 9:*48*
Young Girls Pursuing Fame 9:*48*
Young Women Plucking the Fruits of Knowledge and Science 9:*48*

Modiste, La (Boucher) 5:*91*

Mona Lisa (Leonardo) 2:*18, 28*
stolen 8:*106*

Monforte Altarpiece, The (Van der Goes) 1:*141*

Monsieur Bertin (Ingres) 4:*125*

M. and Mme Auguste Manet (Manet) 7:*13*

Mont-Sainte Victoire (Cézanne) 8:*68*

Moonlight Landscape with Figure at the Door of a Cottage (Gainsborough) 6:*50*

Morning, The (Boccioni) 8:*90*

Morning Toilet, The (Chardin) 5:*51*

Morning Walk, The (Gainsborough) 6:*65*

Moss Roses (Renoir) 7:*115*

Mother Anthony's Inn (Renoir) 7:*109*

Moulin de la Galette, La (Renoir) 7:*114-15, 116-17*

Mountain Stream (Sargent) 9:*97*

Mousehold Heath (Crome) 6:*140*

Mr and Mrs Robert Andrews (Gainsborough) 6:*54-5, 56-7, 65*

Mrs Joseph Hamar (Reynolds) 6:*13, 13*

Mrs Philip Thicknesse (Gainsborough) 6:*59*

Mrs Richard Brinsley Sheridan (Gainsborough) 6:*53, 62*

Muses, The (Le Sueur) 3:*119*

Music (Russolo) 8:*102*

Music Lesson, The (Metsu) 3:*141*

Music Lesson, The (Vermeer) 3:*124*

Music Party, A (sketch, Gainsborough) 6:*47*

Music Party, The (Watteau) 5:*17, 20*
changes to 5:*20*

Musician's Table, The (Braque) 8:*68-9*

N

Napoleon Crossing the Alps (David) 4:*80, 98*

Napoleon Crowning Himself (sketch, David) 4:*80*

Napoleon as Emperor (Ingres) 4:*130*

Napoleon as First Consul (Ingres) 4:*110, 120*

Napoleon at the Pass of St Bernard (David) 4:*80, 99*

Napoleon in his Study (David) 4:*99, 111*

Nativity (Campin) 1:*101, 102, 141*

Nativity (Christus) 1:*140*

Nativity with Cardinal Jean Rolin (Master of Moulins) 1:*141*

Nativity at Night (Geertgen tot Sint Jans) 1:*141*

Nativity Triptych (Van der Weyden) 1:*102*
right wing 1:*81*

Nelly O'Brien (Reynolds) 6:*27*

Night Watch, The (Rembrandt) 3:*88-9, 92-3*
details 3:*88, 89*
watercolour copy 3:*89*

Night Windows (Sloan) 9:*134*

Nighthawks (Hopper) 9:*118-19, 126-7*
details 9:*118, 119*

Nocturne in Black and Gold: The Falling Rocket (Whistler) 9:*14, 15, 15-16*
Ruskin and 9:*73-4*

Nocturne, Grey and Gold – Chelsea Snow (Whistler) 9:*21, 29*

Nocturne, Grey and Gold – Westminster Bridge (Whistler) 9:*28*

Noli Me Tangere (Titian) 2:*120*

Norham Castle; Sunrise (Turner) 6:*122-3*

Nude descending a staircase (Duchamp) 8:*85*

Nude in a Red Armchair (Picasso) 8:*62*

Nude in the Bath (Bonnard) 7:*52*

Nurse and Child (Hals) 3:*56*

Nymphs of Diana Surprised by Satyrs, The (Rubens) 5:*84-5*

O

O Mistress Mine (Abbey) 9:*102*

Oath of the Horatii, The (David) 4:*77, 84, 89, 91, 132*

Oath of the Jeu de Paume (sketch, David) 4:*78, 82*

Oath of Julius Civilis, The (Rembrandt) 3:*82*

Odalisque (Boucher) 5:*87*

Odalisque, The (Renoir) 7:*109*

Odalisque with Red Bloomers (Matisse) 8:*31*

Odalisque with Slave (Ingres) 4:*126-7*

Office at Night (Hopper) 9:*116-17*
detail 9:*117*

Old Man and a Youth, An (Leonardo) 2:*15*

Old Savoyard (drawing, Watteau) 5:*19*

Oliver Goldsmith (copy, Reynolds) 6:*14*

Olympia (Manet) 7:*15, 20, 21, 22-3, 26-7*, 9:*82*
  details 7:*22*
  Matisse on 8:*20*
  sketch for 7:*23*

Omval, The (etching, Rembrandt) 3:*81*

On the Balcony during the Carnival (Cassatt) 9:*56*

Open Window, The (Matisse) 8:*15, 19*

Open Window, Collioure (Matisse) 8:*22*

Opening of the Fifth Seal, The (El Greco) 2:*140*

Opéra Orchestra, The (Degas) 7:*45, 57*

Oyster Gatherers at Cancale, The (Sargent) 9:*82*
  sketches for 9:*78*

P

Pagan Deities: Astarte and Neith (Sargent) 9:*81*

Painter's Daughters Chasing a Butterfly, The (Gainsborough) 6:*51*

Pancake Baker, The (Brouwer) 3:*133*

Pansies (Boldoni) 8:*85*

Parade (drop-curtain, Picasso) 8:*46*

Parental Admonition (Terborch) 3:*141*

Parnassus (Raphael) 2:*98*

Partie Quarrée, La (Watteau) 5:*24*

Parting of Hero and Leander, The (Turner) 6:*115*

Pastoral Caprice with the Arch of Constantine (Claude) 4:*64*

Pastoral Landscape (drawing, Claude) 4:*49*

Paterson Children, The (Raeburn) 6:*21*

Peace, Burial at Sea (Turner) 6:*113*

Pearl Earring, The (Vermeer) 3:*113*

Pearl Necklace, The (Vermeer) 3:*113*

Peasants Smoking at a Cottage

Door (Gainsborough) 6:*67*

Pelletier, Le (copy, David) 4:*87*

Perseus and the Origin of Coral (sketch, Claude) 4:*50-51*

Pesaro Madonna, The (Titian) 2:*10*

Petites Heures, Les 1:*15*
  illustration added by Limbourg brothers 1:*15*

Pietà (Bellini) 2:*140*

Pietà (Botticelli) 1:*85*

Pietà (Titian) 2:*113, 116*

Pietà, Duomo (sculpture, Michelangelo) 2:*49*

Pietà, St Peter's (sculpture, Michelangelo) 2:*46, 54*; 4:*87*

Pig (study, Rembrandt) 3:*80*

Pilgrimage to the Island of Cythera, The (Watteau) 5: *15, 22-3, 26-7*
  details 5:*22, 23*
  preliminary sketch 5:*23*

Pink and Grey: Three Figures (Whistler) 9:*30-31*

Pinks and Clematis (Manet) 7:*19*

Place du Théâtre Français, La (Pissarro) 7:*140*

Plague at Jaffa, The (Gros) 4:*140*

Polish Rider, The (Rembrandt) 3:*84*

Pomegranates (Sargent) 9:*96*

Pomeranian Dogs (Gainsborough) 6:*47*

Pont Neuf (Renoir) 7:*84*

Pool of London (Derain) 8:*14*

Poplars (Monet) 7:*94*

Portinari Altarpiece, The 1:*141*
  (detail, Van der Goes) 1:*101*

Portrait of

Agatha Bas (Rembrandt) 3:*85*

Agnolo Doni (Raphael) 2:*87*

Alexander VI (Pinturicchio) 2:*37*

The Archduke Albert (Rubens) 3:*15*

Aretino (Titian) 2:*113*

The Artist's Mother (Rembrandt) 3:*76*

Aved (Chardin) 5:*47*

Berthe Morisot with a Bunch of Violets (Manet) 7:*17, 140*

Cardinal Richelieu (de Champaigne) 3:*39*

Castiglione (Raphael) 2:*78*

Chardin (La Tour) 5:*48*

Charles the Bold (Van der Weyden) 1:*77*

Charles I (detail, Van Dyck) 3:*16*

Charles V (Titian) 2:*132-3*

Charlotte Pécoul (David) 4:*79*

The Comte de Turenne (detail, David) 4:*83*

Constable (Reinagle) 6:*75*

Delphine Ramel (Ingres) 4:*113*

Desmaisons (David) 4:*76*

The Duc de Montpensier (Boucher) 5:*83*

The Empress Isabella (Titian) 2:*133*

Federico Gonzaga (Titian) 2:*110*

Ferruccio Busoni (Boccioni) 8:*99*

Frank Burty Haviland (Modigliani) 8:*121*

George III (Reynolds) 6:*36*

The Infanta Isabella (Rubens) 3:*15*

Isabella Brandt (Rubens) 3:*14*

Isabella of Portugal (Van Eyck) 1:*43*

Jacques Lipchitz and his Wife (Modigliani) 8:*118-19, 123*
  preliminary drawings 8:*119*

Jan de Leeuw (Van Eyck) 1:*65*

Jan Six (Rembrandt) 3:*87*
  detail 3:*87*

Jeanne Hébuterne (Modigliani) 8:*130-31*

John Constable (Reinagle) 6:*75*

Julius II (Raphael) 2:*79*

A Lady (Van der Weyden) 1:*97*

Leo X and Two Cardinals (Raphael) 2:*80*

A Little Boy (Rubens) 3:*21*

Madame Baudouin (Boucher) 5:*80*

Madame Boucher (Boucher) 5:*79*

Madame de Pompadour (Boucher) (1758) 5:*98*, (1759) 5:*99*
  (Drouais) 5:*103*
  (Quentin de la Tour) 5:*48*

Madame Récamier (David) 4:*85, 96-7*
  (Gerard) 4:*140*

Marguerite Gérard (sketch, Fragonard) 5:*113*

Marquise de Seignelay (Mignard) 4:*141*

Michelangelo (del Conte) 2:*43*

A Musician (Leonardo) 2:*31*

Paracelsus (Rubens) 2:*73*

Paul III and his Grandsons (Titian) 2:*111*

Philip the Good (Van der Weyden) 1:*76*

Philip II in Armour (Titian) 2:*114, 135*

Ranuccio Farnese (Titian) 2:*114*

Robert Kelso Cassatt (Cassatt) 9:*50*

Saskia (Rembrandt) 3:*78, 79*

A Seated Woman (Hals) 3:*48, 49*

Signora Busoni (Boccioni) 8:*80-81*

Signora Massimino (Boccioni) 8:*88*

Sophie Guimard (Fragonard) 5:*111*

Tessin (Aved) 5:*79*

Thomas Carlyle (Whistler) 9:*17*

Titus (Rembrandt) 3:*82*

Vermeer 3:*9,107*

Verrocchio (di Credi) 2:*14*

Vittoria Colonna (Piombo) 2:*49*

Watteau (Carriera) 5:*11*

His Wife? (Van der Weyden) 1:*86*

His Wife? (Van Eyck) 1:*46*

A Young Man (Van Eyck) 1:*59*

A Young Woman (Van der Weyden) 1:*86*

Presentation in the Temple, The (Rubens) 3:*23, 25*

Presentation of the Virgin, The (Gaddi) 1:*17*

Princesse du Pays de la Porcelaine (Whistler) 9:*25*

Procuress, The (Van Baburen) 3:*111, 112, 114, 125*

Procuress, The (Vermeer) 3:*112, 112, 128*

Prodigal Son, The (Rubens) 3:*18-19*

Prodigal Son in a Tavern, The (Hals) 3:*51*

Pursuit of Love, The (Fragonard) 5:*112, 124-5*

Q

Quarrel of the Cabmen (Gillot) 5:*14*

Queen Caroline Murat (sketch, Ingres) 4:*111, 111*

INDEX OF MASTERPIECES

R

Racehorses at Longchamp (Degas)
7:58-9
Rain, Steam and Speed (Turner)
6:113, 117, 129
Raising of the Cross, The (Rubens)
3:15, 20, 22
Raising of Lazarus, The (Lievens)
3:78
Rape of Europa (Titian) 2:131
Raphael and La Fornarina (Ingres)
2:80
Reader, The (Fragonard)
5:115
Reclining Nude (Modigliani)
7:21
Reclining Nude with Necklace
(Picasso) 8:66-7
Red Horseman (Carrà) 8:101
Red Interior, Still-Life on a Blue
Table (Matisse) 8:32
Red Studio, The (Matisse)
9:111
Regatta at Argenteuil (Monet)
7:84-5
Regentesses, The (Hals) 3:47, 49,
50, 86
Resistance (copy, Fragonard)
5:119
Rest on the Flight into Egypt, The
(Patenier) 1:141
Return of Marcus Sextus (Guérin)
4:84
Rhyl Sands (Cox) 6:140
Richard Wagner (Renoir)
7:112
Rinaldo and Armida (Boucher)
5:78-9
Riot in the Galleria (Boccioni)
8:83, 91
Rising of the Sun, The (Boucher)
5:84, 96
Robert Kelso Cassatt (Cassatt)
9:50
Rockets and Blue Lights (Turner)
6:127
Roger Freeing Angelica (Ingres)
4:8-9, 111
studies for 4:115, *115*
Rohan Book of Hours, The
1:21
Romulus and Remus and the
She-Wolf (Rubens) 3:8
Rotherhithe (etching, Whistler)
9:19
Rouen Cathedral in Full Sunlight
(Monet) 7:95
detail *87*
Royal Academicians, The
(Sanders) 6:37
Rubens and Isabella Brandt in a
Honeysuckle Bower (Rubens)
3:18

Rue Montorgueil Decked with
Flags, The (Monet) 7:93

S

Sacre, Le (David) 4:80
preliminary sketch
4:80
Sacred and Profane Love (Titian)
2:110, *118-19*, 122-3
details 2:*118*, *119*
St Barbara (Van Eyck) 1:40
St Cecilia Altarpiece, The
(Raphael) 2:83
St Christopher (Bosch) 1:113
St Christopher (Patenier)
1:141
St Eligius Weighing the Rings of a
Bridal Couple (Christus)
1:140
St Erasmus Altarpiece (Poussin)
4:14
St Francis Receiving the Stigmata
(Van Eyck) 1:48-9
St George and the Dragon
(Rubens) 3:19
St James (study, Leonardo)
2:34
St Jerome (Bellini) 2:140
St Jerome (Leonardo) 2:31
St John the Baptist between a
Pharisee and a Levite (sculpture,
Rustici) 2:32-3
St John the Baptist with Sts
Andrew and Peter (Domenichino)
4:40-41
St John the Baptist in the
Wilderness (Bosch) 1:121,
128
landscape in 1:117
sources for 1:117
St Joseph (School of Campin)
3:116
St Luke Drawing the Virgin (Van
der Weyden) 1:80
St Luke Painting the Virgin
(Deutsch) 1:*102*
St Mark (sculpture, Donatello)
2:52
St Mark Freeing a Christian Slave
(Tintoretto) 2:141
St Mary Magdalen (Titian) 2:*115*,
116
St Michael and the Dragon
(Raphael) 2:82
St Sebastian (Perugino)
2:141
Sainte Geneviève des Ardents
(Doyen) 5:119
Salle du Conseil, The (Boucher)

5:80-81
Salome (Titian) 2:*112*
Samuel Johnson (Reynolds)
6:15
San Giorgio Maggiore (Guardi)
4:106
Santa Maria in Vallicella
altarpiece (Rubens)
3:15
Sarah Siddons as the Tragic Muse
(Reynolds) 6:19, 35, 49
Saskia as Flora (Rembrandt)
3:91
Saying Grace (Chardin) 5:54-5,
63
details 5:55
Rotterdam version 5:54
sketch of lost original
5:54
Saying Grace (Maes) 3:*133*,
134
School of Athens, The (Raphael)
2:78, 84, 90-91, 96-7, 89
cartoon (full-scale) 2:96-7
details 2:97
preliminary study 2:97
Schoolmistress, The (Chardin)
5:50
Screen with Old Battersea Bridge
(Whistler) 9:19
Scullery Maid, The (Chardin)
3:117
Scupstoel (drawing, Van der
Weyden) 1:77, *100*
Seaport with the Embarkation of the
Queen of Sheba (Claude) 4:50,
54-5, 60-61, 63
details 4:54-5
preliminary sketch 4:55
Seaport with the Landing of
Cleopatra in Tarsus (Claude)
4:57
Seaport with Setting Sun (Claude)
4:56
Seasons (series, Watteau) 5:14
Spring 5:13
Seated Man Leaning on a Table, A
(Modigliani) 8:*126-7*
Seated Persian (drawing,
Watteau) 5:18
Seated Woman (Picasso) 8:53,
53
Seated Nude (Modigliani)
8:114
Second-Storey Sunlight (Hopper)
9:131
Self-portrait of
Boccioni 8:89
Bosch (drawing) 1:*111*
Boucher 5:77
Cassatt 7:48; 9:9, 43
Chardin 5:109, (1775) 5:43
Claude (copy of engraving)
4:8, 43

Constable 6:8, 75
David 4:9, 75
Degas 7:9, 43, 44; 9:47
Fabritius 3:*110*
?Fragonard 5:*107*
Gainsborough 6:8, 43
Gros 4:*80*
Hals 3:8, 43
Hopper 9:9, *107*
Ingres 4:8, *107*, 118
Leonardo 2:8, 11 (1513), 19
Leyster 3:46, *46*, 47
Lievens 3:78
?Limbourgs 1:*13*
Manet 7:11
Matisse (drawing) 8:*11*
Michelangelo 8:8
Modigliani 8:*114*
Manet 7:9, 11
Monet 7:75
Poussin 4:9, 11, 46
(drawing) 4:*14*
Raphael 2:8, 75
(drawing) 2:*76*
Rembrandt 3:97
(aged 23) 3:77
(aged 34, detail) 3:*75*
(aged 63) 3:*83*
Renoir 7:*107*
Reynolds 6:9, 11
Rubens, 3:11
Sargent 9:9, 75
Titian 2:9, *107*
Turner 6:9, *107*
Van der Werff 3:69
Van der Weyden 1:*76*, 77, 77,
80
Van Eyck 1:43
Watteau 5:15
Whistler 9:9, 11
as Doctor of Civil Law
(Reynolds) 6:16, 17
with the Duke of Lerma
(Rubens) 3:*13*
with Friends (Rubens) 3:*13*
with Hélène Fourment (Rubens)
3:16
with Isabella Brandt (Rubens)
3:18
as Rembrandt (Reynolds)
6:48
with Saskia (Rembrandt)
3:90
Servant Reading to his Master
(Robert) 5:71
Setting of the Sun, The (Boucher)
5:84, 97
Seven Deadly Sins, The (Bosch)
1:112
Seven Sacraments Altarpiece, The
(Van der Weyden) 1:78, 92-3
Sforza Monument, The
(Leonardo) 2:15-16, 18
She-Goat, The (Picasso) 8:50

72

Shepherd Piping to a Shepherdess (Boucher) 5:*108-109*

Shoshone Cliffs (Hopper) 9:*115*

Shrovetide Revellers, The (Hals) 3:*50*

Shuffleton's Barber Shop (Rockwell) 9:*116*

Sick Child, The (Metsu) 3:*41*

Signora Massimino (Boccioni) 8:*88*

Singel Canal, Amersfoort (drawing, Rembrandt) 3:*80-81*

Sirois and his Family (Watteau) 5:*14*

Sistine Chapel ceiling (Michelangelo) 2:*47, 50-51, 56-9, 64-5, 66-7, 85;* 6:*13*
   copy of nude of Rubens 3:*14*
   restoration of 2:*67*

Sistine Madonna, The (Raphael) 2:*94*

Sitwell Children, The (Copley) 9:*84*

Skate, The (Chardin) 5:*44-5, 46*

Skiff, The (Renoir) 7:*123*

Slave Ship, The (Turner) 6:*114-15*

Sleeping Girl (Vermeer) 3:*116*

Sleeping Kitchen Maid (Maes) 5:*52*

Sleeping Woman (drawing, Rembrandt) 3:*81*

Small Bather, The (Ingres) 4:*118*

Smash the Hun (poster, Hopper) 9:*109*

Smokers, The (Brouwer) 3:*140*

Snowstorm (Turner) 6:*116, 117*

Snowstorm; Hannibal Crossing the Alps (Turner) 6:*121*

Snowstorm; Mount Cenis (Turner) 6:*111*

Society of Dilettanti, The (Reynolds) 6:*15, 15*

Soldier with a Laughing Girl (Vermeer) 3:*121*

Soldier Offering a Young Woman Coins (Terborch) 3:*133, 134*

Sophia Charlotte, Lady Sheffield (Gainsborough) 6:*53*

Spanish Guitarist, The (Manet) 3:*53*

Spring (Watteau) 5:*13*

Square Dining Room at Petworth (Turner) 6:*110, 111*

Stag at Sharkey's (Bellows) 9:*134-5*

Standing Nude (Braque) 8:*68*

Stanza d'Eliodoro (Raphael) 2:*79, 92-3, 99*

Stanza dell'Incendio (Raphael) 2:*80, 81, 99*

Stanza della Segnatura (Raphael) 2:*79, 84, 90-91, 96-7, 98*

States of Mind (Boccioni) 8:*83*
   The Farewell 8:*85, 94*
   Those Who Go 8:*95*

Steeplechase Cracks (Herring) 7:*66-7*

Stephanus Geraerts (Hals) 3:*66*

Steps, The (Renoir) 7:*115*

Still-Life with Oriental Rugs (Matisse) 8:*24-5*

Stolen Shirt, The (Fragonard) 5:*115*

Stonehenge (Constable) 6:*97*

Stormy Landscape (Rembrandt) 2:*33*

Stratford St Mary (sketch, Constable) 6:*82*

Street Enters the House, The (Boccioni) 8:*82-3, 83-4*

Street Scene with Snow (Henri) 9:*132*

Studio in the Batignolles Quarter (Fantine-Latour) 7:*14*

Study of an Old Man (Rembrandt) 3:*77*

Suffering Christ, The (Bellini) 2:*140*

Sulking (Degas) 7:*66-7*

Summer (Poussin) 4:*21, 34*

Sunday, Women Drying Their Hair (Sloan) 9:*132-3*

Sunlight in a Cafeteria (Hopper) 9:*130*

Susan on a Balcony Holding a Dog (Cassatt) 9:*63*

Swing, The (Cazes) 5:*44*

Swing, The (Fragonard)
   (1775) 5:*122, 129*
   (1776-7) 5:*111, 118-19, 121*
   details 5: *118-19*

Swing, The (Renoir) 7:*116*
   detail 7:*116*

Symphony in White, No. 1: The White Girl (Whistler) 9:*22, 22-3, 24*
   details 9:*23*

Symphony in White, No. 2: The Little White Girl (Whistler) 9:*22, 23*

Symphony in White, No. 3: (sketch, Whistler) 9:*23*

Syndics, The (Rembrandt) 3:*98*

Synthesis of Human Dynamism (Boccioni) 8:*79*

T

Tableau de Cébès, Le (Varin) 4:*12-13*

Tarquin and Lucretia (Titian) 2:*116-17*
   detail 2:*117*
   preliminary drawing? 2:*116*

Tempest, The (Giorgione) 2:*110*

Temptation of St Anthony, The (Bosch) 1:*121, 130-31*
   details 1:*114-15*
   sources 1:*117, 130*

Temptation of St Anthony (Ernst) 1:*110*

Ten O'Clock Lecture (Whistler) 9:*16*

Terrace, The (Monet) 7:*76-7*

Thames near Walton Bridge, The (Turner) 6:*114*

Thief on the Cross, The (Campin) 1:*141*

Three Bathers (Cézanne) 8:*20*

Three Crosses, The (etching, Rembrandt) 3:*86, 87*

Three Dancers, The (Picasso) 8:*48, 50-51*

Three Graces, The (Rubens) 3:*20*

Three Ladies Adorning a Term of Hymen (Reynolds) 6:*22-3, 30-31*

Three Trees, The (etching, Rembrandt) 3:*85*

Tintern Abbey (Turner) 6:*114*

Tobias and the Archangels (detail, Botticini) 2:*12*

Toilette, La (Watteau) 5:*17*

Torero and a Young Girl (Cassatt) 9:*45, 57*

Torso Belvedere (sculpture) 2:*51, 67*

Transfiguration (Bellini) 2:*140*

Transfiguration (Raphael) 2:*81, 83, 85, 95*

Transport of the Body of St Mark (Tintoretto) 2:*141*

Très Belles Heures de Notre-Dame, Les (Limbourgs) 1:*16*

Très Riches Heures du Duc de Berry, Les (Limbourgs) 1:*11,*

16-17, 17, 18, 18, 19, 20
   calendar from 1:*17, 18, 24-35*
   details from 'October' 1:*22-3, 22-3*
   influence of Duc de Berry's collection on 1:*19*

Trial of Moses, The (Giorgione) 2:*140*

Tribunal of the Uffizi, The (Zoffany) 6:*141*

Tribute Money, The (detail, Masaccio) 2:*52*

Triptych of the Virgin (Van der Weyden) 1:*80*

Tristesse du Roi, La (Matisse) 8:*34-5*

Triumph of Galatea (Raphael) 2:*79*

Triumph of Pan, The (Poussin) 4:*26*

Triumph of Silenus (Poussin) 4:*15*

Triumph of Venus, The (Boucher) 5:*80, 88-9*

Tub, The (Degas) 7:*53*

Turkish Bath, The (Ingres) 4:*113, 117, 118-19, 129*
   changes in 4:*118*
   details 4:*118, 119*
   study for 4:*119*

Turkish Woman and her Slave (Liotard) 5:*68-9*

Two Comedians (Hopper) 9:*113*

Two Dancers on Stage (Degas) 7:*60*

Two Kinds of Games (Steen) 3:*108*

Two Sisters (Cassatt) see *Little Sisters, The*

Two Studies of Women (drawing, Watteau) 5:*18*

Two Women in an Interior (Matisse) 8:*30*

U

Umbrellas, The (Renoir) 7:*128*

Unique Form of Continuity in Space (Boccioni) 8:*79, 85*

Useless Resistance (Fragonard) 5:*119*

V

Valley Farm, The (Constable) 6:*81*

Valparaiso (Whistler) 9:*18-19*

Valpinçon Bather, The (Ingres)
4:*117, 121*; 7:*52*
Variations in Flesh and Green: The Balcony (Whistler) 9:*21*
detail 9:*21*
Venice from the Giudecca (Turner)
6:*126*
Venice: Moonrise (Turner)
6:*115*
Venus and Adonis (Lemoyne)
5:*76*
Venus Asleep (Boucher)
5:*117*
Venus of Urbino (Titian) 2:*126-7*;
7:*21*
View of La Crescenza (Claude)
4:*45*
View of Delft (detail, Vermeer)
3:*114, 123*
View of the Grande Galerie in the Louvre (Robert) 5:*81*
View of Haarlem from Noorder Spaarne (Vroom) 3:*44-5*
View of Potrel Manor (Griffier)
5:*70*
View from the Luxembourg (David) 4:*79*
View of SS Trinità dei Monti (Claude) 4:*47*
Villa at Rueil (Manet) 7:*16*
Virgin and Child, The (Campin)
1:*78, 78*
Virgin and Child, The (Geertgen tot Sint Jans) 1:*41*
Virgin and Child in a Niche (Van der Weyden) 1:*78, 87*
Virgin and Child with St Anne, The (Leonardo) 2:*29*
Virgin and Child with St Anne and John the Baptist, The

(Leonardo) 2:*26*
Virgin in the Burning Bush (Froment) 1:*140*
Virgin of the Rocks, The (Leonardo) 2:*32* (c.1508)
2:*15, 27*
Visit to the Nursery, The (Fragonard) 5:*111*
Visitation, The (Rubens) 3:*22, 24*
Vollard Suite, The: No. 38 (Picasso) 8:*51*
Vow to Louis XIII, The (Ingres)
4:*112*

W

War (Rubens) 3:*69*
Washerwoman, The (Chardin)
5:*50-51*
Water Urn, The (Chardin)
5:*50*
Waterfall at Tivoli (Dughet) 4:*16, 141*
Waterlilies (Monet) 7:*96-7*
Waterloo Bridge (Monet)
7:*81*
Well of Moses (Sluter) 1:*33*
Western Motel (Hopper)
9:*128-9*
Whistlejacket (Stubbs) 6:*140*
White Duck, The (Oudry)
5:*141*
White House, Chelsea, The (Girtin)
6:*140*
Who Shall Deliver Me?

(Khnopff) 8:*116*
Wild Poppies (Monet) 7:*88-9*
Wilkes and Liberty (Hogarth)
6:*41*
Willem van Heythuyzen (Hals)
3:*49*
Winter (engraving, Boucher)
5:*77*
Winter (Poussin) 4:*21, 35*
Woman with a Balance (Vermeer)
3:*114*
Woman Bathing (Cassatt)
9:*65*
Woman with Blue Eyes (Matisse)
8:*19*
Woman in Blue Reading a Letter (Vermeer) 3:*109*
Woman Carrying a Child (drawing, Rembrandt)
3:*80*
Woman and Child Driving (Cassatt) 9:*60-61*
Woman in a Garden (Boccioni)
8:*82*
Woman with Goldfish (Matisse)
8:*15, 28-9*
Woman at her Mirror (Cassatt)
9:*48-9*
Woman with a Muff (Boucher)
5:*83*
Woman Reading a Book (Fragonard) 5:*127*
Woman Reading a Letter (Metsu)
3:*134*
Woman Taking Tea (Chardin)
5:*45*
Woman Weighing Pearls, A (Vermeer) 1:*47*
symbolism in 1:*51*
Woman's Work (Sloan) 9:*134*

Women of Algiers (Delacroix)
8:*20*
Women in the Garden (Monet)
7:*82, 82*
Women Ironing (Degas) 7:*63*
Women Picking Fruit (Cassatt)
9:*50-51*
Women Running on the Beach (Picasso) 8:*60-61*
Women Sewing (Cassatt) 7:*48*
Woodcutter Courting a Milkmaid (Gainsborough) 6:*58*
Wyndham Sisters, The (Sargent)
9:*95*

Y

Young Couples with Guitarist and Shepherd (Watteau) 5:*28*
Young Draughtsman, The (Chardin) 5:*59*
Young Englishman, The (Titian)
2:*128*
Young Girl (Cassatt) 9:*48*
Young Man, Portrait of a (Van Eyck) 1:*59*
Young Woman, Portrait of a (Van der Weyden) 1:*86*
Young Woman with Blue Eyes (Manet) 7:*19*
Young Women on the Banks of the Seine (Courbet) 7:*117*
Young Spartans Exercising (Degas) 7:*44-5, 50*
Ypres Salient at Night, The (Nash)
9:*104-105*

Glossary

absorbent ground The surface of a canvas which has been treated with chalk to enable it to absorb the oil from paint, so leaving a matt finish.

Abstract Art Art that does not try to represent the appearance of objects, real or imaginary. An old tradition in the decorative arts and in Moslem art – according to the Koran, the human figure may not be depicted – abstract art emerged in Western art in the early 20th century in works by artists such as Mondrian, Kandinsky and Malevich.

Abstract Expressionism School of almost automatic painting developed in New York in the 1940s, marked by spontaneous expression through abstract forms. Jackson Pollock was its most famous exponent.

Academic Art Formal, usually **Classical** art inspired by, or devoted to, the axioms of the Academies that flourished in France, England and other countries from the 17th to 19th centuries. See also **Classical Art, Romantic Art.**

academy figure Depiction of a nude figure used for teaching purposes and not as a work of art.

acrylic paint Quick-drying synthetic paint first exploited by artists in the late 1940s. Because it can be used as a thin wash or as a very thick **impasto**, acrylic paint can be used like both traditional **watercolours** and **oil paints.**

Action Painting This term was used first

in 1952 to describe splashing and dribbling paint on canvas, designed to allow the unconscious mind to produce a work of art.

Aestheticism Theory that the beauty of a work of art justifies its existence – often summarized as 'art for art's sake'. Ideas taken up by the Aesthetic Movement. See volume 9, pp.34-7.

after In imitation of the style of, as in 'after Raphael'.

altarpiece Screen, painting or wall behind a church altar.

American Abstract Artists' Group Founded in New York in 1939 to promote abstract art in America. Founder members included Diller, Bolotowsky and Greene.

Anamorphosis Painting or drawing of an object distorted in such a way that the image is only lifelike when seen from a particular angle or by a special mirror. The skull in the foreground of *The Ambassadors* (1533) by Holbien is a famous example.

Archaic Art Art of Greece from about 650 BC. This era is usually said to end in 480 when the Persians sacked Athens. Followed by the **Classical** era.

Armory Show International Exhibition of Modern Art in New York held in 1913, which showed modern works by, among others, Duchamp, the **Symbolists, Impressionists** and **Post-**

Impressionists, and challenged the **Representational** tradition in the USA.

Art Deco Decorative style popular in 1920s and 1930s. Geometric shapes, smooth lines and streamlining were features of this style.

Art Nouveau Style that flourished from about 1890 to World War 1. Characteristics included asymmetry and flowing lines.

Ashcan School A group of 19th-20th century American **Realist** painters interested in depicting the sordid side of city life, especially New York. See volume 9, pp.132-5.

attribution Term used when assigning a work to an artist when the authorship cannot be definitely stated.

Barbizon School A mid-19th century group of landscape painters who depicted realistic peasant life. The group worked from the village of Barbizon in the Forest of Fontainebleau, and its chief members were Millet, Theodore Rousseau and Diaz.

Baroque The style that emerged from 16th century **Mannerism** and lasted, with many modifications, well into the 18th century. It was concentrated in the High Baroque in Rome from 1620-80, where Bernini united the arts of architecture, painting and sculpture in his work. The blend of light, colour, **illusionism** and movement was intended to overwhelm the spectator by a direct

emotional appeal. The Baroque had little appeal in northern Europe but was used to glorify the French monarchy at Versailles. In the 18th century many south German palaces and abbeys emulated this form of Baroque.

Bauhaus Influential German school of architecture and design founded by the architect Walter Gropius at Weimar, Germany, in 1919.

Biedermeier Style predominant in Germany and Austria from 1815 to 1848, emphasizing a solid, totally unheroic bourgeois comfort.

Biomorphic form Abstract form derived from organic shapes.

bon dieuserie (French: good Goddery). Over-sentimental religious art from France and Belgium.

bust Painting or sculpture showing only the head and shoulders of a sitter.

camera obscura (Latin: dark chamber) Device used as an aid to accuracy in drawing, consisting of an arrangement of lenses in a darkened tent or box, invented in the 16th century. Much used by Vermeer and by Canaletto. See volume 3, pp. 114-15.

caricature Drawing of a person with exaggerated features which make the person appear ridiculous.

cartoon A full-size drawing used to transfer a design to the painting surface, now mainly referring to humorous drawings or animated films.

chiaroscuro (Italian: light-dark) Term used to describe dramatic effects of shade and light in painting, as in the works of Caravaggio and his followers.

Cinquecento (Italian: five hundred) The 16th century, used especially in relation to Italian art.

Classic, Classical Term describing the ordered harmony associated with the art of Ancient Greece and Rome, long considered the ideal art forms. It is also used in a wider sense as the antithesis of **Romanticism,** denoting an art that adheres to accepted canons of beauty and – in most cases – to a particular type of subject matter, rather than relying on personal inspiration. See also **Academic Art, Romantic Art** and p.38.

collage (French: sticking) A picture built up from pieces of paper, cloth or other matter stuck onto a canvas.

Colour Field Painting Description for some of the work of the **Abstract Expressionists,** especially Newman and Rothko, who were interested in the effects created by large areas of colour, often over the entire canvas.

composition Arrangement of objects or figures in a picture to please the eye and make an effective whole. See also p.45.

continuous narrative or **representation** One picture showing several scenes of a complete story, such as the martyrdom of a saint or the events of the life of Christ. See also p.35.

contraposto Pose in which one part of the body is twisted in the opposite direction from the rest of the body. Much used by Michelangelo. See volume 2, p.53.

Constructivism A Russian **abstract** movement headed by Vladimir Tatlin. Materials used included wire, glass and sheet metal.

conversation piece Group portrait with the subjects in an informal, usually domestic, setting. Particularly popular with 18th-century English artists. See volume 6, p.52.

craquelure (French: cracking) Fine cracks on the surface of an old painting.

Cubism Movement that revolutionized 20th-century painting and sculpture by rejecting the **naturalistic** tradition. Inspired by Cézanne's last works, Picasso and Braque abandoned attempts to represent things as they actually appear in favour of a more intellectual approach to form and colour, as seen in their superimposed and interlocking geometric planes. First seen in Paris in 1907, it attracted much opposition. Painters like Malevich and Mondrian took Cubism to its logically **abstract** conclusion. See volume 8, pp.68-71 and also **Abstract Art, Orphism.**

Dada (French: hobbyhorse) A nihilistic precursor of **Surrealism** invented in Zurich in 1915, it set out to be anti-art and irrational. One of its most famous products was Marcel Duchamp's *Mona Lisa* with a moustache, and a typical event was a lecture given by 38 lecturers

simultaneously. It had died out by 1923. See also **Surrealism.**

decorative arts Arts in which decoration is applied to a functional object – for example, hand-painting on fine porcelain – as opposed to the fine arts of painting and sculpture.

diptych A picture in two, normally hinged, parts, usually of a religious nature such as an **altarpiece.** Similarly, a triptych is a three-part picture, and a polyptych has more than three parts.

distemper Powdered colour mixed with **size** to make an inexpensive, impermanent paint **medium.**

drôlerie Humorous picture, or the grotesque drawings in the margins of medieval manuscripts.

Dugento (Italian: two hundred) The 13th century, usually used in relation to Italian art.

eclecticism The practice of selecting different styles or features from various artists and combining them.

engraving Term denoting both the process of cutting a design into wood or metal and the print taken from the plate or block so cut. The former refers properly to only two processes of printmaking – metal engraving or line engraving, and wood engraving. The latter is a **relief** method in which negative parts of the design are cut away from a block of hardwood, leaving raised lines for inking. Metal engraving, with hard, clear lines, is an **intaglio** process in which the design is cut into a smooth metal plate with an engraving tool, and paper is pressed into the ink furrows. Metal engraving was both an independent art form and the main method of reproductive printing from the 16th to 19th centuries.

etching The process of biting out a design in a metal plate with acid, also the resulting print.

Expressionism A quality of expressive emphasis and distortion that may be found in art of any period. More specifically it is a term used for northern European, 20th-century art, deriving from Van Gogh, especially German art. The *Brucke* and the *Blaue Reiter* are two principal subgroups, major artists being Beckman, Ensor and Nolde.

fancy picture Idealized rural **genre** picture, most notably in 18th-century England. Gainsborough was an exponent. See volume 6, pp.50-53.

Fauvists (French: 'wild beast') A group of artists associated with Matisse from 1905 to 1907, noted for their luminous use of colour. See volume 8, p.14 and also **Cubism.**

fête champêtre Genre painting set in an idealized garden or parkland. Giorgione's *Fête Champêtre* is the best-known Renaissance example. The genre's popularity continued until the 18th century with Watteau's fêtes galantes. See also p.40.

Figurative Art Art representing figures or other recognizable objects. Also known as Representational Art. See also **Abstract Art.**

fine arts See **decorative arts.**

Fontainebleau School Name given to artists associated with the French court in the 16th century, mainly Italian Mannerist painters like Rosso and Primaticcio. See also **Mannerism.**

foreshortening Perspective applied to an object – for example, an arm is foreshortened when it is painted pointing directly out of the picture so that only the hand can be seen.

folk art Art based on the traditional designs of a particular country.

fresco (Italian: fresh) Wall-painting using water-based paint on lime plaster. For the true or *buon fresco* method, perfected in Italy in the 16th century, the wall is first rough plastered, then a coat, known as the *arriciato*, is applied on which the outlines of the design or cartoon are drawn. Fresh plaster mixed with lime covers one day's work area and then the painting is done with pigments mixed with plain water, while this layer, the *intonaco*, is still damp. Frescoes are more suited to dry than to damp climates.

Futurism Movement founded in Italy in 1909 by the poet Marinetti, concerned with fusing modern technology with art. The first exhibtion in Milan in 1911 was followed by a tour through northern Europe. It contemptuously rejected 'museum' art. See volume 8, pp.100-103 and also **Dada.**

genre In general terms, any type of art – landscape, portraits, etc. – but normally applied to paintings of everyday life. Most notable examples occur in 17th-century Dutch art. See volume 3.

gesso The bright white ground used in **tempera** and **oil** paintings.

gilding Method of applying precious metals such as gold and silver to another material. The precious metal is held in place with **size.** See also p.34.

Golden Mean or Golden Section Near mystical definition of a line divided in such a way that the smaller part is to the larger as the larger is to the whole, in practice on the ratio 8:13.

Gothic Style of architecture and painting that dominated Europe from the mid-12th to the 16th century. Characterized by pointed arches in architecture, in other arts by its rejection of Renaissance humanism, as in the work of Grünewald and Notke. See also **Classic** and **Renaissance.**

gouache Opaque, fast-drying **watercolour** paint, once widely used by manuscript illuminators and French watercolourists.

Grand Manner In **Academic Art,** the only way to portray themes from the Bible or ancient history was this elevated, heroic style of **history painting.** Sir Joshua Reynolds was a notable exponent. See volume 6, pp.18-35.

graphic art Art which depends less on colour than line, such as engraving.

grisaille Painting executed entirely in monochrome shades of grey.

grotesque A form of fanciful decoration dominated by linked festoons and decorative frames containing **figurative** or floral ornaments. In the 16th century, Raphael and his followers were inspired by the recently discovered 'grotta', meaning caves, of the Emperor Nero's Golden House in Rome. Only later did the term become perjorative.

ground The surface on which a design or painting is made.

hatching Shading carried out in parallel lines, a series of fine lines being laid close together.

herm Sculpted head or bust on top of a tapering, rectangular column. Also known as term.

High Renaissance The period from approximately 1495 to 1520 when **Renaissance** art attained a perfect balance between the ideal and the real in the works of Leonardo, Michelangelo and above all Raphael. See volume 2, and also **Mannerism, Renaissance.**

History painting Pictures of real or imaginary ancient historical scenes. In **Academic Art,** the first in the hierarchy of types of subject.

hot colour tone Colours and tones at the red end of the spectrum.

Hudson River School Group of mid-19th century American landscape painters, including Cole and Durand.

icon Image of saint or other religious figure particularly applied to Russian and Greek Orthodox images.

iconography Branch of art history dealing with the subject matter of **Figurative Art.**

illumination Decoration of manuscripts, with borders or ornamental letters, especially common in medieval Europe.

illusionism Use of virtuoso techniques such as **perspective** and **foreshortening** to make a painted object seem three-dimensional; as in the paintings of the **Baroque** era. See also **trompe l'oeil,** and p.39.

imago pietatis (Latin: image of pity). Depiction of the dead Christ standing in the tomb.

impasto (Italian: paste) Describes the thickness of paint on a canvas or panel, suitable only to oil paints or acrylics.

Impressionism The most important artistic movement of the 19th century, originating in the 1860s. Influenced by scientific findings that colour was not inherent in an object, but the outcome of the way light reflects from it, the Impressionists reacted against **Academic** doctrines and **Romantic** ideas alike, trying to depict life in an objective manner. Monet, Renoir, Sisley, Pissaro, Cézanne and others held the first of eight Impressionist Exhibitions in 1874. At first generally attacked and mocked

for the flickering touches with which they applied paint in small brightly coloured dabs, they caused painters everywhere to lighten their palettes.

intaglio Concave 'relief' formed by cutting areas out of a surface.

International Gothic Essentially a courtly style of painting and sculpture that flourished in the late 14th and early 15th centuries, marked by a refined elegance, as in the works of the Limbourg brothers. See volume 1, pp.11-42.

intimisme Domestic interior scenes rendered in **Impressionist** style.

intonaco See **fresco.**

Jugendstil German term for **Art Nouveau** derived from the review *Die Jugend* founded in Munich in 1896.

Junk Art Modern art forms using débris for artistic purposes.

Kinetic Art (Greek: moving) Art based on the idea that light and movement can create a work of art. Objects may be made to gyrate or create patterns of light and shadow.

limner See **miniature.**

linocut A relief printing process begun in the 20th century using thick linoleum, and allowing bold images to be cut in a negative form for printing.

lithography A method of surface printing in which a design is drawn or painted directly on to a limestone block or metal plate. It was invented in 1798 by Aloys Senefelder.

local colour The actual colour of an object, uninfluenced by reflected light or colour.

Luminists American landscape painters of the mid-19th century. Their concern with light and atmosphere connects them with the **Barbizon School** and **Impressionism.** Cole, Lane and Durand were all Luminists.

maestà (Italian: majesty) Describes a work of art portraying the Virgin and Child enthroned, surrounded by saints or angels.

Mannerism The dominant style in European art from about 1520 to 1600. Characterized by elongated or otherwise unnatural figures, it was a self-conscious reaction against the serene **Classicism** of the **High Renaissance.** See also **Renaissance.**

masses The fundamental shapes to which paintings, sculptures or buildings can be reduced.

Master of Term used to label anonymous artists who seem to have a distinct style; the name usually refers to their most famous work.

masterpiece Work of generally acknowledged greatness, or the greatest work of a particular artist.

mastic Resin from trees, used to make varnish and paint **media.**

medium The physical material of which a work of art is made: oil paint, clay, ink, wood, etc.

Metaphysical Art The movement founded by Giorgio de Chirico in 1918, now seen as a bridge between a certain type of **Romanticism** and **Surrealism.**

miniature Very small painting, usually a portrait. The artist is called a limner.

Minimal Art Type of **Abstract Art** that uses only very basic, strictly geometric shapes and flat colours, free of personal overtones.

montage (French: mounting) Picture made by arranging images from newsprint or photography. Main reason for the choice of images is the subject matter. See also **collage.**

mosaic Picture or decorative pattern made by setting small fragments of marble, glass or ceramic materials into cement or plaster.

mural A painting or decoration on a wall. See also **fresco.**

Naive Art Painting in a style that looks untrained or child-like, often rejecting perspective and tending to use bright colours, as with Rousseau.

Naturalism The representation of objects in an accurate, objective and unstylized way. See also **Realism.**

Nazarenes A group of German painters active in Rome in the early 19th century who advocated an art based on the inspiration of primitive Christianity, led by Overbeck and Pforr. See also **Pre-Raphaelite Brotherhood.**

Neo-Classicism The dominant style in the late 18th and early 19th centuries, notable for its severely **classical** forms and high moral ideas, in reaction against **Rococo.** It was initially inspired by archaelogical discoveries at Pompeii.

Neo-Impressionism A development of **Impressionism,** also called **Divisionism** or **Pointillism,** pioneered by Seurat and employing small touches of pure colour so that they mix not on the canvas but in the viewer's eye. See also p.47 and **Impressionism.**

Neo-Plasticism An extension of **Cubism,** also called *De Stijl,* founded by Mondrian, in which the action of colour and forms was reduced to utter simplicity by adherence to geometric forms. See also **Cubism.**

Neue Sachlichkeit (German: new objectivity) A group of German painters active in the 1920s and 1930s, whose work made strong social comments. Dix and Grosz were among its leaders.

New York School Group of artists based in New York in the mid-20th century, who wanted to discover a uniquely American form of artistic expression. Members of the school include Pollock, Rothko and Still.

Nocturne A night scene – a term first used by Whistler for his paintings. See volume 9, pp.19-20.

ochre Name of **pigments** made from natural earths.

oil paint Paint produced by mixing **pigment** and a medium of drying oils; the dominant **medium** in Western painting from the late **Renaissance** to the present day.

Op Art Painting, particularly that of the 1960s, which depends on dazzling optical effects to create visual illusions. Vasarely and Riley were among its leading exponents.

Orphism Term coined by Apollinaire in 1912 to describe a development of **Cubism** pioneered by Robert Delauney. It was mainly concerned with the primacy of colour over form.

painterly Technical term meaning the opposite of linear – Botticelli was a linear painter, Titian a painterly one.

palette The surface on which an artist sets out his paint, and so the range of colours used by an artist. See also p.33.

pastel A picture executed with crayon sticks made of coloured powder that has been mixed with gum and moulded into finger shapes.

pastiche Imitation or forgery which combines sections of various works of one artist to produce a supposedly original work by that artist.

Pastoral Idealized landscape painting, often influenced by pastoral poetry and populated with nymphs and other mythological beings. See also p. 41.

pendant paintings Companion paintings meant to be hung together. See volume 5, pp.66 and 67 for examples by Chardin.

pentimento (Italian: repent) An alteration made by the artist while painting which later shows through the new work.

perspective Means of representing three-dimensional forms on a flat two-dimensional surface, invented in the 15th century. See also **vanishing point.**

Picturesque Aesthetic attitude, common in 18th-century Britain, which found delight in ruined buildings, wild or irregular landscape (as in Claude – see volume 4, pp.43-72). Only later did it come to mean 'pretty'. See also p.42.

pietà (Italian: pity) Sculpture or painting of the Virgin Mary supporting the dead Christ on her lap. See Volume 2, p.54 for Michelangelo's *Pietà.*

pigment Mineral or organic, coloured material which is mixed with a **medium** – for example, oil – to produce paint.

plein-air (French: open air) Paintings done outside rather than in the studio. A central feature of **Impressionism.**

Pointillism See **Neo-Impressionism.**

polyptich See **diptych.**

Pop Art Art movement originating in the 1950s and drawing its imagery from popular culture and commercial art. Andy Warhol's famous paintings of soup cans are typical images.

Post-Impressionism Term referring to the art of Cézanne, Van Gogh, Seurat and Gauguin and first used by Roger Fry, the English critic, in 1910. See also **Impressionism.**

Post-Painterly Abstraction Group of abstract artists working in the 1960s who reacted against the extreme subjectivity of **Abstract Expressionism** to create more objective paintings. Members of this **School** include Noland, Stella, Kelly and Olitski.

Precisionism American style of painting of the 1920s, in which urban and industrial scenes were painted in a precise, simplified way. Precisionist artists include Demuth and Spencer.

Pre-Raphaelite Brotherhood (PRB) Short-lived (1848-54) group of young British painters formed with the aim of reviving what they considered the high moral tone of painting before Raphael. Millais, Collinson Stephens and Rossetti were among the founder-members. The movement proved very influential. See also **Nazarenes.**

primary colours Red, yellow and blue; by mixing them, all the other colours can be made.

priming A layer, or layers, of material applied to a canvas or other painting **support** in preparation for painting.

Primitive (1) Netherlandish and Italian painters working before about 1500. (2) Unsophisticated, **naive art** produced by amateur, self-taught painters – for example, Edward Hicks, John Kane and Grandma Moses.

Prix de Rome (French: Rome prize) Four-year scholarship for study in Rome awarded by the French Academy. Notable winners were David and Ingres. See volume 4.

props Objects or costumes that identify the characters portrayed in a painting. See also p.44.

putto (Italian: little boy) Plump, naked, cupid-like children often featured in Italian art of the 15th and 16th centuries. The plural is putti.

Quattrocento (Italian: four hundred) The 15th century, used especially when referring to that century's Italian art and literature. See also **Renaissance.**

Realism Fidelity to natural, sometimes depressing, appearances dating back to Gustave Courbet in the 1850s. See also **Naturalism** and **Impressionism.**

Regionalism Movement in American art during the 1930s. The style was often conservative and aimed to celebrate small-town, rural America. Members of the school included Benton and Wood.

relief Carving or moulding in which the design projects from, or is sunk into, the surface, the degree of projection varying from low relief *(basso-rilievo)* to high relief *(alto rilievo).*

Renaissance Art (French: rebirth) Art of the period from 1400 to 1520 but sometimes traced back to Giotto (1300). During the 14th century, Italian art moved towards greater realism. Spurred in the 15th century by the rediscovery of ancient **classical** art, it reached its climax from 1500 to 1520 with Raphael, Leonardo da Vinci and Michelangelo (see volume 2), spreading outwards to Northern Europe, where it is called the Northern Renaissance. See also **Gothic** and **Mannerism.**

Representational Art See **Figurative Art.**

Rocky Mountain School American artists of the 19th century who painted the mountains. Leading artists were Bierstadt and Moran.

Rococo Frothy, elegant style developed out of **Baroque** early in the 18th century, Boucher and Fragonard being typical Rococo artists (see volume 5). See also **Baroque** and **Neo-Classicism.**

Romanesque Art Style of art and especially of architecture prevailing in the 11th and 12th centuries in Europe, characterized by its massive stone vaults. See also **Gothic.**

Romanticism Intellectual and artistic movement flourishing from about 1780 to 1840, in which the imagination and intuition predominated. Fired by the writings of men like Rousseau, Byron and Goethe, painters turned with new enthusiasm and vision to nature and to historical scenes. Turner (see volume 6,

pp.107-29), Friedrich and Delacroix were typical Romantic painters. See also **Academic Art, Classicism.**

sacra conversazione (Italian: holy conversation). Representation of the Madonna and Child with angels, painted as a group united by some common action in a single scene. See also p.36.

Salon The annual art exhibition held in the Louvre of the French academy, which originated in the 17th century. The *Salon des Réfusés* was established by Emperor Napoleon III after protests at the number of paintings rejected by the increasingly conservative jury. The Salon was taken over in 1881 by the *Société des Artistes Français*.

sanguine Red chalk, one of the most common materials used by drawing.

School Group of painters connected by style, period or a specific town or country – for example **Rocky Mountain School, Ashcan School.** Also used to describe artists working with a master – for example, School of Titian.

Secession or Sezession Name taken by several groups of artists in Germany and Austria at the end of the 19th century who broke away from traditional **academic** institutions. Klimt was a leader in Vienna.

sfumato (Italian: smoke) Tones blended with imperceptibly subtle transitions, as in the works of Leonardo da Vinci. See volume 2, p.29.

size A form of glue used to **prime** canvases or panels.

Social Realism Painting in **Realist** style in which the subject has overtly political or social meanings, not to be confused with Socialist Realism: official Soviet state art.

stippling Technique of shading in drawing and painting, using closely spaced dots rather than lines.

still-life Painting of inanimate objects, such as fruit or flowers.

support The untreated surface to which paint is applied.

Surrealism Originally a literary movement, inaugurated in 1924, it sought to reveal the reality behind appearances, especially in dreams. Hence the use of bizarre dream imagery, automatism and **symbolism,** under the influence of Freudian ideas. Magritte, Dali, Ernst and Miró were prominent surrealists. See also **Dada, Metaphysical Art** and **Symbolism.**

stucco Light plaster, mixed with powdered marble, used as decoration on buildings. Used to its fullest extent during the **Mannerist, Baroque** and **Rococo** periods.

Superrealism British and American style of sculpture and painting of the 1960s in which the subject matter was reproduced very exactly with a smooth, featureless surface. Because these works of art resemble photography, the style is sometimes known as Photorealism. Chuck Close and Duane Hanson are members of this school.

symbolism The representation of something immaterial by a material object – ripe fruit representing sensual pleasure. See also p.48.

Symbolism It started as a French literary movement of the 1880s inspired by writers like Baudelaire and his 'Fleurs du Mal', in reaction against **Impressionism** and **Realism.** Literary painters such as Moreau and Puvis de Chavennes used the striking imagery of the Symbolists – the severed head and the *femme fatale*. Painters like Gauguin and Van Gogh took a more formal, stylized aproach. See also **Surrealism.**

tempera Paint using egg as the **medium,** superseded for the most part by **oil paint** during the **Renaissance.**

Tenebrists Caravaggio and his 17th-

century Dutch, Neapolitan and Spanish followers, and La Tour in France, who painted interior scenes dramatically lit by candles or torches.

term See **herm.**

tondo (Italian: round) Circular painting or sculpture.

tone Term describing the degree of darkness or lightness of a colour.

tooth The degree of roughness of canvas or other support.

Trecento (Italian: three hundred) the 12th century in Italian art.

triptych See **diptych.**

trompe l'oeil (French: deceive the eye) The skill used to make a painted object appear to be a real, three-dimensional one. See also **Illusionism.**

underpainting Early stage in oil painting when the design and colour tones are worked out on the canvas. See also p.37.

value The gradations in **tone** seen on any solid object under light.

vanishing point The point on the horizon at which receding parallel lines seem to meet and disappear. See also **perspective.**

vanitas work (Italian: vanity) Still-life of a collection of objects meant to symbolize the brief span and uncertainty of human life – for example, skulls, clocks, smoking candles, petals falling from flowers. Vanitas elements can also be found as details in other paintings.

viewpoint Position from which a scene is depicted by an artist. See also p.43.

wash A thin, usually broadly applied, layer of transparent **pigment** such as **watercolour** or ink.

watercolour A pigment bound with gum and diluted with water, used to create translucent effects. See also p.46.